Effective Document Management

Unlocking Corporate Knowledge

Grateful acknowledgement to
'Podge'
who wandered in regularly to greet me at work
and ensure that I was still at it.

Effective Document Management

Unlocking Corporate Knowledge

Bob Wiggins

Gower

© Bob Wiggins 2000

All rights reserved. No part of this publication may be reproduced, stored in a retrieval system or transmitted in any form or by any means, electronic, mechanical, photocopying, recording or otherwise without the permission of the publisher.

The Publisher makes no representation, express or implied, with regard to the accuracy of the information contained in this book and cannot accept responsibility or liability for any errors or omissions that may be made.

First edition published in the UK by Elan Business Publishing as *Integrated Document Management*, 1996.

Figures 4.1 and 4.2 are UK Crown copyright material and are reproduced with the permission of CCTA and the Controller of Her Majesty's Stationery Office.

Hyperknowledge is a registered trade mark of Logical Water Ltd; PRINCE is a registered trade mark of CCTA; Docbase is a registered trade mark of Documentum.

In Chapter 9, the case studies remain the copyright of (in the order in which they are printed): Documentum, Altris, Open Text, SER Systems Ltd, *Information Age*. They have been reproduced with their permission from their Web sites.

Published by
Gower Publishing Limited
Gower House
Croft Road
Aldershot
Hampshire GU11 3HR
England

Gower
Old Post Road
Brookfield
Vermont 05036
USA

Bob Wiggins has asserted his rights under the Copyright, Designs and Patents Act 1988 to be identified as the author of this work.

British Library Cataloguing in Publication Data
Wiggins, Bob
    Effective document management : unlocking corporate
    knowledge
    1. Business records – Management 2. Business records –
    Management – Data processing
    I. Title
    651.5

ISBN 0 566 08148 2

Library of Congress Catalog Card Number: 99-75347

Text designed by David Brown. Printed in Great Britain by MPG Books Ltd, Bodmin, England.

CONTENTS

LIST OF FIGURES	IX
LIST OF TABLES	XI
PREFACE	XIII

1 INTRODUCTION 1

1.1	Why is document management of significance?	2
1.2	What is its potential?	3
1.3	What are the risks?	4
1.4	How can this book help?	5
1.5	Who is the intended readership?	5
1.6	How to use this book	6

PART 1 ENTERPRISE KNOWLEDGE – THE BUSINESS RESOURCE

2 INFORMATION, STRATEGY AND THE CORPORATE CONTEXT 11

2.1	What constitutes an organisation?	11
2.2	Challenges for managers in the information age	12
2.3	New technology	13
2.4	Gaining competitive advantage	13
2.5	Information's strategic importance for knowledge workers	15
2.6	Managing information resources	16
2.7	Developing an information systems strategy	25
2.8	Information systems development	31
2.9	Information content	33
2.10	Information sciences and skills	33
2.11	Managing the information life cycle	34

3 APPROACHES FOR IMPROVING BUSINESS PERFORMANCE 41

3.1	Structured systems development	41
3.2	Dealing with unstructured problems	44
3.3	Approaches based on quality	48
3.4	Business process re-engineering	54
3.5	People approaches	57

3.6	Organisational cultures	59
3.7	Automated support tools	59

4 RECORDS MANAGEMENT AND DOCUMENT MANAGEMENT 63

4.1	What are records?	63
4.2	The need for records management	64
4.3	Records management and document management	66
4.4	*Infobuild*: an information life cycle management approach	67
4.5	management data	73
4.6	Records system design	74
4.7	Forms management	76
4.8	Reports management	77
4.9	Devising retention schedules	79
4.10	Storage and retrieval systems	81
4.11	Implementation, administration and control	83

PART 2   TECHNOLOGY AND RETRIEVAL

5 TECHNOLOGY – PROMISES FULFILLED AND UNFULFILLED 87

5.1	Client/server technology	86
5.2	Communication networks	90
5.3	Buses and interfaces	98
5.4	The Internet and the World Wide Web	100
5.5	Input devices	104
5.6	Storage technologies	116
5.7	Display technologies	125
5.8	Information and document storage and interchange standards	127
5.9	Document management standards	136
5.10	Operating system software	139
5.11	Programming and software development languages	140
5.12	Authoring software	141
5.13	Document viewers	142
5.14	Co-operative working technologies	143
5.15	Information security	145

6   INFORMATION AND KNOWLEDGE RETRIEVAL   149

6.1   The information-seeking problem   149
6.2   The value of information   151
6.3   Speed of retrieval   152
6.4   Document or information retrieval?   152
6.5   Document or information storage?   154
6.6   Indexing – the key to retrieval   155
6.7   Software for information retrieval   166

PART 3   PROJECT MANAGEMENT AND SOLUTIONS – IDEAS INTO ACTION

---

7   DOCUMENT MANAGEMENT – THE PROJECT FOCUS   175

7.1   Choosing the project area   175
7.2   User needs and system functionality   179
7.3   Business case and justification   191
7.4   Project management   195
7.5   Requirements definition   201
7.6   The invitation to tender   204
7.7   The project for real!   207

8   THE DOCUMENT MANAGEMENT MARKETPLACE   211

8.1   Sources of information   216
8.3   Supplier profiles   219

9   SUITABLE CASES FOR TREATMENT   231

Brown & Root Energy Services' common enterprise repository for key documents speeds time to construction, delivers high ROI   231

BP Schiehallion information management and the challenge of cultural change   234

BASIS – putting power to work   238

Two-hundred seat PAFEC EDM system gathers speed at Railtrack Property   242

Granada Ghia – Granada Media's switched-on view of information retrieval   244

INDEX   249

LIST OF FIGURES

1.1	Elements of a compound document	2
2.1	Organisational model	12
2.2	Illustrative business services and associated information systems in the value chain	14
2.3	Relative information needs of planning and control	15
2.4	Flows of information used for goal setting and management planning	16
2.5	A Rich Picture of the information scene	18
2.6	The knowledge hierarchy	20
2.7	Information, knowledge and enterprise knowledge management	24
2.8	Constituent elements of enterprise knowledge management	24
2.9	Basic questions for an IS strategy study	26
2.10	An information model	27
2.11	Information system development life cycle elements	32
2.12	The information life cycle	35
3.1	Logical data model	43
3.2	Data flow diagram (process model)	43
3.3	The stages of the soft systems methodology	45
3.4	Business excellence model	50
3.5	A simple supply chain process model	51
3.6	An expanded supply chain	52
3.7	A comparison of TQM and BPR	56
4.1	The elements of records management	65
4.2	A standard data page for reports	78
5.1	Technologies and the information life cycle	88
5.2	The hierarchy of information management standards	135
5.3	Authoring activities for online documentation	142
6.1	Sources of information – a general outline	150
6.2	Generalised flow diagram for document indexing	160
6.3	Contrasting DBMS and information retrieval systems	167
7.1	Technology options	177
7.2	Document management functionality	180
7.3	Simplified example of a software life cycle	196

7.4	The PRINCE process model	198
7.5	PRINCE project management structure	199
8.1	Sales revenues of document management vendors	219

LIST OF TABLES

2.1	Likely contribution of specialists to information activities	19
2.2	Gartner's view on knowledge and information management	23
2.3	Techniques to aid strategic planning for information systems	30
3.1	Techniques to aid quality and process improvement	53
3.2	A comparison of conventional and laboratory approaches to systems development	57
3.3	An analysis of organisational cultures	60
4.1	A comparison of records and document management	66
4.2	Informatrix1	68
4.3	Informatrix2	70
4.4	Detailed survey questions	70
4.5	Document types and usage patterns	71
4.6	Physical and structural characteristics of paper documents	72
4.7	Forms management programme	77
4.8	Report management programme	79
4.9	Guidelines for determining retention	80
4.10	Typical retention schedule for engineering function	82
5.1	Software that comes under the middleware banner	91
5.2	LAN technologies	94
5.3	WAN technologies	95
5.4	Packet-switching technologies for WANs	96
5.5	Connection technologies	97
5.6	Simplified categorisation of cabling	96
5.7	Bus types	98
5.8	SCSI specifications	99
5.9	Standardised URL prefixes for the Internet	102
5.10	Comparisons of ISIS and TWAIN	111
5.11	Typical scanning resolutions for different applications	112
5.12	Typical file size (megabytes) for raster images, vector and ASCII text	112
5.13	Available RAID levels	119
5.14	DVD variants	120

5.15	Colour and bit depth	126
5.16	Firewall techniques	146
6.1	Generalised information-seeking problem	151
6.2	Basic range of information types to be handled	154
6.3	Key retention and indexing criteria	156
6.4	Comparative features of natural and controlled language	159
6.5	Retrieval aids	161
6.6	Retrieval software - representative products	169
7.1	Pre-project actions taken	176
7.2	Classification of document management applications	178
7.3	Document management functional models and sub-functions	181
7.4	Comparison of storage media for different requirements	189
7.5	Elements of a business case	193
7.6	Typical target benefits	194
7.7	Activities for a software quality plan	197
7.8	Roles and responsibilities for a PRINCE project	200
7.9	Types of user	202
7.10	Project management activities	207
8.1	Industry acquisitions	212
8.2	Opposites attract?	216
8.3	Sources of information on document management technologies	217

PREFACE

Every organisation deals with some form of document - reports, correspondence, electronic mail, cheques .... Documents contain 'information' - that which is available in recorded form independent of humans - and together with 'knowledge' - information that individuals know and hold in their brains - they are vital elements of an organisation's 'enterprise knowledge'. Document management is a discipline supported by an increasing range of information technologies for dealing with this material in a more effective and efficient manner, whether the documents are on paper or electronic media.

While many organisations will commence with localised projects, there are strong moves towards enterprise-wide integrated systems for managing both recorded information and that drawn from the intellectual capital embodied in staff and management. This is because the flow of information and knowledge in support of business activities need not, and should not, be constrained by functional boundaries. Document management can therefore be a key contributor to enhancing business performance in support of other improvement approaches focused, for example, on information system development, quality systems, process re-engineering and people themselves.

Unfortunately, the latest technologies and 'guru-management' speak, and the ways in which they are often promulgated, tend to confuse those seeking to deal with their 'real-world' business problems. In writing this book I have aimed to avoid such obfuscation. Also, whilst giving detailed consideration to such topics as information survey and analysis techniques, document indexing, project management, the supplier scene and real-life benefits, as illustrated in the case studies, I have set document management in the broader organisational, information and technological context. This should help readers to understand better how document management can be 'fitted' into other initiatives that their organisations may be pursuing.

1
INTRODUCTION

'I may truly say it is a novelty to the world'.

Lafeu, All's Well that Ends Well, Act 2, Scene 2:
William Shakespeare

Document management (DM) must be seen as one of the contributors to business efficiency and effectiveness. Ideally it should take its place alongside other candidate information system investments having this aim, and be considered in the context of a broader information system strategy. Document management involves the integration of new and existing information technologies, and as such it is a key approach which potential users need to assess as an aid to achieving their business objectives.

It has been noted *'that the trouble with many of the latest developments to spring from the computer industry is that their purposes can seem so grand and all-embracing that, when it comes to making real decisions about real implementations of workable solutions, it is not always possible to make the grand concepts square with the requirements of a specific application. For example, while a spreadsheet is a spreadsheet, and definitely not a word processor, just what is a document management system?'.*[1]

Broadly interpreted, documents comprise coherent records of information meaningful to their relevant users. Thus correspondence, reports, meeting minutes, engineering drawings, form work, purchase orders and cheques fall readily into this definition. Documents are typically associated with paper, although they may be stored on other media such as microfilm, hard (and floppy) disks or optical disks. Less obviously, perhaps, one can include photographic, video and sound recordings, any of which may be equally, or more important to an information user than the aforementioned document types; hence the growing interest in multimedia systems. Documents can, therefore, be highly complex mixtures of these objects where not only the information content, but also the format, layout and appearance of the information are of equal importance. For so-called rich text, one must be able to deal with attributes such as type size, font, kerning and proportional spacing. Overall the term 'compound' document symbolises this complexity (see Figure

Compound document content →	List	Document	Spreadsheet	Image	Drawing	Audio	Video
	Data file	Text file	Spreadsheet file	Raster graphics file	Vector graphics file	Sound file	Video file
Format (as seen by user)	Records	Pages	Rows and columns (cells)	Bitmap	Vectors (line co-ordinates)	Digitised voice	Multiple bitmaps
	Fields	Words					
Underlying structure (used by computer)	Bytes							
	Bits							

Figure 1.1 Elements of a compound document

1.1).

Document management is one of several IT buzz-words. Thus those supplying scanners, optical character recognition software, work group software products and text retrieval facilities will often contend that they are supplying into the DM (and now the knowledge management) market. On a broader scale DM can be considered as just one component of information or knowledge management or of business process re-engineering (BPR). Thus when managing documents it is important to understand the life cycle processes through which the documents pass, and the wider issues of information or knowledge management within the organisation.

Integrated document management (IDM) implies use of the technology beyond isolated islands of automated functionality to provide, for example, the tight integration of internally generated and externally sourced documents, or its application in product data management (PDM) to support the product cycle from design, development and production to sales and service.

1.1 WHY IS DOCUMENT MANAGEMENT OF SIGNIFICANCE?

The results of various surveys have supported the simple evidence of most employees' eyes that paper is still the principal medium of information exchange in organisations. Why this reliance on paper in the age of IT? Various factors combine to explain this situation. Readily produced, easy to handle and with a history harking back to the Egyptians some 5,500 years ago, paper is a familiar, uncomplicated medium on which to record information. It requires no special technology or skill to use, and facilitates review and browsing of information.

However, paper takes up increasingly costly space in organisations, is labour-intensive to handle, liable to be mis-filed and lost, and is heavy. For example saving the weight of paper documentation on board naval ships enables additional weaponry to be accommodated. The current, and increasing demand for paper also has environmental implications. These relate to the need for more trees and wood pulping facilities on the production side and to the problems of disposal and recycling of waste paper.

If the management of information within organisations is to succeed, a major focus must be the management of paperwork, its movement into, within and beyond the organisation, and its integration with other information media and information systems. The technologies associated with document management aim to address these issues, and the ongoing requirement to manage documents in digitised form.

More fundamentally, document management technology can help support key business processes as exemplified by:

- vetting and approval of engineering design documents and drawings
- processing insurance claims
- document version control
- controlled document distribution (e.g. via the Internet, Intranet or Extranet)
- quality management procedures such as those associated with ISO 9000.

1.2 What is its potential?

Document management involves the integration of new and existing information technologies, and as such it is just one of many developments which potential users need to assess as an aid to achieving their business objectives. What sets it apart from other IT advances, however, is that it tackles the problem of paper as the principal carrier of business information, provides means to integrate ALL information-carrying media, and maintains the natural concept of a document, as broadly defined.

With the increasing prevalence of microcomputers and word processors, for example, much of the documentation generated within organisations is in electronic form. Two key problems often encountered by organisations wishing to capitalise on electronic means of managing their information relate to:

- externally-generated information which is still largely paper-based (correspondence, publicity literature, purchase orders, books, etc.) and

- backlogs of paper-based information created or received within the organisation before it adopted computer technology for information generation.

Where business requirements justify the conversion, imaging such documents enables them to be more readily managed, not just as static objects which can be stored more compactly, but more importantly as dynamic and transactional carriers of information. These can then be processed and manipulated as an integral part of businesses activities and the flow of work amongst and between individuals, work groups and organisations.

As to the benefits to be gained, those who have adopted document management have found that both strategic and tactical benefits arise. These have ranged from increases in quality, timeliness and management control (all strategic in nature) to improved productivity and cost reduction as regards both personnel and storage space (tactical benefits).

1.3 WHAT ARE THE RISKS?

The introduction of document management may have major implications across the enterprise for the way business is organised, for staffing levels, skills and training and for the computer hardware, software and communication infrastructure. This impact may be felt beyond the organisation by its customers and suppliers as the demand increases for similar treatment to be applied to the information flowing between them, i.e. electronic commerce.

Document management is not an end in itself. However, the allure of the technology can all too easily dazzle the unwary and generate a blinkered approach to the development of a document management project. For example, insufficient thought is frequently given to such factors as the preparation of paper documents prior to scanning and to the need for proper indexing. The latter issue is particularly crucial as inadequately indexed documents are effectively lost for ever. Furthermore the benefits that can be derived from the Internet's web-based technology can too easily go unrealised if uncoordinated strategies are pursued.

This all argues for a carefully planned approach as would (or should) be adopted for any technologically-based projects. In assessing the merits and demerits of document management, the risks involved need to be identified and built into the planning and decision-making process.

Additionally, skills and experience must be harnessed from all those (e.g. computer network administrators, process analysts, records managers, librarians, data analysts, business managers, end users) that are in some way concerned with managing and using information throughout its life cycle. This is because the technology continues to blur the boundaries between these functions. There is the danger that the organisation's information resources will be put at risk if proper consideration is not given to such factors as the retention and safeguarding of vital records, indexing and retrieval mechanisms and records design within the electronic environment.

1.4 How can this book help?

For the introduction of document management to be successful, it needs more than an understanding of the technology. It requires an awareness of the business objectives that need to be achieved and of the information that supports the business activities which underlie the objectives. Furthermore the organisation's technological framework into which the system will be fitted has to be comprehended along with broader IT industry trends.

The choice of document management system is facilitated by knowledge of such issues as the capture process, storage media, indexing and retrieval options, technical standards and key selection criteria.

Over and above all these detailed considerations is the need for a project framework covering, for example, the specification of user requirements, system selection and design and implementation.

Suffice to say, this book is not intended to provide answers to all the questions that a reader might pose. Nor is it a product review guide. Nevertheless, the book aims to provide guidance on the topics noted above, and in a way that enables the reader to address such questions as :

- What are the strategic issues that need to be considered?
- What technologies are involved?
- How can a document management project be justified and initiated?
- Who are the potential types of solution providers?
- What are user experiences?

1.5 Who is the intended readership?

As a guide, it is hoped that the book will be helpful to readers from across the organisation. This will facilitate attaining a common framework of understanding within the enterprise between those who may be affected by the introduction of a document management system. Particular targets are noted below.

- Business managers

    Managers responsible for line functions need to be sufficiently aware of technological developments and the way they can impact and support their business activities.

- ◆ System designers, developers and implementers

   Those concerned with the various stages of a document management project need to understand not just the strengths and limitations of the technology but also the information and knowledge management context in which it has to operate.

- ◆ Records managers, librarians and information managers

   Information professionals, particularly those who have long been concerned with managing mainly paper-based documents, need an appreciation of the impact of the technology and of how their particular areas of expertise can best be applied. Such professionals often have a key role to play in the management or operation of document management systems.

- ◆ End users

   The ultimate user who is seeking information is generally only concerned with receiving the right information in the right form and at the right time (irrespective of the method of access or delivery). Nevertheless if a document management system (or for that matter any new information system) is to be introduced, the user must be suitably involved and in control in the appropriate system project stages, including such aspects as the specification and agreement of requirements. An appreciation of the significance and potential of such systems, and of the scope of their facilities provides the user with confidence in dealing with system designers at the outset, and with system implementers at the conclusion of the project.

1.6 HOW TO USE THE BOOK

The book is divided into three parts each of which is designed to be read largely independently of the others.

Part 1 -   ENTERPRISE KNOWLEDGE - THE BUSINESS RESOURCE

considers the importance of recorded information and personal knowledge in the organisational context, the development of a strategic approach, the contributions to be made by business improvement approaches such as those based on process re-engineering and quality, and the role of records management as compared with document management.

Part 2 -   TECHNOLOGY AND RETRIEVAL

provides an overview of information technology and industry trends relevant to document management, and highlights indexing and information retrieval concepts.

Part 3 -   PROJECT MANAGEMENT AND SOLUTIONS - IDEAS INTO ACTION

outlines the elements of a document management project, including choosing the target area, project justification and managing the project. It presents an overview of the supplier market and snapshots of some of the main suppliers, describing user experiences of the technology. The whole of the last chapter is dedicated to suppliers' case studies exemplifying the range of organisations that are adopting different technologies and the type of business problem to which they can be applied.

References to sources of information are contained in each part.

REFERENCES IN CHAPTER 1

1   Banks, Martin, 'Document Decisions', *Information Age,* September 1995, pp. 39-40, 42, 45-46

PART 1

ENTERPRISE KNOWLEDGE - THE BUSINESS RESOURCE

2

INFORMATION, STRATEGY AND THE CORPORATE CONTEXT

*'All men can see the tactics whereby I conquer,
but what none can see is the strategy out of which victory is evolved'.*

On the Art of War: Sun Tzu

Before one can sensibly focus on the detailed implementation of a document management system it is helpful to be aware of the broader strategic business and information systems framework in which the new technology will be deployed. Without this knowledge it is more likely that isolated and incompatible islands of technology will appear which will hamper the development of coherent and co-operative information systems. This chapter deals with some of the broader issues that should be considered to help ensure that document management is an enabling, rather than a disabling technology.

2.1 WHAT CONSTITUTES AN ORGANISATION?

While this is no place to present a dissertation on organisational theory, there is merit in drawing on Leavitt's '60s view of an organisation since it has stood the test of time and provides a useful backdrop when the issues which surround document management are considered. Leavitt viewed an organisation as a dynamic and a human system comprising of four basic elements:[1]

- ◆ Processes (Leavitt referred to 'Tasks' here)
    - the organisation builds or designs things or provides services by undertaking an organised assembly of tasks that transform inputs into outputs, subject to particular controls

- ◆ Structure
    - the organisation has some broad, more or less permanent framework; some arrangement of processes and material resources and people in some sequence and hierarchy

◆ Tools
  • the organisation utilises technological advances and provides tools that enable people or machines to perform tasks and to effect administrative control

◆ People
  • the organisation is populated by, as Leavitt expressed it *'these sometimes troublesome, but highly flexible doers of work'*.

These organisational elements (or organisational levers of change as they are often now called[2]) are interdependent in that any change in one will affect the others (Figure 2.1).

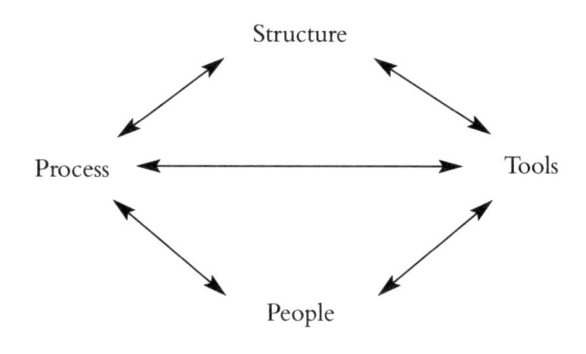

Figure 2.1 Organisational model

Leavitt viewed information as the glue which holds an organisation together.

2.2 CHALLENGES FOR MANAGERS IN THE INFORMATION AGE

The management and staff of businesses face increasing challenges, and the forces of change can be considered from three viewpoints.

First, there are economic and commercial challenges that relate to such factors as fluctuating economic environments and changes in international trade and competition. This situation is exacerbated by the political changes in the former Eastern European block countries and beyond, and the dramatic downturn in Asian and Far Eastern economies during 1998.

Second, there are the changes in social and governmental attitudes arising largely from improved and more numerous communication channels to the public and legislators and the loosening of state control of key industries. Businesses are faced with increasingly complex and abundant environmental and consumer legislation from government and political blocks such as the European Community (EC). This is coupled with the concerns of employees faced with the implications of takeovers, mergers, down-sizing and re-engineering.

Third, there are technologically- and scientifically-oriented developments. The computer and microprocessor have a profound effect on information handling in administrative and business-support areas and, when incorporated in machinery, revolutionise the productive capacity and speed of manufacture with commensurate reduction in costs. This in turn is encouraging the earlier replacement of products by new or improved versions.

2.3 NEW TECHNOLOGY

Many observers refer to the accelerating speed of technological change in recent times as something which is quite unprecedented. However, Drucker[3] in the early '80s is one who challenged this view. He believed that what accelerated was the awareness of the change, and that the change itself may even have slowed. Furthermore he saw the period to the end of the century being one *'of structural change rather than one of modification, or extension or of exploitation'*.

So what sort of society is management faced with now, and how is it developing and changing? Much has been made[4,5] of the transformation from an industrial society to an information society and more recently from the concept of 'information' to that of 'knowledge'. However, these apparently recent phenomena are not unique in the history of the western world. As an example, the introduction of the typewriter (which originally referred to the female operator rather than the machine itself) had a more dramatic effect.[6] It greatly influenced female employment prospects, and social and physical arrangements in the office. Its impact was certainly greater than that encountered more recently with the implementation of word processing.

Nevertheless, persuasive evidence that technology is contributing to increasing office productivity proved difficult to find. In the decade to 1993 service companies in the US were estimated to have spent $860 billion on information technology, while the service sector (which employed three-quarters of US workers) was only increasing its productivity by 0.5% per year. *Fortune* magazine's survey of 1991 found that office productivity fell far behind that in factories. In fact the most productive companies tended to spend less per employee on management systems than those companies with average productivity.[7] The contribution of IT to productivity has been described as *'a trillion-dollar experiment'*, while acknowledging that *'the fact that you can't see the productivity benefit doesn't mean that you don't have to make the investment'*.[8] Workflow software is one technology that is demonstrably delivering productivity benefits in many organisations.

2.4 GAINING COMPETITIVE ADVANTAGE

To be successful businesses need to achieve sustainable competitive advantage relative to their competitors. Porter sees competitive advantage being achieved in two basic ways:[9]

- ◆ lowering the cost of product design, manufacture and marketing, or of service provision
- ◆ differentiating the product or service by its uniqueness or superior value in the eye of the customer.

At the heart of these processes is innovation whose success or otherwise is often crucially dependent on the new technologies of the information industry based around computer hardware, software and communication systems.

14   Enterprise Knowledge – the Business Resource

While emphasis in the past has been on standalone computer systems and office products such as telex, facsimiles, photocopiers and the telephone, the major thrust now is on integration of these technologies via digital communication. Companies are increasingly seizing on this opportunity to conduct their internal activities and external business through these new electronic channels, for example by forging electronic data interchange (EDI) and, increasingly, Extranet links with both their suppliers (purchasing partnerships) and customers. The degree to which competitive advantage is gained depends largely on how successfully the organisation manages this entire scenario. This constitutes a series of value chains, with associated information systems as exemplified in Figure 2.2 (adapted from Porter[9]).

However, despite the advantages claimed by the use of information technology,[10] they can be ephemeral unless businesses continue to identify and exploit new opportunities. It is

Firm infrastructure	• Financial services • Accounting	• Management consulting • Legal services	• Conflict resolution services			M
Human resources management	• Compensation consulting • Health services	• Education & training • Temporary help	• Employment agencies			A
Technology development	• Contract research • Calibration services • Design services	• Testing services • Custom software	• Market research			R
Procurement			• Rating services • Telecoms consulting			G
Core services and Information systems	• Transportation services • Warehousing services • Supplier databases	• Engineering services • Building maintenance • Equipment maintenance and repair • Security services • Industrial laundry services • On-line data capture • CAD/CAM • Product data management systems	• Waste disposal • Transportation • Warehousing services • Credit reporting • Environmental management systems	• Advertising • Direct response marketing • Coupon processing • Contact databases	• Installation and testing services • Repair and overhaul • Maintenance management systems • Asset database	I N
	INBOUND LOGISTICS	OPERATIONS	OUTBOUND LOGISTICS	MARKETING & SALES	SERVICE	

Figure 2.2 Illustrative business services and associated information systems in the value chain

not surprising, therefore, that organisations seize upon fresh approaches to gaining competitive advantage as expounded by the latest breeds of management gurus.

2.5 Information's strategic importance for knowledge workers

Beyond the automation of manual tasks, emphasis is increasingly focused on the knowledge workers whose main activities revolve round the utilisation and exploitation of information; an activity crucial to the success of innovation. Such people are found not just in businesses whose main line activity is finance, insurance, journalism, advertising or publishing for example, but also within productive industry where they are concerned with strategic planning, market research or scientific research and development.

Zuboff[11] coined the word 'informating'. Unlike 'automating' which implies the use of technology to replace people, informating exploits the technology of smart machines to increase an organisation's thinking or intellective capacity. In developing this view Zuboff was presaging the recognition of knowledge as something different from information, a topic to which this chapter returns later in section 2.6.2.

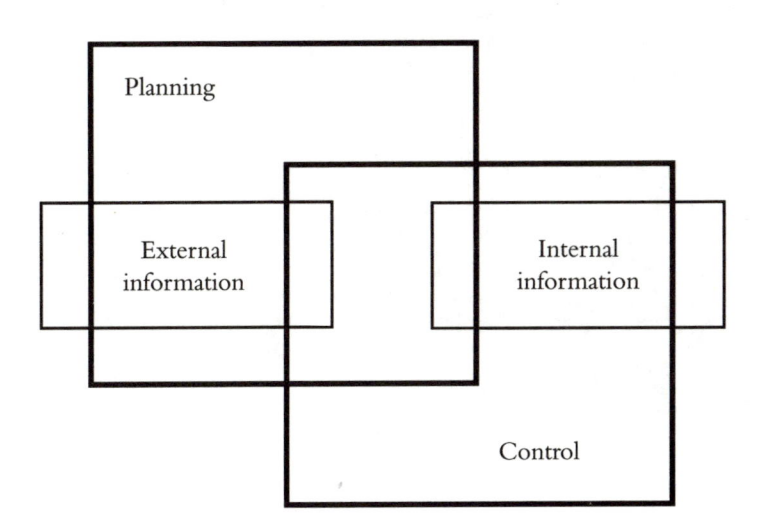

Figure 2.3 Relative information needs of planning and control

In this context information is the life blood of the organisation with internally-generated information much concerned with management and control of the business, and externally-sourced information contributing more to planning and strategic decision-making (Figure 2.3). One organisation estimated that the percentage of its company records relevant to the classic four levels of the corporate pyramid amounted to around:

◆ Executive decision support and strategic information: 1%

◆ Audit and Control: 4%

◆ Planning and Analysis: 20%

◆ Transactional: 75%.

However, if one looks at the requirement for external information, the picture is somewhat different, with the outward-looking business strategist requiring a variety of information from the external environment, much of it being text-oriented and much being interpersonally communicated.

16   Enterprise Knowledge – the Business Resource

The diversity of information and information flows used for setting the goals of an organisation is exemplified in Figure 2.4, which derives from a classic study undertaken in the mid '60s[12] relating to the chemical industry.

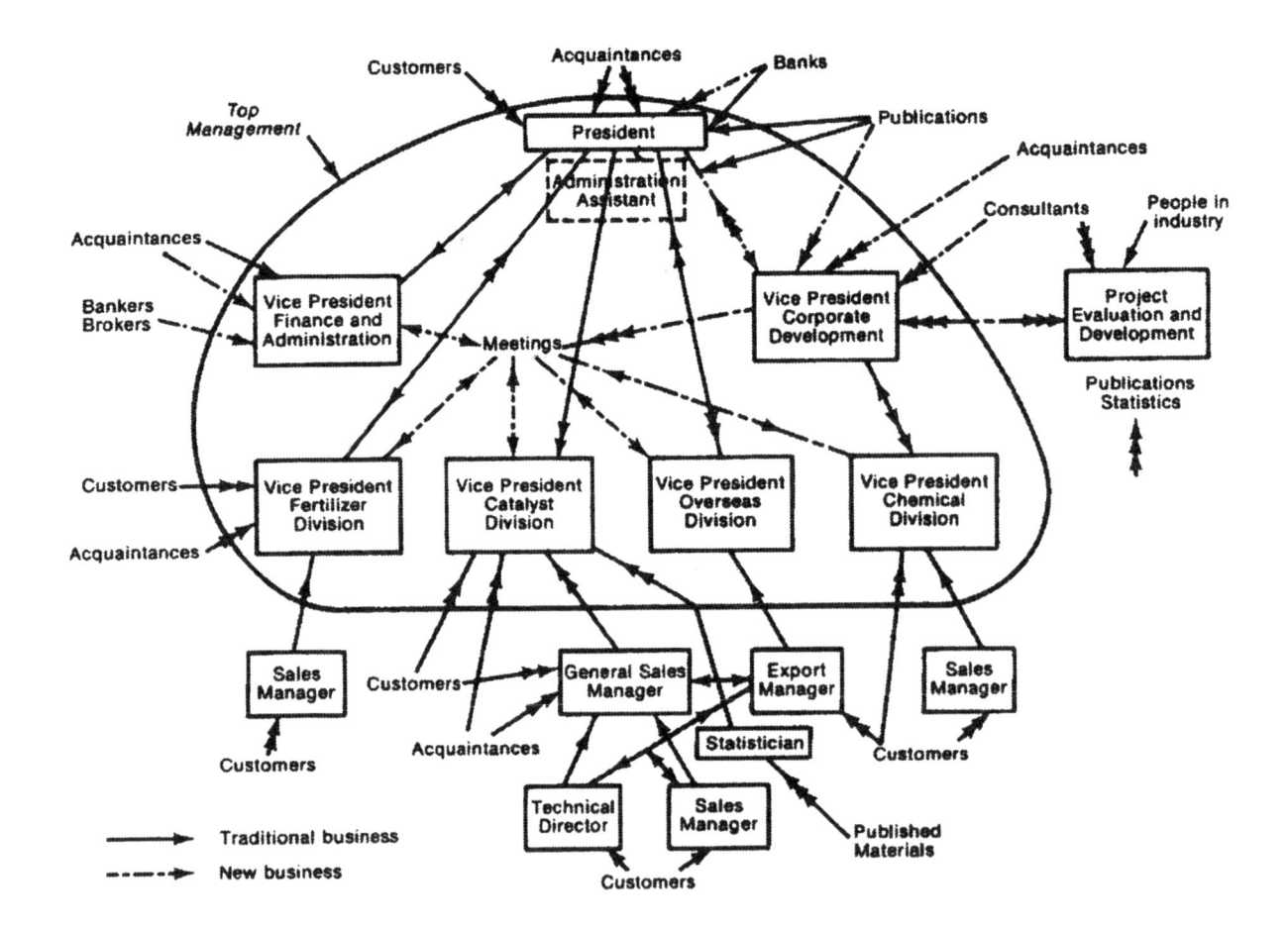

Figure 2.4 Flows of information used for goal setting and management planning

2.6 MANAGING INFORMATION RESOURCES

Even a brief review of the literature[13] highlights the variety of complex attitudes, perceptions and philosophical and practical issues surrounding attempts to define not only information itself but also the areas of expertise concerned with information and its management.

To exemplify this, I produced the Rich Picture on page 18 (Figure 2.5[14]) which aims to capture the essence of the situation. Although focused on the UK information scene, and produced some years ago, it still seems valid today, particularly as regards the 'somewhat confused user'.

The picture includes:

◆ 'professions and disciplines';

- skill areas which relate to services provided;
- the impact of new (and traditional) technology;
- information and the corporate pyramid;
- flows and processes, and
- the user.

It is worth highlighting some of the general themes that can be drawn from the picture.

2.6.1 The contribution of specialists

The traditional practitioners in such fields as computing, records management and libraries have become increasingly aware of each other's existence within organisations, if unclear as to their respective roles, functions and inter-relationship. This situation has been accelerated by the convergence of data processing, telecommunications and office technologies. No longer can individual experts such as data analysts, management scientists, records managers, or librarians afford to isolate themselves into watertight service compartments. An example is the emphasis now being placed on records management when designing and implementing document management systems.

Furthermore, professional information bodies are seeking closer ties, and even mergers, as exemplified by the discussions between the Library Association and the Institute of Information Scientists in the UK. There is a need to capitalise on the skills and experience of all such information specialists and the services they can provide by fostering and undertaking broad-based information-related studies which draw on this expertise.

Studies[15] have shown that if both information systems (IS) specialists and users heighten awareness of their respective power bases this can facilitate the parties working in unison for the development of effective systems. It is also important to recognise that '*IS development and politics are inextricably intertwined... An IS specialist who approaches the systems development process in a clinical, methodological and completely detached manner is not being constructive*'.

The particular specialists depicted in Figure 2.5 refer to their interests in terms of the 'message', 'media' or 'elements', the first two being adapted from a McLuhan quote.[16] One can equate 'message' to information as understood by (most) users and 'media' as the physical medium on which it is held. If one accepts this analogy then data can be considered to be the 'elements' (words, phrases, numbers, even characters) which make up the message. Given this somewhat artificial basis one can suggest (Table 2.1)[17] the contribution of specialists to information management based on the activities which make up the information life cycle.

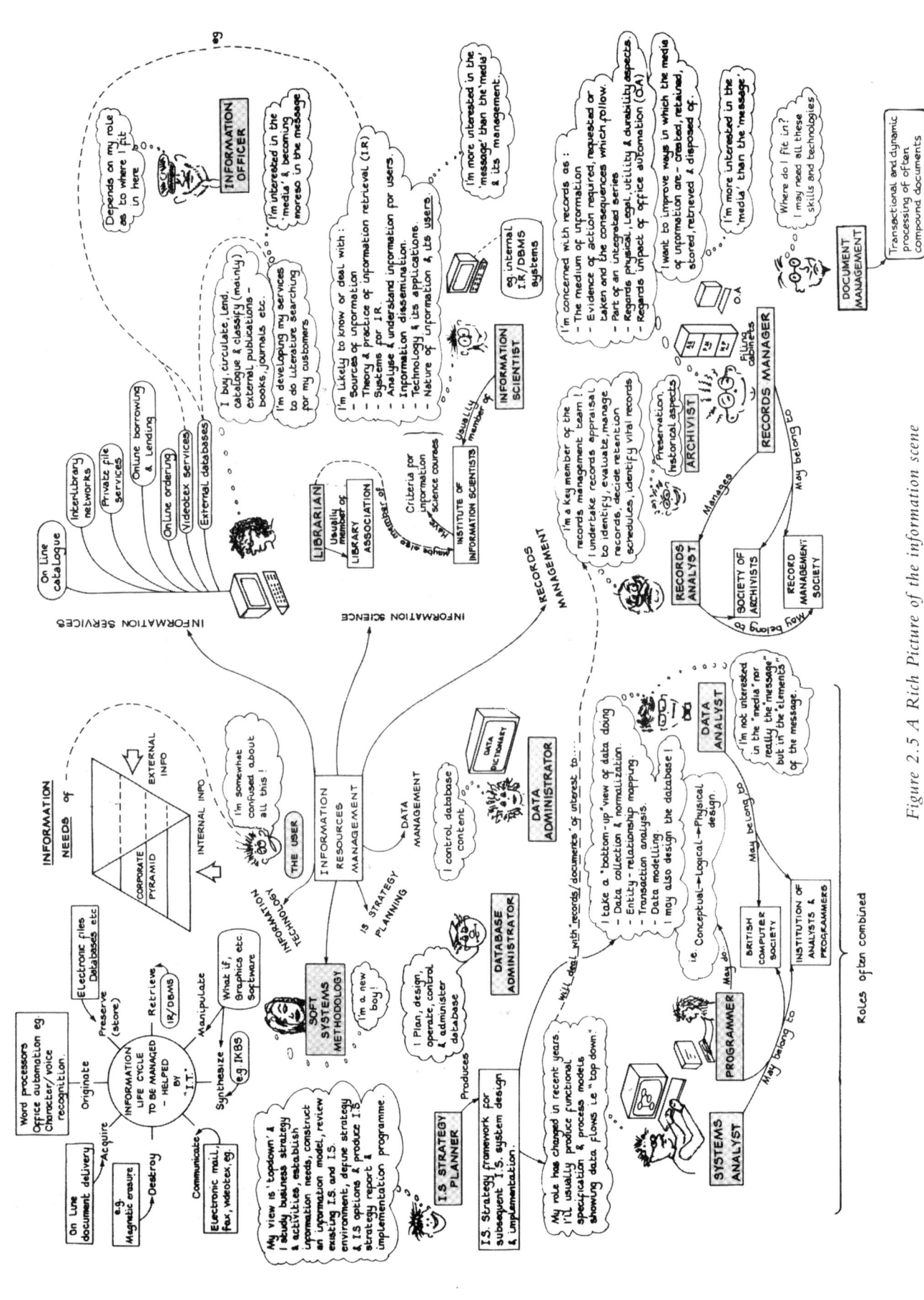

18   *Enterprise Knowledge – the Business Resource*

Figure 2.5 A Rich Picture of the information scene

SPECIALIST	IS strategy planner	DP Manager	Data analyst	Database administrator	Data administrator	Records manager	Archivist	Information scientist	Librarian[1]	End user[2]
INFORMATION TYPE										
'Message'	P	N	S	N	S	S	P	P	P	P
'Elements'	N	S	P	S	P	N	N	S	N	N
'Media'	N	S	N	S	N	P	P	S	S	N
External information	P	S	S	S	S	S	S	P	P	P
Internal information[3]	P	P	P	S	P	P	P	P	S	P
ACTIVITIES										
Determine business strategy	P	N	N	N	N	N	N	N	N	P
Identify relevant information	P	N	P	N	P	S	P	P	P	P
Acquire	S	N	S	N	S	S	S	P	P	S
Create	N	N	N	N	N	N	N	S	N	P
Retain	S	S	N	S	P	P	P	S	S	S
Store	N	P	N	S	N	P	P	S	P	S
Retrieve	N	S	S	S	S	S	S	P	P	S
Communicate	S	S	S	S	S	S	S	P	S	P
Revise	S	N	S	N	S	S	S	S	S	P
Utilise	N	N	S	N	S	S	S	P	S	P
Destroy	N	S	N	N	P	P	P	S	P	N

Key: P= Primary concern; S= Secondary concern; N= No real concern

[1] Many 'librarians' are more proactive than is indicated here. The title given to a post-holder is not necessarily descriptive of their information activities.

[2] The answers provided will depend on the seniority of, and activities undertaken by, a particular end user.

[3] Brought-in external information is typically integrated with internal information. Thus it is not always possible clearly to distinguish between the two.

Table 2.1 Likely contribution of specialists to information activities

2.6.2 Data, text, information and knowledge

Much is often made of the differences between data and information. A data analyst, for example, may view data as information coded and structured for subsequent processing - the subtle difference being that information is in context, data is not.[18] Was this definition intended to cover discursive text in documents or published literature? It would mean that text may also not be considered information until it is placed in context. On the other hand, a user does not refer to text as data, while he may refer to information in an engineering handbook as useful data.

Another differentiating factor is that data is usually associated with facts and figures in some structured form as exemplified by customer databases made up of database records and database fields incorporating names, addresses, telephone numbers, etc. The text in documents, however, can be of any length and of varying structure.

Others[19] have instead referred to information holdings and divided these into data (facts, figures, numbers), documents (reports, records - not database records -, messages and memos) and literature (monographs, periodicals). To some this definition will be more understandable than that used by computer specialists.

What about the term 'knowledge'? One organisation's exposition of information management included the statement *'information is the knowledge about a subject which forms the basis of decision making'*. This conflicts somewhat with a dictionary definition *'familiarity gained by experience; a person's range of information; the sum of what is known'*, which fits in with the development of knowledge-based systems whereby the experience of specialists, such as medical practitioners, is captured in a computer-based system for use independent of the specialist.

This hierarchy of data, information and knowledge has often been represented as a pyramid, as shown in Figure 2.6.[20]

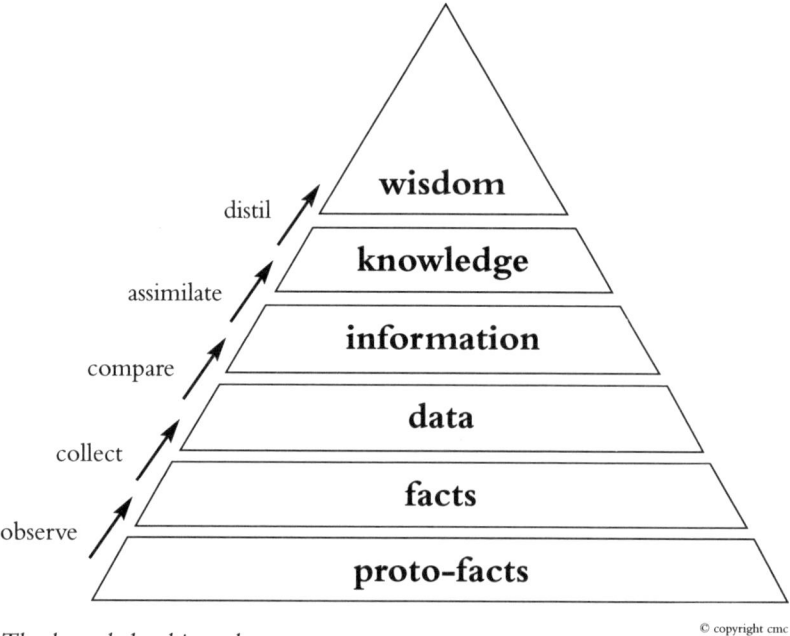

Figure 2.6 The knowledge hierarchy

The general point that emerges from this is that there are no correct definitions. As Checkland has pointed out,[21] *'Making sense of the field of IS (Information Systems) requires a very clear concept of what "information" is, but given the present confused state of the field it is perhaps not surprising that there is at present no well-defined definition of such terms as "data" and "information" upon which there is general agreement'*.

In order to minimise the chances of misunderstanding it is important to speak and understand to a sufficient extent the language of those with whom we are communicating and, in turn, be able to translate clearly and unambiguously our language into that of the recipient. Many of the failures of computer-based systems to deliver what was expected of them can be attributed to a lack of communication and understanding between computer personnel and the users of the systems for whom they were developed. Jargon terms such as 'down-sizing' and 're-engineering' and 'outsourcing' are now more likely to conjure up less attractive thoughts in the minds of staff and management, such as 'redundancy' and 'increased work loads'.

Unfortunately most suppliers to the document management market have confused users further by simply replacing the word 'information' with 'knowledge' in their product literature. Despite these problems of definition, information can be seen to possess somewhat peculiar characteristics as an organisational resource, for example:

- its usefulness, relevance or value can vary with time

- it can be used simultaneously by more than one person

- it can exist independently of physical form, i.e. in one's mind (as knowledge)

- it can be open to different interpretations and degrees of acceptability depending on such factors as social and cultural background, gender and one's state of motivation.

2.6.3 Distinguish 'information' from 'system'

It is important to distinguish between the information aspect of information systems and the systems themselves be they based on new technology or traditional paper-based ones.

All too often IT-oriented personnel, involved for example in the design and development of a computer-based solution to a business problem, are seduced by the technology and their familiarity with it. Hence they fail properly to take account of the real business needs and the business information which the system stores and processes. In contrast those who utilise information in their day-to-day activities often have a cavalier attitude to the systems and data management aspects.

Information systems that aim to address the information problems facing organisations are increasingly computer-based, but can never be totally comprehensive or all-inclusive, since human beings are a necessary part of these systems.

It is a well-known adage that an information system should deliver information which is:

- relevant
  - appropriate to the goals of the organisation and the individual users
- timely
  - available as and when needed
- comprehensible
  - readily absorbable by those who have the need for it.

Furthermore the total cost of this information provision, as incurred by the 'process', 'structure', 'people' and 'tools', should not exceed the value of the benefits that its use will generate.

2.6.4 So is there a difference between information management and knowledge management?

While many, under the banner of 'information management' (or 'information resources management') and titles such as Chief Information Officer (CIO), have for years been happily managing and exploiting recorded information (in books, reports and other documents), intellectual capital (information that people know) and the systems that support these activities, there are now moves to rename these roles. Thus staff titles that were once CIO are now Chief Knowledge Officer (CKO) to the extent that already in 1997 it was estimated that a third of US organisations had one.[22]

Gartner notes that *'knowledge management enables individuals and collaborative groups to identify, capture and share information, while information management uses specialised IT staff to identify, capture and process information'*.[23] Gartner proposes differences between two approaches, as shown in Table 2.2.

This division seems to confuse rather than clarify. It tends to compartmentalise and further separate from one another computer professionals and users of information (knowledge workers), when there should be a coming together and cross-fertilisation. Also, defining a characteristic of information management as being 'dependent on well-defined enquiries for retrieval' renders it more akin to (structured) data management. In fact, if one substituted 'information' for 'knowledge' in the lefthand column, and 'data' for 'information' in the other, the table entries still make sense, and would be recognisable to 'pre-knowledge management' information professionals.

What is important is that the management process must encompass both recorded information (which is independent of individuals) and the information that they know (which is dependent on individuals). Elsewhere Gartner recognises this by defining knowledge management (KM) as:

> *'a discipline that promotes an integrated approach to identifying, capturing, retrieving, sharing and evaluating an enterprise's information assets. These*

KNOWLEDGE MANAGEMENT	INFORMATION MANAGEMENT
Captures existing knowledge	Centres on recording and processing information
Takes information from one source and promotes re-use in other situations	Takes information from multiple sources and organises into database systems
Designed for distributed access, storage and control (empowers the end user)	Designed for centralised information storage and control (empowers the IT function)
Emphasises collaboration and sharing	Emphasises enquiries to highly structured repositories
Enables end-user defined information relationships and needs	Concerned with information collection, classification and distribution
Employs technologies for knowledge discovery	Dependent on well-defined enquiries for retrieval
Adds value for growth, innovation and leverage	Required to maintain mission-critical enterprise data
Increases productivity for innovation	Good productivity for efficiency

Table 2.2 Gartner's views on knowledge and information management

> *information assets may include databases, documents, policies and procedures as well as the uncaptured, tacit expertise and experience resident in individual workers'.* [24]

But 'knowledge is power', and in this uncertain organisational world employees will not willingly share knowledge as it may literally make them redundant. Hence the greater emphasis being given to human resources management in companies.

Although widely recognised as being over-hyped (and over here), knowledge management cannot be ignored. If you can clarify what your colleagues, suppliers or customers mean when they refer to KM and a commom understanding is reached – all to the good.

The intention in this book is to be consistent by using the words 'knowledge' to mean information that individuals know and hold in their brains, 'information' to cover that which is available in recorded form independent of humans, and 'enterprise knowledge management' (EKM) to embrace both information and knowledge in the corporate context. To put it another way, knowledge implies 'awareness', 'understanding'. Thus 'I have knowledge of the information', and 'I have information about this knowledge'. The relationship between these elements is shown in Figure 2.7.

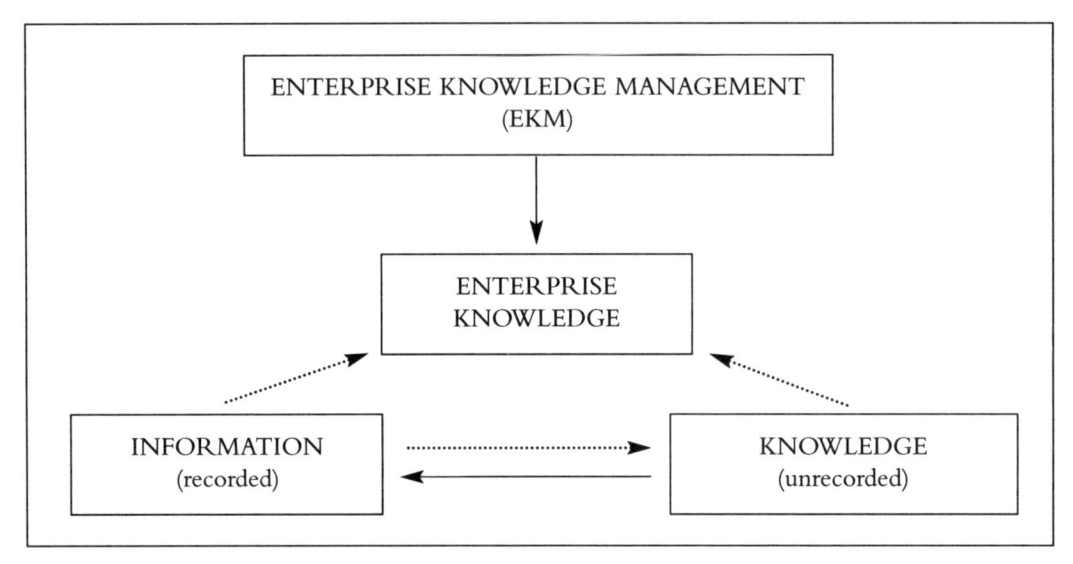

Figure 2.7 Information, knowledge and enterprise knowledge management

Given this viewpoint, one can identify the key constituent elements of EKM based on those of Leavitt – namely 'process', 'people', '(organisational) structure' and 'tools' (Figure 2.8).

PROCESSES
Processes to capture knowledge and information and manage its life cycle

STRUCTURE
Framework and policies for business operations, human resources management and supporting tools

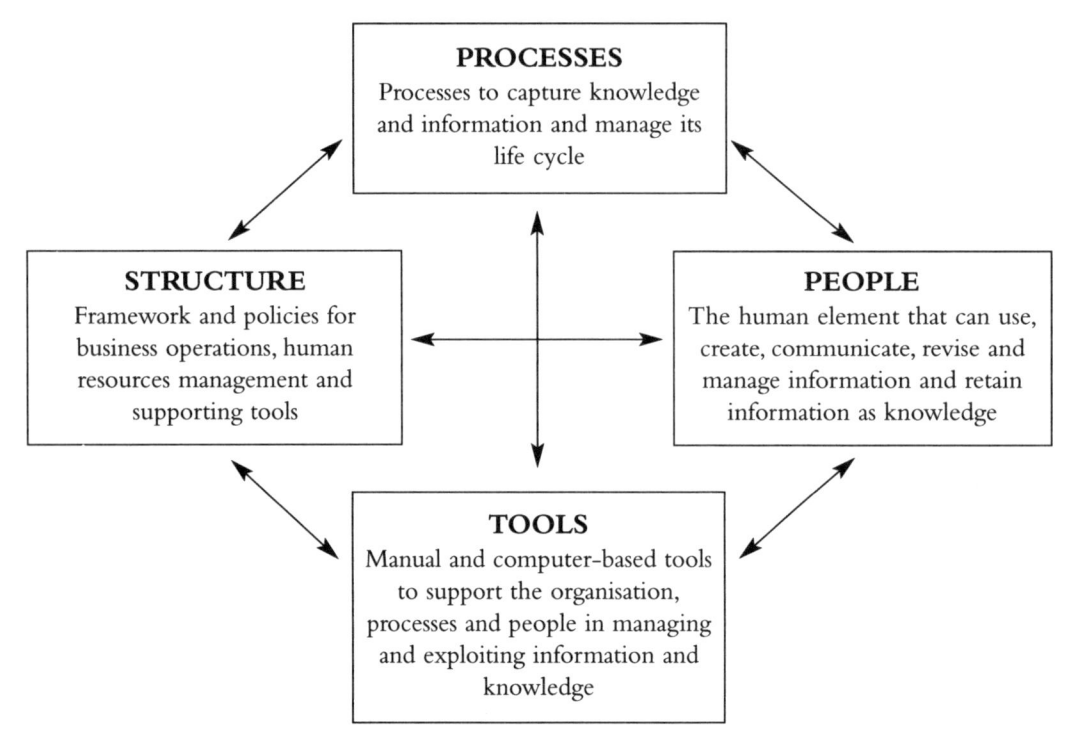

PEOPLE
The human element that can use, create, communicate, revise and manage information and retain information as knowledge

TOOLS
Manual and computer-based tools to support the organisation, processes and people in managing and exploiting information and knowledge

Figure 2.8 Constituent elements of enterprise knowledge management

2.7 DEVELOPING AN INFORMATION SYSTEMS STRATEGY

A person's knowledge is only accessible to others if it is either communicated orally or stored as information in some recorded form such as a document or database. A strategy for enterprise knowledge management must include one for the enterprise's informaton and supporting systems.

Over the years computing, communications and office systems technologies have developed and converged to the point where their use can impact all types and sizes of organisation and all levels of staff. The power and potential of such developments continues to increase as their relative costs decrease. Companies are realising that significant proportions of their staff and of expenditure on technology are now concerned with information activities. If information and information technology (IT) are to be managed as a resource in the same way as money, materials or people, then managers need to apply similar criteria in the management process. In particular, the resources utilised must support the business by helping managers and staff achieve their business objectives.

The importance of this approach is increasingly recognised at national level as instanced by the various publications from the UK's CCTA Information Management Library[25] and from DISC, which was set up within the British Standards Institution to help accelerate operational effectiveness in enterprises through the promotion of standards for information systems.[26] In the United States the Paperwork Reduction Act[27] is explicit about Federal agency responsibilities and includes coverage of the paperwork clearance process, information dissemination and information resources management.

The importance of valuing information assets is increasingly being recognised, not only in relation to brand names, but also from a financial perspective.[28] In the UK a new accounting standard for intangible assets requires that from the end of 1998 UK companies must capitalise such assets in their company accounts.

At the organisational level an information systems strategy plan (ISSP) is a way to determine in general terms what information systems an organisation should have in place over the medium to long term (typically around three to five years - although planning horizons are shortening) to help achieve the company's business objectives. The IS strategy should be aligned with the business planning cycle and should be supported by top management who must therefore be involved in the planning process.

Information systems in this context are not simply computer-based but will include any assembly of information which is, or may be used by the organisation.

Ideally such a strategic approach should be applied across the whole organisation. For large organisations it may not be politically possible to gain immediate acceptance for such a broad-based top-down study. In such circumstances approval may more readily be gained, for example, by limiting the study to the particular department or function where the need has arisen, but plan the approach so that business process interfaces are identified and the exercise can, as necessary, be expanded later to other parts of the enterprise.

A holistic and creative approach should be adopted in developing the overall strategy so that it encompasses captured knowledge as well as information. The ISS plan should include appropriate use of process re-engineering/process redesign and modelling of the data and information approaches at the more detailed level.

An ISSP report is written for senior management, not for the IS specialist. Once the plan is approved it provides the general framework within which the design and development of the individual information systems can proceed.

2.7.1 Typical stages of an information systems strategy study

Although different consultants will offer their own particular approaches to undertaking an ISSP, the key elements (Figure 2.9[29]) will involve answering the questions:

- What it the scope of the IS strategy?
- Where are we now?
- Where do we want to be?
- How do we get there?

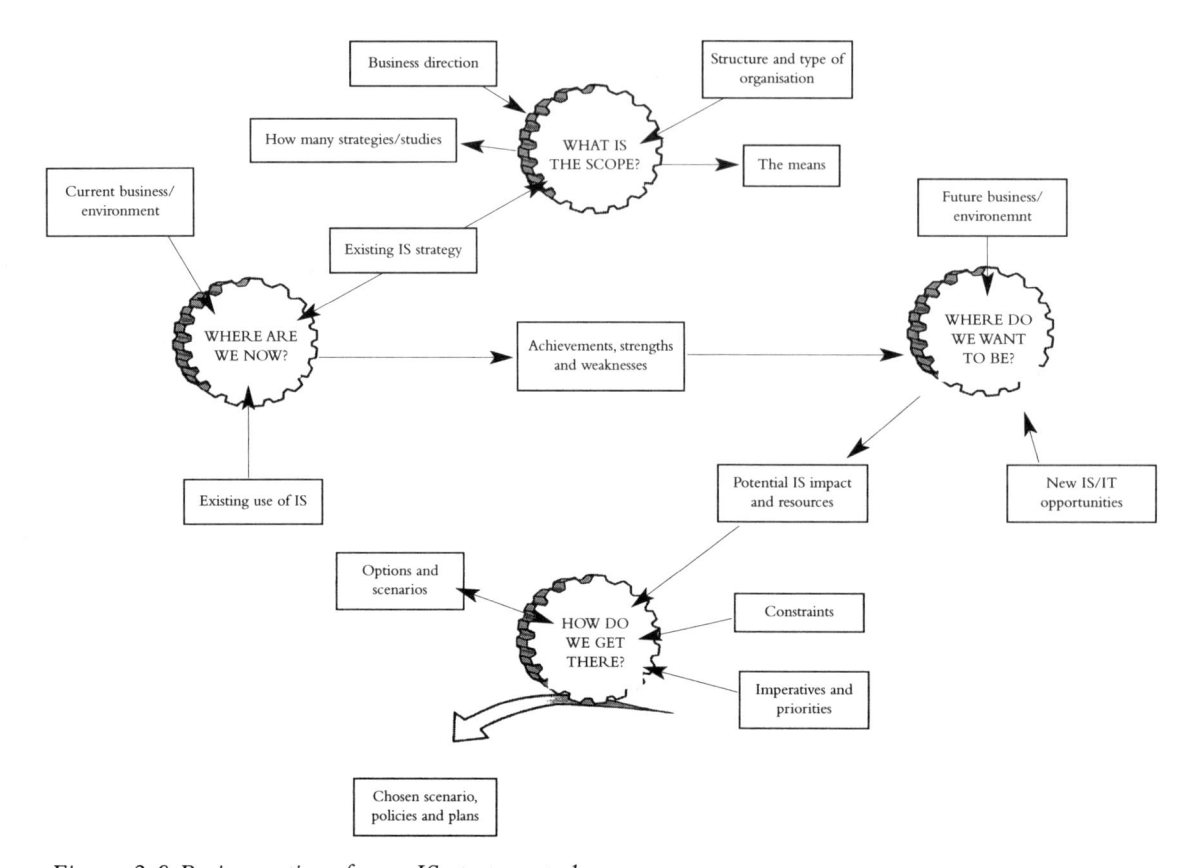

Figure. 2.9 Basic questions for an IS strategy study

Figure. 2.10 An information model

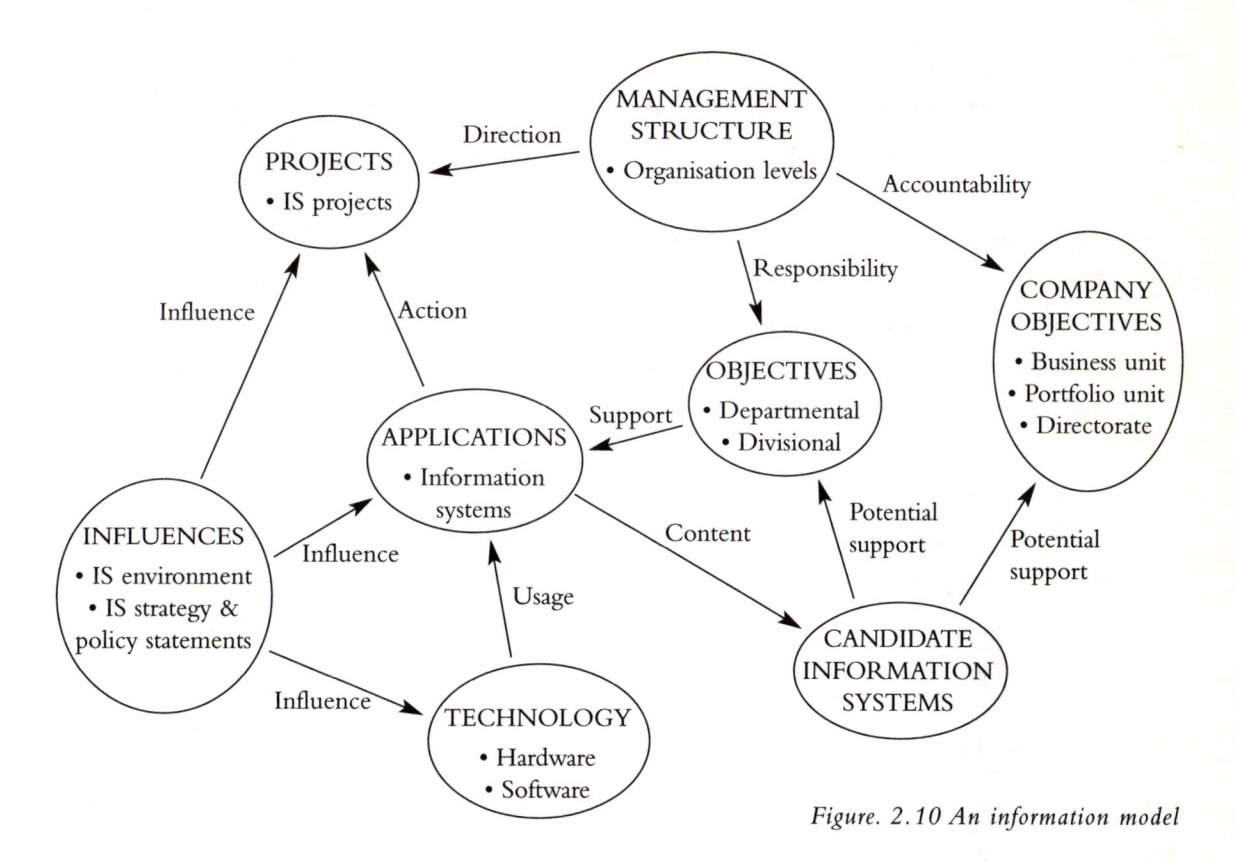

In this context, the following stages will be present in one form or another:[30]

Stage 1 - Diagnosis

Business objectives and information needs are identified. Available resources, including current information systems (manual and computer-based), are documented. Various influences (company policies, technological advances, national considerations, etc.) which might affect decisions are noted. Opportunities for using information technology may be outlined in general terms (costs, effort, timescales). The foregoing elements combine a top-down approach focusing on business strategy with a bottom-up viewpoint concentrated on business activities and existing systems. A detailed information model (Figure 2.10) covering these findings may be produced. A report is prepared for the client's Management Review Board.

First Management Review

The Management Review Board consider and, after any necessary amendments, agree the business objectives, information needs and the general scale of possible investment.

Stage 2 - Planning

Various information system options are considered and evaluated. Selected options are incorporated in alternative costed IS plans (say minimum 2 to maximum 4 plans) and presented in a report along with relative benefits and disadvantages.

Second Management Review

> The Management Board consider the options presented and, subject to any amendments, select an option to form the agreed IS strategy plan.

Stage 3 - Action

> The plan is documented in sufficient detail so if necessary others (often the company's Information Systems Department) can implement the plan. The plan must therefore indicate resources required, time-scales, priorities and responsibilities for all the plan's constituent information systems.

Stage 4 - Evaluation

> Progress must be reviewed regularly and at key decision points by senior management as well as by the client management concerned with individual projects within the plan. The assessment must be against the objectives that were originally set.

2.7.2 Approaches to ISSP

When information systems strategy planning is expressed in the above terms, it might appear to be a straightforward exercise. However, experience in conducting such studies has often proved otherwise.

Detailed consideration of the barriers to achieving a successful strategy has been undertaken by various researchers. Thus Wilson, supported by Arthur Anderson & Co. undertook a survey of *The Times* 500 companies and 47 financial services companies in the UK[31] and identified the following key features of IT strategies as being most likely to cause problems for companies:

- ◆ difficulties in recruiting appropriate staff
- ◆ lack of resources to engage in user education
- ◆ the nature of the business
- ◆ difficulties in measuring benefits.

Earl[32] reported the following problems experienced in IS strategy formulation:

- ◆ inadequate business plans
- ◆ agreeing priorities
- ◆ lack of planning experience
- ◆ rate of business/user change

- organisation structure

- discovering competitive advantage.

Martin[33] highlighted the power struggle between IT managers and users in a survey of the UK and Ireland. The ultimate objective in employing those with information management skills and experience is to facilitate the attainment of the business objectives of users. This means, for example, that users must be suitably involved in information systems development, while IT personnel must have adequate awareness of the users' business. The survey found that the main obstacles to success were:

- organisational constraints

- poor communication between users and IT staff (compounded by the fact that the majority of respondents had no plans to re-deploy IT staff to user departments)

- insufficient understanding of systems development methodologies

- lack of standards.

There is evidence that the relationship between IT and the business is improving, as was shown by *Information Week* pan-European research of the top IT spenders in December 1997.[34] Of the respondents, 70% believed that IT goals and business were better aligned than two years previously. Furthermore, 77% reported a collaborative relationship between IT and the business.

However, it is noteworthy that many of these barriers include several which are not solely related to IS strategy planning. Thus staff recruitment problems, inadequate business plans and lack of communication will adversely affect many an innovation. Nevertheless the choice of methodology (or more likely a combination of approaches) will be a key contributing factor to the success or otherwise of the strategy that emerges.

For example, the hard, systems engineering approaches to introducing mechanised or computerised systems either ignore or give insufficient consideration to qualitative, soft aspects.[35] Some practitioners of ISSP concentrate on technology to the exclusion of manually-based information systems. They are in fact undertaking information technology (IT) rather than information system (IS) strategy planning.

As can be surmised, methodologies exist in great numbers, some addressing strategic business issues, others being applicable at the sharper end of system design and development. Examples of techniques and methodologies which can be drawn upon when undertaking strategic planning are shown in Table 2.3.

TECHNIQUES AND METHODOLOGIES	DESCRIPTION
Arkush Square	Assesses the style of investment likely to be required by comparing the extent to which IS is accepted against the rate of business change.
Boston Square	Provides a framework for classifying information technology. Helps identify the rate at which demand for IS is growing and how much of the need is being met.
Business systems planning (BSP)	Developed by IBM it provides a data-oriented view of the organisation.
Business impact analysis	Assists in comparing the extent to which current IS support meets current and likely future business needs.
Business modelling	Typically involves construction of models for business functions, major entities and information flows. Can be the basis for systems development using structured methodologies such as SSADM.
Critical success factors	Identifies those key factors where resources must be concentrated to ensure corporate success.
Goal and problem analysis	Goals (specific targets achievable in a given time) and problems are associated with information needs and information systems.
Linkage analysis	Developing a strategic business vision by considering waves of information system growth, experience curves, industry power relationships, external enterprise interaction and electronic channel support systems.
McKenny Square	Assesses the importance of IS to the business, both past, current and future so that future strategic directions can be identified.
PEST analysis	Helps gain a better understanding of the organisation's environment viewed from a Political, Economic, Social and Technological (PEST) viewpoint.
Porter's value chain analysis	Analyses an organisation in terms of a linked set of primary functions such as design, manufacture, storage, sales, etc. as supported by secondary functions such as personnel and finance.
Portfolio analysis	Typically based on the Boston Square (see above) it assists obtaining the best result from an evolving number of products in a competitive environment.
Soft systems	Aimed at addressing 'fuzzy' ill-defined problem situations, it involves conceptual modelling and comparing the results with the real world to identify areas for improvement.
Stakeholder analysis	Identifies the major external influences, their likely perceptions of the organisation, and their potential interactions with it.
Systems assessment	An objective assessment of the resources (people, finance and technical) consumed by a system and how well it performs. This approach is typically used in conjunction with the user needs survey.
SWOT analysis	Strategic analysis of internal strengths and weaknesses, and external opportunities and threats.
Technology impact reviews	Mapping a taxonomy of new technology against opportunities for new products, services etc.
User needs survey	A variety of approaches can be adopted; one involves contrasting the assessed real system needs of users against the IS providers views of the same systems.

Table 2.3 Techniques to aid strategic planning for information systems[36,37]

Information management methodologies are ultimately concerned with effecting some degree of change in the organisation, and change is not a rational, analytical and mechanistic process. To be effective, ISSP must take account of less tangible factors such as the attitudes, perceptions and value systems of the management concerned and of the staff who will be affected by change. Those conducting the study must therefore have not only business and technical skills but also an awareness of social and political factors. There is therefore growing interest in combining hard and soft approaches in the design of IS.[38,39] The literature concerning effective information systems management is too vast to cover in more detail here. An excellent treatise on strategic management of IS is provided by Wendy Robson.[40]

Within the subject framework for this report the focus is on such topics as records and documents, their management and flow through their life cycle and the business processes conducted within the organisation. In order to assist with the design and development of such information systems, an approach which I have called *Infobuild* is introduced in Chapter 4. It is not a replacement for other methodologies, but is intended to complement them by focusing on the concept of the information life cycle as outlined in section 2.11 below.

2.8 INFORMATION SYSTEMS DEVELOPMENT

The IS strategy plan should identify the manual and computer-based information systems which need to be reviewed, developed or dispensed with during the planning period concerned.

Controlled systems development, as typically based on the well-known development life cycle (Figure 2.11) should ensure that the operational system:

- Satisfies the user's real information requirements

- Is easy to use and to operate

- Is easy to maintain (i.e. to correct problems that occur)

- Is easily modified or enhanced.

The execution of the life cycle stages can be facilitated in a co-ordinated and coherent fashion, by the use of systems development methodologies. These have certain common features:[41]

- An underlying philosophy about how a system should be modelled

- Use of a set of techniques for modelling the system

- Possible use of tools to produce output (e.g. requirements definitions models or programming code) from the various design and development stages

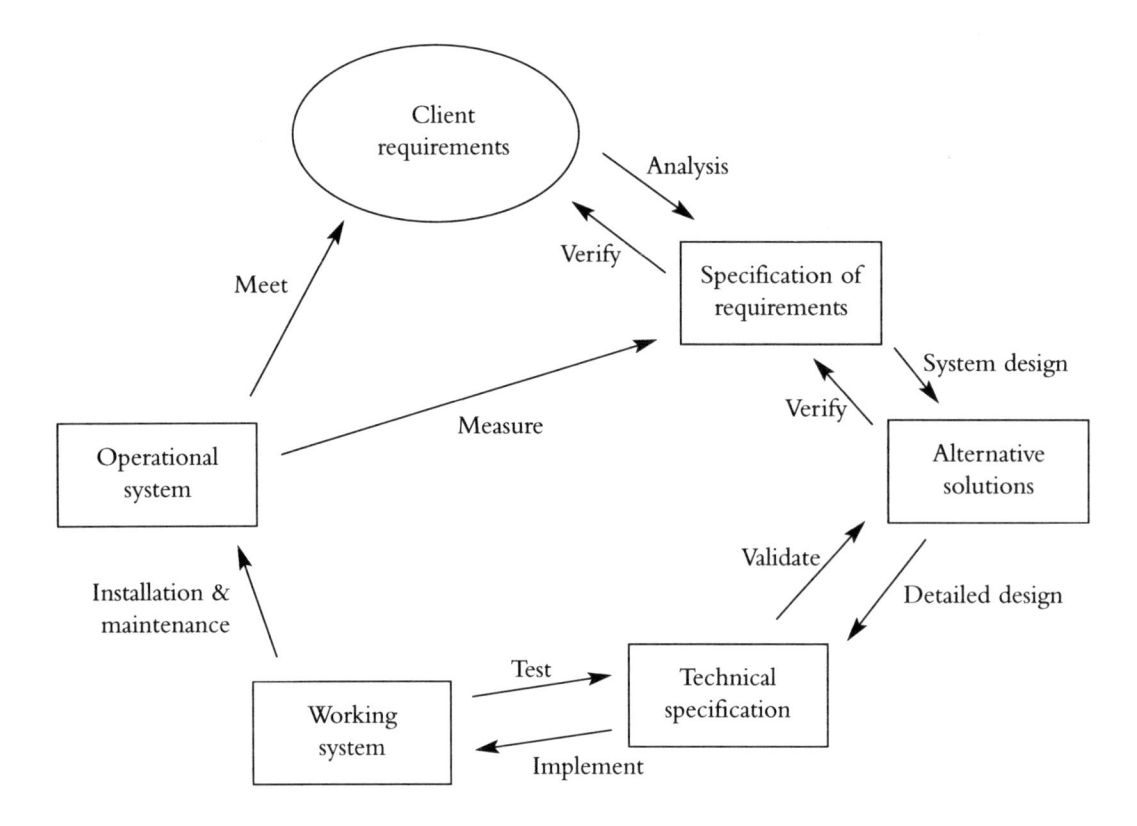

Figure. 2.11 Information system development life cycle elements

- Procedures for the use of the techniques and tools
- Procedures for planning and controlling the development process
- May make recommendations about the allocation of systems people to development tasks.

2.8.1 Data management

Data management has long underpinned the development and maintenance of computer-based systems and is concerned with

- The development of a data management strategy
- Data analysis to determine such facts as the existence, ownership, source, type, volumes, currency and redundancy of data and to produce logical models of the data system and associated processes
- Selection of appropriate database management systems and physical design of the database
- Implementation planning and data control including the loading of any backlog
- Administration of the data and of the database system itself.

Data management helps to ensure the delivery of cost-effective computer-based solutions, facilitates systems integration and complements and contributes to any associated records management studies inside the organisation.

The use of data and process models is considered further in Chapter 3 in the context of structured system development methodologies.

2.9 INFORMATION CONTENT

Effective and efficient use of information in organisations requires that all aspects of the information handling process are properly managed. The *Infobuild* approach facilitates this by focusing on the life cycle of information from its acquisition and creation through to its possible destruction.

Elements of *Infobuild* include:

- ◆ Reviewing present and potential methods of undertaking each life cycle activity. This will include access to and acquisition of both external and internal information

- ◆ Mapping technology onto these activities to help identify ways of improving efficiency and effectiveness

- ◆ Mapping available and needed skills onto these activities to see where improvements in information handling and exploitation can be achieved (see Table 2.1)

- ◆ Identifying the potential for integration or elimination of activities.

The use of such an approach helps to ensure for example, that no links are left unconsidered in the information activity cycle, that the benefits of specialist skills and technologies are maximised and that sources of under-exploited information are identified.

Underlying *Infobuild* is the discipline of records management. This is an important issue in the design of document management systems and is considered in more detail in Chapter 4.

2.10 INFORMATION SCIENCES AND SKILLS

The development, implementation and operation of particular information systems may require the application of specialist skills beyond those traditionally employed. Such skills will include:

- ◆ Management science which involves, for example, mathematical programming, linear programming and modelling

◆ Library and information science concerned with the acquisition, processing and exploitation of information both from inside and outside the organisation

◆ Human factors dealing with the way people and machines interact within systems and optimisation of this interaction based on the strengths and weaknesses of humans and computers

◆ Artificial intelligence relating to the development and practical application of artificial intelligence and knowledge-based systems including expert systems, natural language processing and computer-aided instruction

◆ Systems theory approaches to facilitate the management of change in human systems such as organisations.

2.11 MANAGING THE INFORMATION LIFE CYCLE

Planning and development of an information management system must take appropriate account of all the stages in the life cycle of information. A generalised information life cycle model is depicted in Figure 2.12 which incorporates these stages including the strategic planning approach dealt with above, and can serve as a framework for detailed planning and development.

Some of the points to note concerning the life cycle stages are presented below.

1. **Determine objectives**

    There is no business value in establishing information systems unless they will help achieve specified and agreed business objectives.

2. **Identify information to satisfy objectives**

    Once objectives are known it is necessary to determine what information (or knowledge) is required to help achieve them. Particular attention should be given to identifying the type of information which has to be available for success to be achieved; the so-called critical success factors.

3. **Acquire information and knowledge**

    Once the type of information needed is known, possible information sources can be sought. Decisions must be made, for example, as to whether it would be beneficial to acquire certain information rather than consult the external source as and when required. The information seeker has two basic sources available – other people's knowledge and recorded information. Direct interpersonal contact is

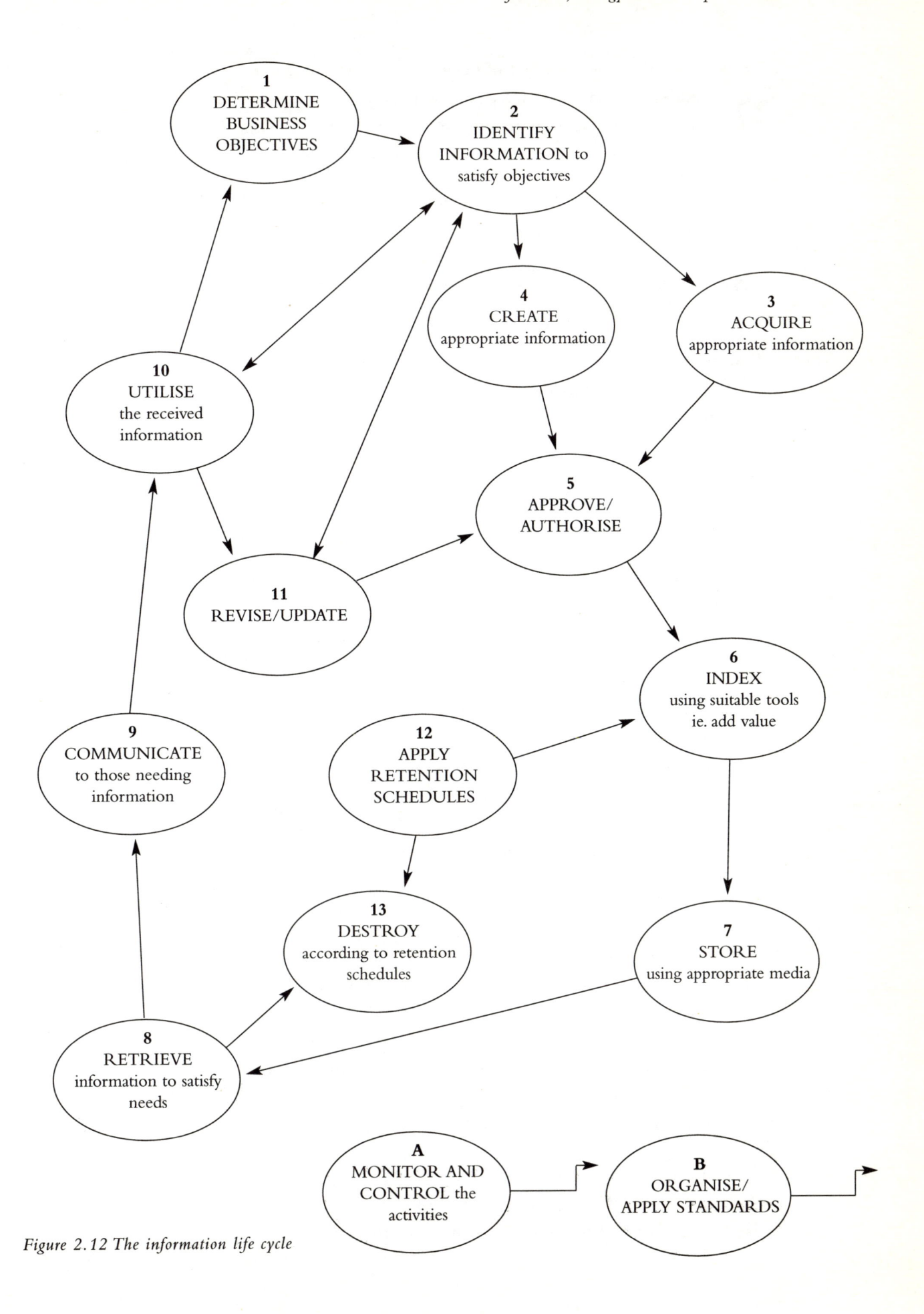

Figure 2.12 The information life cycle

often the quickest and best method of obtaining what is required. It has the advantage that the problem can be discussed and misunderstandings possibly resolved. Aside from people, there is the vast variety of recorded information which is at least theoretically available to the information seeker.

4. **Create information**

    Where the information does not exist, or its acquisition is too difficult or costly, it may need to be created through intellectual effort by knowledgeable people.

5. **Approve/authorise**

    Created, acquired or revised information will need to pass through some approval or authorisation procedure before it is processed or distributed further. The make up of this procedure will depend on the type of document (e.g. quality management manual or engineering drawing) and its intended usage and promulgation.

6. **Index**

    Without adequate indexing and referencing, the information may not be able to be subsequently found.

7. **Store**

    The information acquired or created should be stored using suitable media and storage systems. Thought should be given to the location of the stores, the need for conversion between media, storage life, the legal acceptability of the various media and provision for making security copies (backups) of the information in case the main store of information is destroyed. The knowledge stores of individuals need to be protected by having them recorded in some external physical form available to others.

8. **Retrieve**

    Retrieval systems which enable one to search and extract required information should be appropriate for the particular requirement. Some of the searching will be of acquired and created information held by the person or organisation for example. However, the availability of externally-held information and access methods should be known so that these sources can also be exploited. Publicly available external databases are cases in point.

9. **Communicate**

    Information is of no use if it is not communicated to those who can make use of it. Impediments to information transfer can occur at the source of information, in the transfer channel and with the recipient of the information. These impediments are not simply technologically-based. Thus the originator may have recorded his or her information in a way which the recipient cannot understand, for example by using technical jargon or a foreign language. The overall aim is to ensure that the communication system (source - transfer channel - recipient) will help the information arrive at the right time and in the right form.

10. Utilise

Information and knowledge are of no value unless they are exploited to help achieve particular ends. This is the key activity in the model since it justifies the existence of the whole system. Utilisation may involve simply consulting source information (e.g. by reading recorded information or talking to those with the required knowledge), adding to it, copying or deleting it - or otherwise integrating it in some way to render it more useful and applicable to solving current problems.

11. Revise/update

As necessary, information and knowledge will be updated or revised and will need, as appropriate, to pass through the same approval, indexing, storage cycle as noted above. It may be needed to apply strict version control so that an audit trail is available covering superseded versions, and users may only see the latest, current version, for example.

12. Apply retention schedules

Information that is to be held personally or corporately for example, should have records management principles applied such as retention schedules and security classifications in the case of confidential material. This ensures that information will be available as required to those that have the appropriate right of access, information that is needed is not destroyed and that redundant information can be weeded out of the system.

13. Destroy

Information over which the individual or the organisation has control should have had retention schedules applied to it. This then makes it possible as part of the records management programme to review and as appropriate destroy information which is no longer required for personal, business, legal or historical reasons for example.

A. Monitor and control the life cycle

Irrespective of how efficiently and effectively the above individual activities have been undertaken, the enterprise knowledge management function as a whole will not achieve its potential unless its operation and performance are monitored and controlled. This means that performance measures must be established appropriate to the activity to be monitored. Typical measures might be the speed of response of a computer-based retrieval system, the degree of satisfaction of users with the answers to their queries, the number of documents accessed per week or the percentage of projects completed on time and within budget.

B. Organise/apply standards

The total life cycle must be properly organised as regards people, technology, policies, procedures and tasks and their inter-relationship. Other necessary resources such as finance must be catered for.

REFERENCES IN CHAPTER 2

1. Leavitt, Harold, H., Dill, William R. and Eyring, Henry B., *The Organizational World - A Systematic View of Managers and Management* (New York: Harcourt Brace Jovanovich, 1973)

2. Youngblood, Mark D., *Eating the Chocolate Elephant - Take Charge of Change through Total Process Management* (Richardson, Texas: Micrografx Inc., 1994)

3. Drucker, P.F., *Managing in Turbulent Times* (London: Pan Books, 1981)

4. Naisbitt, J., *Megatrends* (New York: Warner Books, 1982)

5. Strassman, P.A., 'Overview of Strategic Aspects of Information Management', *Office Technology and People,* 1 (1) (March 1982): pp.71-89

6. Delgado, A., *The Enormous File: A Social History of the Office* (London: John Murray, 1979)

7. Reported in Sampson, Anthony, *Company Man - the Rise and Fall of Corporate Life* (London: HarperCollins, 1995), pp. 201-202.

8. Dowler, Rod, reported in 'Future Imperative', *Computing* (18 August 1994), p. 18

9. Porter, M.E., *The Competitive Advantage of Nations* (London: Macmillan Press, 1990)

10. Cronin, B., Cavaye, A. and Davenport, L., 'Competitive Edge and Information Technology', *International Journal of Information Management,* 8 (3) (September 1988), pp. 179-187

11. Zuboff, S., *The Age of the Smart Machine: The Future of Work and Power* (Oxford: Heinemann, 1988)

12. Aguilar, F.J., *Scanning the Business Environment* (New York: Macmillan, 1967)

13. Machlup, F. and Mansfield, U. (eds.), *The Study of Information: Interdisciplinary Messages* (New York: Wiley-Interscience, 1983)

14. Wiggins, B., *Document Imaging - A Management Guide* (Westport: Meckler, 1994)

15. Ang, J. and Pavri, F. A., 'Survey and Critique of the Impacts of Information Technology', *International Journal of Information Management,* 14 (2) (April 1994), pp. 122-133

16 'In a culture like ours long accustomed to splitting and dividing all things as a means of control, it is sometimes a bit of a shock to be reminded that, in operational and practical fact, the medium is the message.' Marshall McLuhan in *Understanding Media,* Part 1, Chapter 1, 1964.

17 Wiggins, R.E., 'A Conceptual Framework for Information Resources Management', *International Journal of Information Management,* 8(1) (March 1988): pp. 5-11.

18 *A Glossary of Computing Terms,* The British Computer Society (Harlow: Longman, 1995)

19 Horton, F.W., Jr., *Information Resources Management: Harnessing Information Assets for Productivity Gains in the Office, Factory and Laboratory* (Englewood Cliffs, N.J.: Prentice Hall, 1985)

20 Varney, J., 'Using a Higher Level of Knowledge', *Business Consultancy* (July 1998), pp. 58-59

21 Checkland, P. and Holwell, S., 'Information Systems: What's The Big Idea?', *Systemist* (The Publication of the United Kingdom Systems Society), 17 (1) (February 1995): pp. 7-13

22 *Computing* (16 April 1997), pp. 36-37

23 *Computing* (28 May 1998), pp. 46-49

24 *European E-Work and Knowledge Management '98,* Rome, March 30-31, 1998, Gartner Group

25 *Managing Information as a Resource* (London: CCTA, 1990)

26 *Principles of Good Practice for Information Management,* DISC PD0010 (London: BSI, 1997)

27 Paperwork Reduction Act, Public Law 104-13 (1995)

28 Oppenheim, C., 'Valuing Information Assets in British Companies', *Records Management Bulletin* (of the UK Records Management Society), Issue 91 (April 1997), pp. 3-7

29 *Guidelines for Directing Information Systems Strategy* (London: CCTA, 1988)

30 The Butler Cox Foundation, *Developing and Implementing a Systems Strategy,* Report Series No.49 (London: Butler Cox, 1985)

31 Wilson, T.D., 'The Implementation of Information Systems Strategies in UK Companies: Aims and Barriers to Success', *International Journal of Information Management,* 9 (4) (December 1989), pp. 245-258

32 Earl, M.J., *Management Strategies for Information Technology* (London: Prentice Hall, 1989)

33 Martin, J., *IT Trends in the Leading 2000,* Applied Learning International (1992).

34 Flood, G., 'Surveying the Foundations', *Information Week,* 18-31 March 1998, pp. 18-25

35 Checkland, P. and Scholes, J., *Soft Systems Methodology in Action* (Chichester: John Wiley & Sons, 1990)

36 Martin, J. and Leben, J., *Strategic Information Planning Methodologies* (Englewood Cliffs, NJ: Prentice-Hall, 1989)

37 *Strategic Planning for Information Systems: ensuring that the business benefits* (Norwich: CCTA, 1989)

38 Avison, D.E. and Wood-Harper, A.T., *Multiview: An Exploration in Information Systems Development* (Oxford: Blackwell Scientific, 1990)

39 Doyle, K.G. and Wood, J.R.G., *Doing the Right Thing Right: A Comparison between Soft Systems Methodology and Jackson System Development,* Proceedings of the ISCR conference, Edinburgh, 1989

40 Robson, W., *Strategic Management of Information Systems* (London: Financial Times Management, 1997)

41 Loucopoulos, P., Black, W.J., Sutcliffe, A.G. and Layzell, P.J., 'Towards a Unified View of System Development Methods', *International Journal of Information Management*, 7 (4) (December 1987), pp. 205-218

3

APPROACHES FOR IMPROVING BUSINESS PERFORMANCE

'I am at my wits' end.' 'Tut, tut; we have solved some worse problems. At least we have plenty of material, if we can only use it.'

The Adventure of the Priory School: Sir Arthur Conan Doyle

In the drive to improve the efficiency and effectiveness of businesses, a variety of methods and methodologies have been developed and applied. (While not wishing to draw a precise distinction between the two - a **method** is more of a **technique** - this being a precise specific programme of action which will produce a standard result. A **methodology** is more of a set of principles which guide action[1]). Each method or methodology has its own particular focus, some being oriented towards business data and its processing, others look out from the organisation to the customer and their needs, while others look inwards at the human resources to see how their contribution to success can be maximised.

In this chapter some of these business improvement approaches of relevance to the application of document management are introduced.

3.1 Structured systems development

The elements of a structured methodology were outlined in section 2.8. Perhaps the best known example is the Structured Systems Analysis and Design Method (SSADM) developed by the United Kingdom Government in 1982 for use in government departments. Since that time it has been adopted by the commercial market and applied in other countries.

SSADM is a data-driven methodology based on the assumption that underlying each business is a relatively unchanging data structure, although processing requirements may change[2]. SSADM provides three main views of the data:

- Logical data structures (LDSs)
- Data flow diagrams (DFDs)
- Entity life histories (ELHs).

Logical data structures (also known outside SSADM as entity-relationship diagrams) are diagrams that specify the information requirements of a system. An LDS shows the entities (objects about which the system must maintain information) and the relationships (associations) that link them.

Data flow diagrams depict the functional requirements of the system being modelled. They partition these requirements into processes and data stores, interconnected by flows.

Entity life histories show how the information is changed during its lifetime.

Each of these views of data has equal importance. They are validated against one another as they are developed in the Requirements Analysis and Requirements Specification modules of SSADM through to detailed logical process design and the conversion to a physical design that can be implemented by suitably written software on the target hardware. A 'logical' design is one which is independent of any physical real-world constraints. The aim of such modelling is to understand the underlying business logic of current practices and processes rather than slavishly represent the actual procedures that are followed, since these may be inappropriate.

Such modelling is invaluable as it provides a far easier means of communicating information than reams of text. The use of automated tools (generally called CASE tools - computer-aided software (or systems) engineering) greatly facilitates the creation and updating of the models.

Figures 3.1 and 3.2 provide examples of a simple data model and process model from the online tutorial for a PC-based CASE tool.[3] (A pack containing an outline data model for a document management system, together with associated guidance material is available from the author. This can assist in designing and developing one's own specification for a document management system.[4])

Beyond these key models, SSADM provides for other types of diagram, for example:

- Enquiry access paths (EAPs) showing the path taken through a logical data structure to satisfy a business enquiry
- Effect correspondence diagrams showing all the entities affected by an event within the system and how these effects impact one another (an event is something which happens to trigger a process on a data flow diagram to update the values or status of the system)

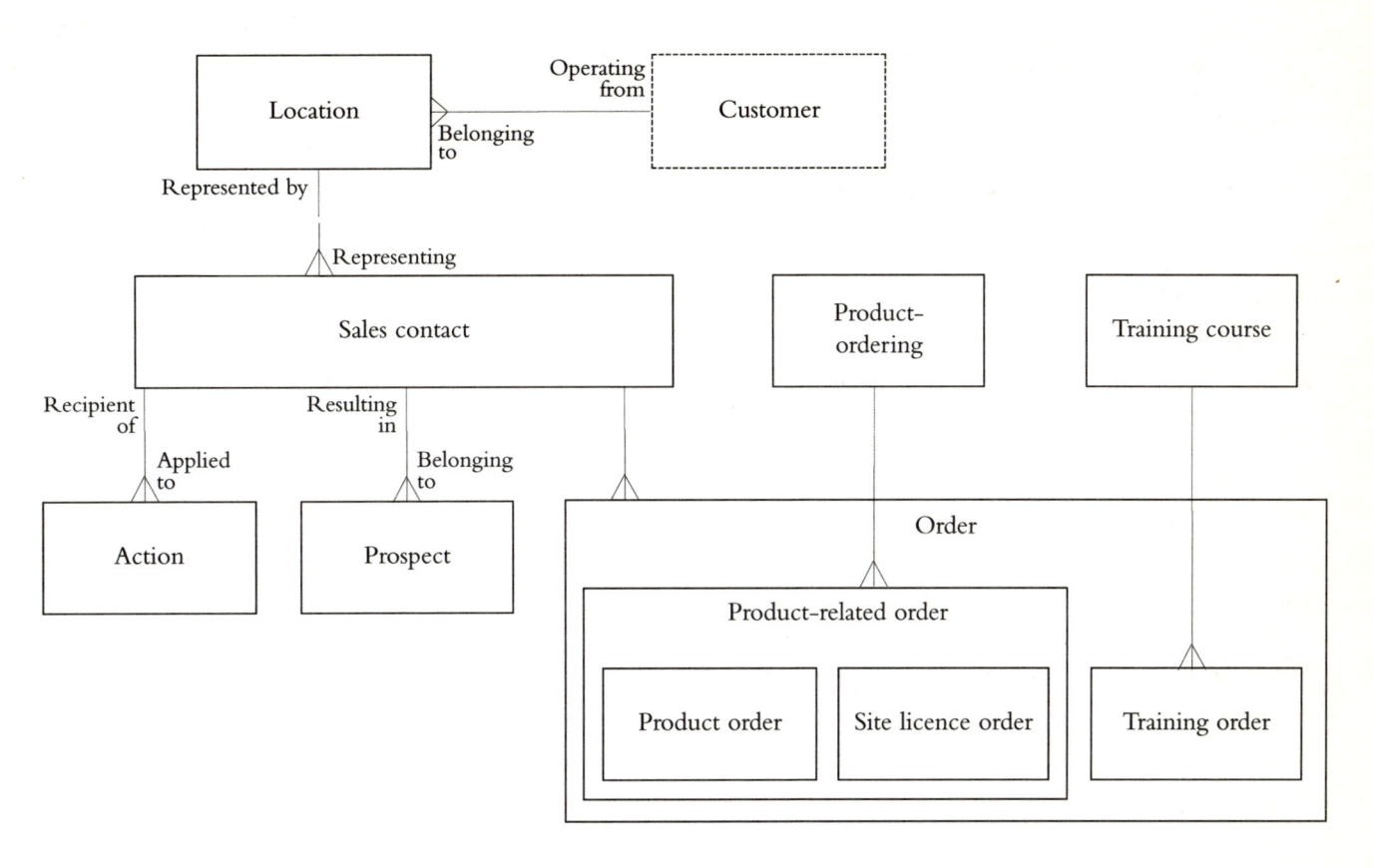

Figure 3.1 Logical data model

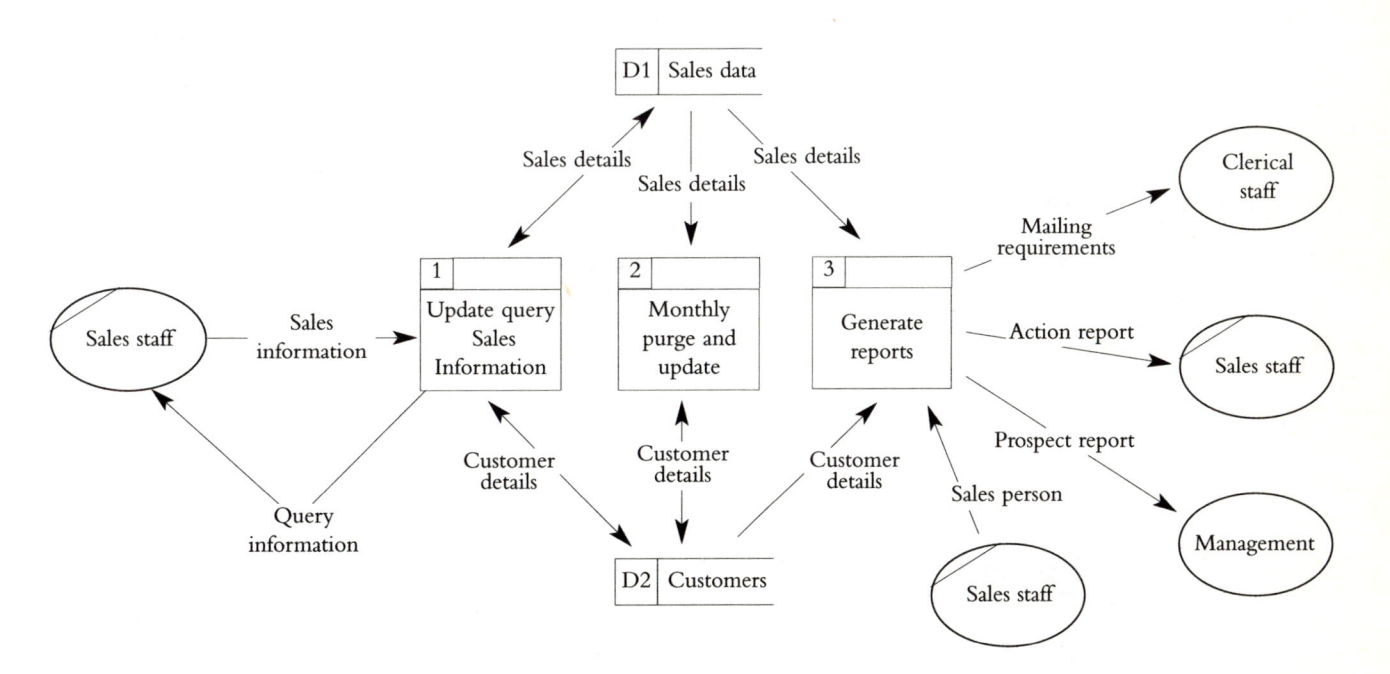

Figure 3.2 Data flow diagram (process model)

◆ Enquiry process model (EPMs) depicts the processing of an enquiry

◆ I/O structures document the input and outputs from a function, or part of a function (a function is a set of system processing which the users wish to schedule together to support their business activity).

Although SSADM, when applied in its full-blown form is a daunting methodology, the two techniques of data and data flow modelling are widely used with minor variations when analysing business information and processing needs. Furthermore SSADM is supported by a range of CASE tools (see section 3.7) and has defined links to the project management technique PRINCE®, which was also designed for use by the UK government and has been adopted elsewhere[4] (see also Chapter 7).

3.2 Dealing with unstructured problems

The focus of most methods and methodologies is on objective and quantitative aspects of a problem area often to the detriment of subjective and qualitative issues. These latter may be the more important factors in deciding the success or otherwise of a project. This problem is compounded if, for example, there is uncertainty in the first place about what are the issues and concerns that need to be addressed. It is in this context of human activity systems that the Soft Systems Methodology (SSM) developed by Checkland has a role to play.[1]

An overview of SSM is provided in Figure 3.3 in which are depicted various stages, some being in the real world, others in the abstract world of systems thinking.

The stages are usually undertaken iteratively rather than in series and comprise the following:[1]

Stage 1 (Real World): The Problem Situation: Unstructured

◆ The first stage involves recognition of a messy situation, identifying elements of relatively slow-to-change *structure* and of continuously-changing *process*. It is important to avoid imposing a particular form to the situation; it is necessary to think about the roles of the client, problem-owner and problem-solver.

Stage 2 (Real World): The Problem Situation: Expressed

◆ Here a 'Rich Picture' (a hand-drawn cartoon) is produced which incorporates hard factual and soft subjective information; structure and processes and their interaction; people and players involved; tensions and conflicts. The aim of the Rich Picture is to help identify new ways of viewing the situation and to draw from it *primary tasks* (these being tasks that the organisation in question was established to

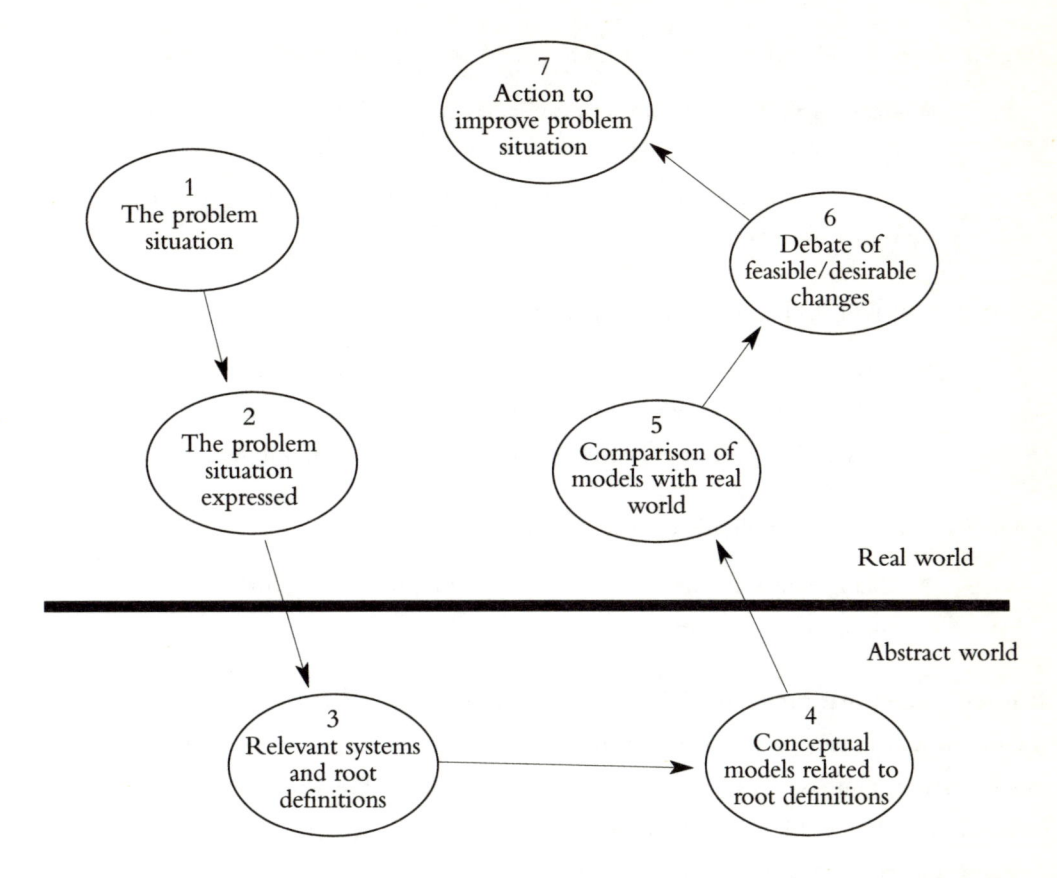

Figure 3.3 The stages of the soft systems methodology

perform, or tasks which are essential for survival) and *issues* (matters of concern or which are the subject of dispute). Figure 2.5 (p. 18) has many of the elements of a Rich Picture for the problem domain of managing information resources.

Stage 3 (Abstract World): Relevant Systems and Root Definitions

◆ Here the aim is not to identify what systems need to be engineered or improved, but rather what are the names of notional systems which from the analysis phase seem relevant to the problem. Having identified such systems they are defined more formally by way of *root definitions* (RD) - a concise, tightly constructed description of a human activity system which states what the system is.

Stage 4 (Abstract World): Conceptual Models

◆ A graphical model is built on the basis of the chosen root definition and comprises a structured set of *activities* expressed as verbs. They are justified purely on logical terms, not by mapping on to the real world.

Stage 5 (Real World): Comparison of Conceptual Model with Reality

- Back in the real world one now looks for similarities and differences between the conceptual model from Stage 4 and the real-world situation from Stage 2; the results of the comparison are recorded and topics are identified for discussion.

Stage 6 (Real World): Debate Feasible and Desirable Changes

- A structured discussion is undertaken with those involved - e.g. client, problem-owner(s) and problem-solver(s) - with the aim of identifying ideas which are both systemically desirable and culturally feasible.

Stage 7 (Real World): Implement Agreed Changes

- Changes may involve changes in structure, procedures or in attitudes and are implemented if agreed.

It is recognised that the methodology does not provide explicit advice concerning implementation as the problem areas that may be the subject of study can be completely different in nature. Thus one problem may relate to human conflicts in an organisation, while another may be to identify the most suitable business area for piloting a document imaging project. The actions that need to be taken following agreement at Stage 7 will therefore differ widely.

SSM is a well-established methodology and has had wide application across government and commerce.[5] It is an assembly of principles applied at different stages, and it is perfectly possible to utilise parts of the process in isolation, such as drawing a Rich Picture to clarify issues, or formulating a root definition to firm up on the scope of a software development project. The intellectual process of devising a root definition is worth considering further.

3.2.1 Root definitions

As mentioned earlier, the root definition is a concise, tightly constructed description of a human activity system which states what the system is. It needs to contain certain elements, these being:

- Customer(s) of the system - those who will benefit (or be the victim of) the system's activities

- Actor(s) - person(s) who carry out one or more of the activities in the system

- Transformation - this is the key feature of the definition and refers to the core transformation process of the human activity system, i.e. the process of converting input(s) into output(s)

- ◆ Weltanschauung (or world view) – the unquestioned image of model or the world which makes the particular human activity system a meaningful one to consider

- ◆ Owner(s) of the system – those who have sufficient power over the system to cause its demise

- ◆ Environment – constraints which the system has to take as given.

The initial letters of these elements form the mnemonic CATWOE to identify these six crucial characteristics which should be included in a well-formulated root definition.

To demonstrate its use, the following root definition was devised for an Oil Company wishing to establish an engineering document management project (names have been changed):

> *'The Operations Technical Document Management System within ABC Oil Company PLC is a facility run on behalf of the Engineering Directorate, by the Operations Documentation Unit, to provide accurate and up-to-date technical documentation to satisfy the business needs of Operations Division. The system ensures the effective storage, ready availability, easy access and timely provision of the required documentation whilst operating within legislative and company policy constraints'.*

Analysing the RD using CATWOE indicates:

- ◆ Customer(s) – staff of the Operations Division

- ◆ Actor(s) – staff of the Operations Documentation Unit

- ◆ Transformation – to take inputs of documentation (possibly inaccurate, out-of-date, poorly stored and not readily available) and transform into outputs of accurate and up-to-date documentation readily accessible and delivered when required

- ◆ Weltanschauung – the view that a system (in this case envisaged to be computer-based) will improve the management of engineering documents

- ◆ Owner(s) – the Engineering Directorate

- ◆ Environment – legislative and company policy constraints.

Another example (again sanitised) relates to a text and publishing study undertaken for a UK government department:

> *'A system with responsibility owned by Business Services Department concerned with internally-generated and externally-sourced text-based information (and founded on the developed and promulgated Departmental information*

management strategy) to ensure that the active and passive needs of Departmental staff and management for text-based information are determined and satisfied, assisted by computer-based technology to integrate text/information life cycle activities across the Department consistent with overall Departmental strategy, policy, resource constraints and the requirements of Open Government.'

Analysing the RD using CATWOE indicates:

- Customer(s) - departmental staff and management

- Actor(s) - Business Services Department (and departmental staff and management, e.g. to indicate relevance of information)

- Transformation - presently poorly defined user needs are determined and unsatisfied needs are satisfied assisted by IT and integration of the text-based information across the information life cycle

- Weltanschauung - the application of information technology and improved strategic relationships will facilitate information provision

- Owner - Business Services Department (the precise ownership was still subject of debate)

- Environment - strategy and resource constraints and the pressure placed on the department by policy changes and the need to balance internal and external requirements through open government.

3.3 APPROACHES BASED ON QUALITY

Quality as typically associated with quality systems[6] and total quality management (TQM)[7] has not always had a good press for it is often held to be synonymous with bureaucracy and the burden of unnecessary paperwork. Given the adage that 'every problem presents an opportunity', it is now well recognised that document management technology can help ease this burden by providing automated support for quality system records. However, the application of such technology in this way is not the immediate intended focus of this section, but rather how the principles behind the quality movement are helpful in improving business performance and providing opportunities to deploy document management systems.

Quality can be simply stated as *'Conformance with user's requirements'* and a quality management system as *'An integrated business system to ensure that quality products or services are produced or supplied'*.

Quality management standards provide the necessary models of quality management systems for one's own use.

The models can:

- ♦ facilitate the design, implementation and improvement of one's quality management system

- ♦ serve as a yardstick against which to test one's quality management system

- ♦ serve as a benchmark to demonstrate competence to others.

There are two main types of quality standard:

- ♦ those produced for guidance; an example being that for TQM[7]

- ♦ those produced as specifications; these are more demanding and involve achieving proved compliance as exemplified by that for quality systems.[6]

In addition to these quality standards, companies striving for world class status have available to them a wider range of approaches to measure their activities against best practice and best-in-class performance. The past few years have seen a dramatic increase in the number of award programmes throughout the world, generally as a result of increased awareness of the need for quality as a key factor in productivity and competitiveness. Hence many governments, associations and organisations have implemented quality award programmes.

For a few companies, quality awards present the opportunity for national or international recognition. For most, however, the application process itself has been seen as worthwhile because it requires a thorough examination of the company's strengths and identifies opportunities for continuous improvement.

In the UK a study was undertaken[8] to identify the main types of award - each or all of which can contribute to the development of world class companies. It was estimated that there are now over 80 quality award programmes in 33 countries and over half of these have been created since 1990.

The study identified:

- ♦ The Deming Prize

- ♦ The European Quality Award

- ♦ The Malcolm Baldrige National Quality Award

- ♦ Investors in People National Standard in the UK

50   *Enterprise Knowledge – the Business Resource*

- The UK Quality Award
- The UK Citizen's Charter - Charter Mark Scheme
- The Best Factory Awards
- The National Training Award
- ISO 9000 (BS5750) Quality Systems.

There is some commonality of approach. For example the UK Quality Award is administered by the British Quality Foundation, which is a not-for-profit membership organisation that promotes business excellence to private and public sector organisations in the UK. Winners of the 1998 award included Nortel networks and BT.

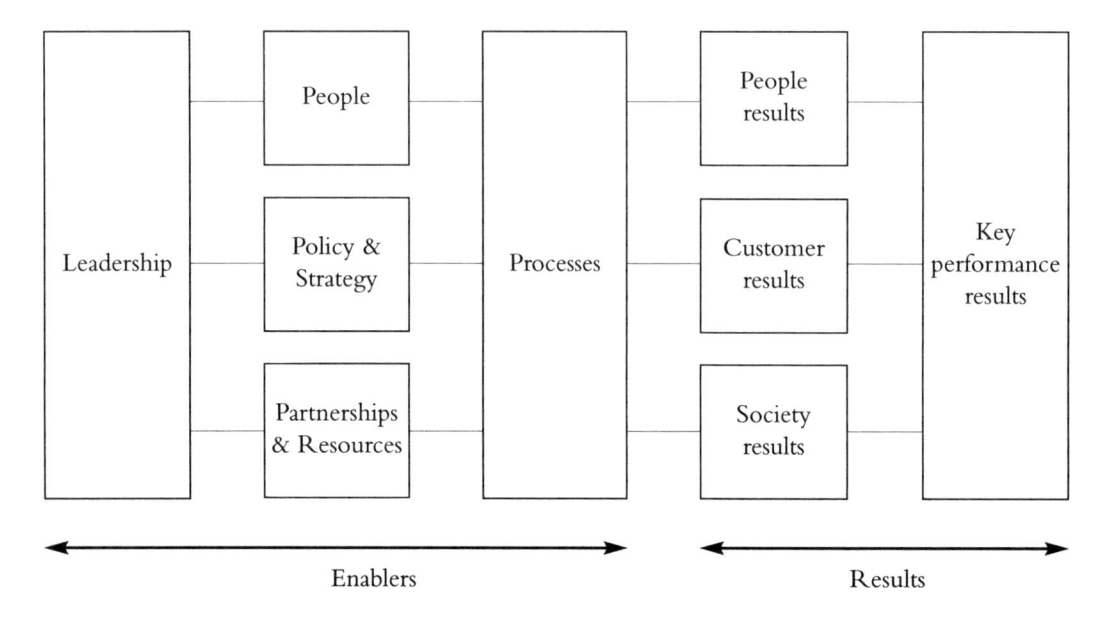

The foundation's business excellence model (see Figure 3.4) is based on that developed by the European Foundation for Quality Management for its European Quality Award. The model has been validated by several hundred companies throughout Europe, and its nine elements are identified as the key components of business excellence. The enablers are concerned with what is done to run the organisation and how it is operated. The results are concerned with what the organisation has achieved and is achieving, as seen by the stakeholders: customers, employees, the community and those who fund the organisation.

The foundation also provides three software tools called ASSESS RapidScore, TeamScore and ValidScore. They are designed to help self-assessment by organisations and to develop planned improvement activities.

A useful summary of approaches to achieving business excellence and of associated user experiences was documented by The Industrial Society.[9]

Figure 3.4 Business excellence model

For many organisations obtaining certification to ISO 9001 (or ISO 9002 if one is not concerned with the design process) is just the first step in a process of continuous improvement. As an aid to improving customer satisfaction and reducing costs within an organisation, a new guide on how to determine the relevant quality management techniques was issued in 1999.[10]

It should be noted that the current ISO 9000 family, which comprises over 20 standards, will be reduced to three quality management standards:[11]

◆ ISO 9000: 2000 (QMS - Fundamentals and Vocabulary)

◆ ISO 9001: 2000 (QMS - Requirements)

◆ ISO 9004: 2000 (QMS - Guidance for Performance Improvement).

A small number of additional standards, technical reports and brochures will address specific issues. Publication of the final documents is scheduled for the fourth quarter of 2000.

The revisions will draw upon the results of a survey in which users were asked to give their priorities for improving on the current standards and incorporation in the revisions. The top seven requested improvements covered: simpler language and terminology, easier integration into one management system, continuous improvement, a process model approach, better compatibility with other management system standards, customer satisfaction and business orientation.

3.3.1 *The process orientation of quality*

The basic building block is the 'business process', defined in the TQM standard, as:

> *'an activity that accepts an "input" of some kind, adds value through doing something and produces an "output"'.*

The process will require some resources to operate such as people or machinery and will also need some form of management control. A simple supply chain is depicted in Figure 3.5.

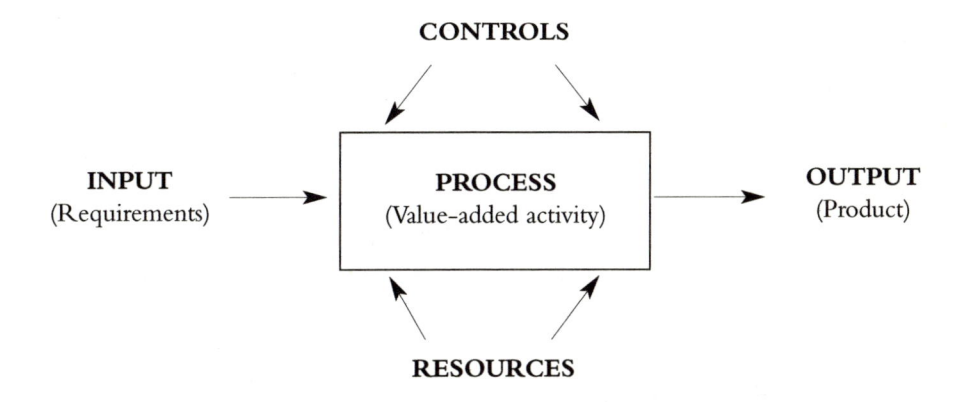

Figure 3.5 A simple supply chain process model

Even from a superficial examination this model is insufficiently rich to mirror the complexities of real life in a business. For example:

- Who are the suppliers?
- Who designs the product or service?
- Who is controlling the processes so that things are produced on time to budget and to specification?
- Is there compliance with regulatory requirements?

A more complete supply chain is shown in Figure 3.6 and incorporates, for example, specification of customer requirement, planning, training and delivery.

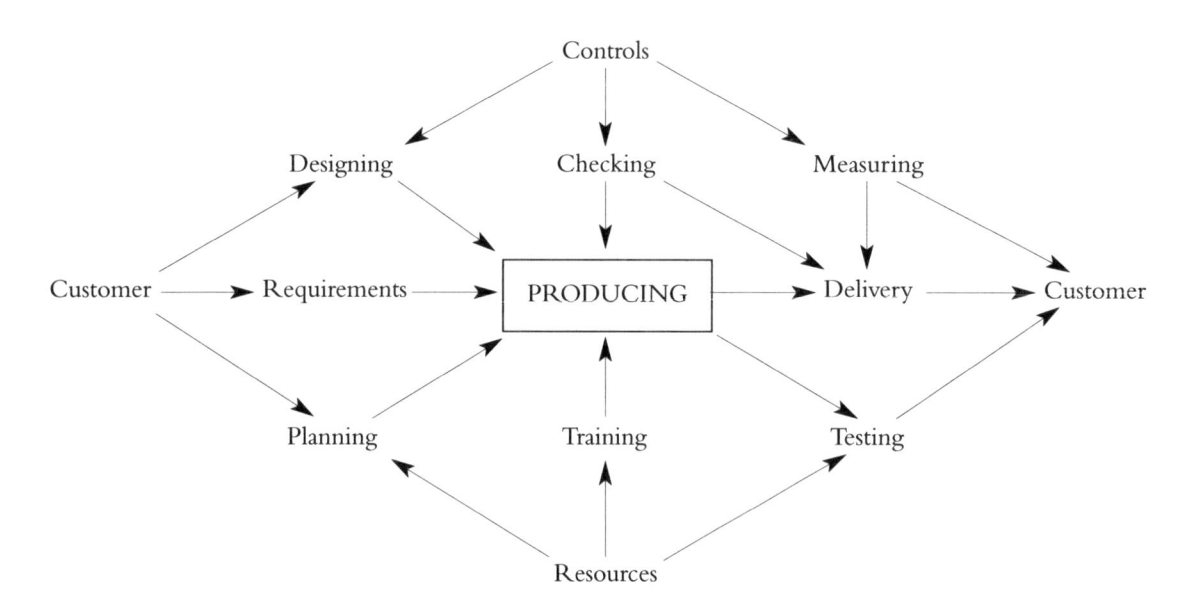

Figure 3.6 An expanded supply chain

The topic of business processes is returned to in section 3.4 which covers business process re-engineering.

3.3.2 Tools and techniques

The TQM standard[7] states that *'Decisions based on the analysis of situation and data play a leading role in quality-improvement projects and activities. Success of quality-improvement projects and activities is enhanced by proper application of tools and techniques developed for these purposes'*.

To this end the standard includes details of tools and techniques as summarised in Table 3.1.

TECHNIQUES	DESCRIPTION
Data collection form	A method of systematically gathering data to provide a clear picture of the facts.
Affinity diagram	Used to organise a large number of ideas or issues to form a picture.
Benchmarking	Comparing a process against those of recognised leaders to identify opportunities for quality improvement.
Brainstorming	Identifying possible opportunities and possible solutions to problems.
Cause and effect (fishbone) diagram	Analysis of relationships to assess possible causes of defects
Flowchart	Displays a process pictorially for improved understanding.
Tree diagram	Displays logical relationships of elements to identify root causes.
Control charts	Monitor performance of a process against a statistical background to help set and assess improvement actions.
Histograms	Display of data to show variables against a common background.
Pareto diagram	Display of data ranking significant factors in priority order.
Scatter diagram	Graphical technique for assessing data to establish a relationship.

Table 3.1 Techniques to aid quality and process improvement[7]

3.3.3 Quality records

Clause 4.16 of ISO 9001[6] includes the requirement that:

> *'The supplier shall establish and maintain documented procedures for identification, collection, indexing, access, filing, storage, maintenance and disposition of quality records.'*

> *'All quality records shall be legible and shall be stored and retained in such a way that they are readily retrievable in facilities that provide a suitable environment to prevent damage or deterioration and to prevent loss. Retention times of quality records shall be established and recorded.'*

> A note to this Clause states *'Records may be in the form of any type of media, such as hard copy or electronic media.'*

Clause 4.5.2 of the standard covers 'Document and Data Approval and Issue' and includes the requirement that:

> *'The document and data shall be reviewed and approved for adequacy by authorised personnel prior to issue. A master list or equivalent document control procedure identifying the current revision status of documents shall be established and be readily available to preclude the use of invalid and/or obsolete documents.'*

These requirements are no more, or no less than good, common sense practice for managing a company's recorded information; a topic returned to in Chapter 4 when records and document management are considered.

3.4 BUSINESS PROCESS RE-ENGINEERING

Defining what is meant by 'business process re-engineering' (BPR) presents almost the same problem as defining 'information' or 'data' since there is no general agreement or standardisation of the terminology. Originating from the pen of Michael Hammer[12] BPR has been variously defined as:

> 'The provision of techniques for re-designing the processes needed for change (limited by some to radical change)'[13]

> 'The dramatic and discontinuous change to business processes; a complete re-invention of how work is done'[14]

> 'The fundamental analysis and radical redesign of everything - business processes and management systems, job definitions, organisational structures - to achieve dramatic performance improvements to meet contemporary requirements'[15]

> 'The constant search for, and implementation of, radical new approaches to business practice leading to step change improvements in productivity and customer service'[16]

In this volatile context there is a need to clarify the meaning of BPR and its application. Thus the US Government General Sciences Administration (GSA) created the Government Business Process Reengineering (BPR) Readiness Assessment because *'of the critical need for Federal agencies to identify factors essential to successful BPR at the earliest possible stage before making major investments in time, money and human resources'* [17] The GSA go on to caution against taking

> 'a project labelled "BPR" or "reengineering" at face value. Some of these actually represent a more incremental approach to change, while others change administrative, rather than core processes. The "process improvement" industry has so broadened the definition of "BPR" as to render it nearly meaningless. So let the BPR buyer beware of case studies of BPR projects that aren't BPR at all'.

Readiness assessment is based upon the following key definitions:

- ◆ Business process is a specific ordering of work activities across time and place, with a beginning, an end, and clearly defined inputs and outputs that deliver value to customers.

- ◆ BPR is the fundamental rethinking and radical redesign of business core processes to bring about dramatic improvements in performance.

Despite the confusion over BPR, there have been attempts to draw out some fundamental characteristics, for example re-engineering projects are seen[18] to have five main objectives:

- achieving step changes in performance
- moving from functional to process capability
- emphasising customers' importance
- integrating work
- developing a process-management culture.

Viewing these objectives dispassionately, many of them are the focus of attention in other approaches as noted in earlier sections, thus:

- The concept of process is key in TQM
- Processes are important in structured system development methodologies as exemplified by data flow diagrams in SSADM
- Transformation of inputs into outputs is at the core of root definitions in the soft systems methodology
- The soft systems methodology considers processes independently of any real world functional structures
- SSADM focuses on logical rather than real world physical processes thereby encouraging integration of work
- The emphasis on processes in these other business improvements approaches encourages changes in management culture
- Meeting customer requirements is central in quality system and quality management standards.

The main differentiating factor between BPR and these other approaches is the emphasis it places on achieving 'step changes', i.e. dramatic, shorter term improvements. It is probably this factor more than the others that has caused BPR to catch the imagination of business managers and executives - helped also by having a catchy title and a three letter mnemonic that rolls readily off the tongue. Presenting BPR in this way is not in any way intended to downgrade the contribution it has and can make. The aim is merely to set BPR in context as one approach to improving business performance.

BPR can be seen as a complementary approach to TQM with benefits of applying them together in an integrated way.[13,14] A comparison of BPR and TQM is presented in Figure 3.7.

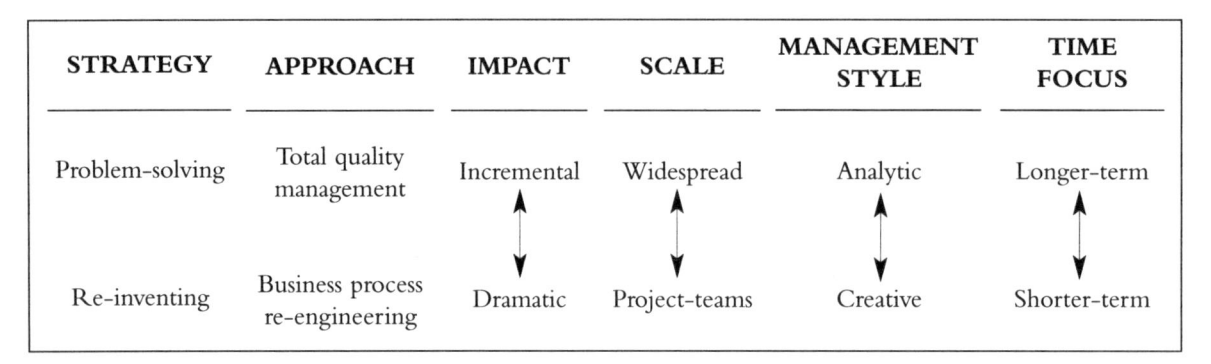

STRATEGY	APPROACH	IMPACT	SCALE	MANAGEMENT STYLE	TIME FOCUS
Problem-solving	Total quality management	Incremental ↕	Widespread ↕	Analytic ↕	Longer-term ↕
Re-inventing	Business process re-engineering	Dramatic	Project-teams	Creative	Shorter-term

Figure 3.7 A comparison of TQM and BPR

Notwithstanding the relatively high rates of failure that BPR projects have suffered, the emphasis on process analysis and improvement in organisations continues. This has tended to mask and effectively devalue the importance of the esssential complementary approach of data analysis and data modelling (see reference 4), defects which are less easy to correct than those encountered in processes. Without proper consideration of such factors as indexing and retrieval requirements in support of business processes, the underlying data model will be inadequate for the task. This can impair the ability to integrate systems: for example, linking seamlessly document management systems with line-of-business systems, such as those concerned with enterprise resource planning (e.g. SAP and PeopleSoft).

3.4.1 Information technology and BPR

Appropriate deployment of information technology is undoubtedly one of the critical success factors in improving business performance (recall from section 2.1 the importance of 'tools' - long recognised as one of the four structural elements of an organisation). However, as already noted in section 2.7, it is important to have a business-driven strategy for deploying technologies. The lessons learnt from BPR are not new, but are now more coherent and capable of application, thanks to:

◆ the availability of more flexible and configurable systems development environments (both in terms of software and project management)

◆ the increasing realisation by IT staff and their management that they can no longer remain aloof from the business but must be intimately involved with their 'customers' in systems development and responsiveness to change – if appropriate by adopting a 'laboratory approach' (see Table 3.2).

BPR is potentially addressing any, or all of the processes undertaken in an organisation, hence the full gamut of IT may need to be drawn upon. However, some technologies are more relevant than others, these having been identified by one study[19] as groupware technologies encompassing:

CONVENTIONAL APPROACH	LABORATORY APPROACH
Business people know what they want in advance	Business people know what they want only when they experience it
Requirements are right first time	Requirements evolve through learning
Changes are minimised or even frozen during development	Major changes will be introduced throughout development
IT development teams meet periodically with system users	IT and business staff develop the system and procedures in joint teams
The user organisation adjusts to the needs of the new system	Organisational changes are modelled long before implementation

Table 3.2 A comparison of conventional and laboratory approaches to systems development[18]

- workflow management
- information sharing
- scheduling
- electronic conferencing
- task management
- computer-aided decision making.

Processes such as workflow, information access, distribution and sharing are key elements of many document management applications. It is clear then that document management can have an important place in delivering benefits from BPR projects. However, for success the emphasis should not so much be on managing existing documents 'better', but rather on eliminating documents in the first place.

3.5 PEOPLE APPROACHES

Noteworthy in the definitions for BPR reproduced above are words like:

- radical
- redesign
- dramatic
- discontinuous

- re-invention
- step-changes
- productivity.

Such words are highly emotive, and coupled with the concept of down-sizing - attributed to Stephen Roach, a US government economist - are not normally ones thought to engender hope, enthusiasm and commitment in the hearts of employees. Down-sizing is not now viewed favourably having increasingly received a bad press, and Roach himself has since recanted.[20,21]

The Business Intelligence report[18] in a survey of those who have completed BPR programmes found that:

- 58% recorded either no increases in job motivation or satisfaction or improvement of up to only 10%
- 22% of organisations have reduced jobs by a quarter or more (although 55% of organisations experienced no job reductions or only 10% or less of the original workforce)
- loss of jobs, changes in authority, responsibilities, and career prospects pose problems at every level
- the stiffest resistance to change is likely to be encountered in the ranks of middle management.

Clearly any move to improve business efficiency along the lines of BPR, that is the 'process' element of Leavitt's 4-element model (see section 2.1), will have a major knock-on affect on the organisation's staff and management. To help ensure a balance between process, tools, people and structure considerable attention will need to be given to people.

One move on this front is the Investors in People National Standard influenced by the UK Confederation of British Industry and derived through examining the human resources practices in business. The standard is founded on four principles:

- commitment
- planning
- action
- evaluation.

Assessment for an award involves a review of a portfolio of written evidence and on-site interviews and is undertaken by independent, trained assessors. The award is managed by

Investors in People UK Ltd and co-ordinated by a network of training agencies across the UK. The principles of Investors in People overlap with key aspects of various other awards.[8]

3.6 Organisational cultures

Whenever change is involved it is important to undertake the process in a way which takes account of the particular culture of the organisation. This is not the place to enter into detail on this topic and readers are referred to the works of others.[22,23] As a taster, Table 3.3 provides an overview of organisation cultures based largely on Handy's study of organisations.[24] This included three main cultures based on power, role and task. It would seem acceptable to equate role with 'function' and task with 'process'.

3.7 Automated support tools

So-called CASE (computer-aided software - or systems - engineering) tools have long been available to provide automated support for system development methodologies. When initially introduced, CASE tools were marketed as the solution to the development backlog. Although these early promises of vast productivity increases were not wholly fulfilled, CASE technology is maturing and becoming more widely available as the power of affordable PCs increases.

With the coming of BPR and workflow, and the continuing interest in quality and other business excellence models, the range of tools to support analysis, design and development continues to expand. These range from relatively inexpensive flow charting packages often with in-built data capture and process analysis capabilities supporting the kinds of techniques summarised in Table 3.1, to simulation packages, knowledge and process repositories and workflow products, the latter often being embedded in document management systems.

Information about the low-end tools may be found in the occasional reviews undertaken by many of the computer magazines found on newsagents' shelves. More detailed reviews of the higher-end power tools that support re-engineering, redesign and management of business processes are available from those focused on watching this specialised sector.[25]

Culture	Description	Factors affecting the choice of culture					
		History & ownership	Size	Technology	Goals & objectives	The environment	The people
Power	Web-like structure. Depends on: - central power source - trust and empathy for effectiveness - telepathy & personal conversation for communication Characteristics: - few rules/procedures - reacts well to threat & danger - resources are main power base - take pride in their results. Suited to: Policy and Crisis activities in organisation	Centralised ownership. Family firms. Aggressive & independent new organisation.	Small entrepreneurial. Grow by web-linking series of role (temple) structures.	Non-continuous discrete operations; unit production. Rapidly changing technologies.	Growth goals important.	Threat or danger (e.g. mergers, economic disaster).	Power-oriented. Politically minded. Risk-taking. Skills and talents have greater impact.
Role (Function)	Temple-like structure. Depends on: - functions or specialities as its pillars - procedures for roles and communication - rules for settling disputes Characteristics: - succeeds in stable environment where economies of scale more important than flexibility - slow to react to change - frustrating for power-oriented individuals - take pride in their process Suited to: Steady-state activities in organisation	New generation of managers espousing 'systems instead of politics'.	Larger organisations.	Routine programmable operations. High-cost technologies requiring monitoring, expertise. Integrated tasks requiring co-ordination.	Product quality important.	Stable environment. Standardisation	Persons with low tolerance for ambiguity. Those seeking clear career ladder. Position-oriented people. Technical expertise.
Task (Process)	Net-like structure. Depends on: - expert power rather than position or personal power - unifying nature of teams Characteristics: - adaptable, reactive - works quickly - control difficult - inherently unstable - tends to change to a power or role/function culture Suited to: Innovation activities in organisation	Flexible, adaptive new organisations. New generation of managers espousing 'efficiency not bureaucracy'.	Smaller organisations. Project-oriented departments.	Non-continuous discrete operations; unit production. Rapidly changing technologies.	Growth goals important.	Changes in the market or the product. Diversity in the environment.	Judgement by results.

Table 3.3 An analysis of organisational cultures (based on Handy[24])

REFERENCES IN CHAPTER 3

1. Checkland, Peter, *Systems Thinking, Systems Practice* (Chichester: John Wiley & Son, 1985)
2. Goodland, Mike and Slater, Caroline, *SSADM - A Practical Approach* (Chichester: McGraw-Hill, 1995)
3. Select SSADM Professional CASE Tool, From: Select Software Tools (acquired by Princeton Softech Inc., see http://www.princetonsoftech.com)
4. *Document Management Data Model - A Starter Pack* (details from Cura Consortium Ltd, Timbers, Broadlands Road, Burgess Hill, West Sussex RH15 0BG, UK)
5. Checkland, Peter and Scholes, Jim, *Soft Systems Methodology in Action* (Chichester: John Wiley & Sons, 1990)
6. *BS EN ISO 9001: 1994, Quality Systems - Model for Quality Assurance in Design, Development, Production, Installation and Servicing* (ISO 9002 covers the same ground but excludes Design)
7. *BS 7850 Part 2: 1994, Total Quality Management Part 2 Guidelines for Quality Improvement*
8. *Towards World Class Performance* (Humberside Training and Enterprise Council, 1994)
9. 'Business Excellence', *Making Best Practice,* No. 25, July 1996 (The Industrial Society)
10. *PD ISO/TR 10014: 1999, Guidelines for Managing the Economics of Quality*
11. See ISO Website http://www.iso.ch
12. Hammer, M., 'Re-engineering Work: Don't Automate, Obliterate', *Harvard Business Review* (July-August 1990), p. 107
13. Born, Gary, *Process Management to Quality Improvement* (Chichester: John Wiley & Sons, 1994)
14. Youngblood, Mark D., *Eating the Chocolate Elephant - Take Charge of Change through Total Process Management* (Richardson, Texas: Micrografx Inc., 1994)
15. Definition provided by Lucas Industries in Harvey, David, *Re-engineering: the Critical Success Factors* (London: Business Intelligence Ltd, 1995)
16. Quoted in Miers, Derek, *Process Product Watch, Volume 3, Business Modelling & Analysis Tools in BPR* (Richmond: Enix Ltd, 1994)
17. See Website http://www.itpolicy.gsa.gov/mkm/bpr/
18. Harvey, David, *Re-engineering: the Critical Success Factors* (London: Business Intelligence, 1995)
19. Bartram, Peter, *The Groupware Report 93* (London: Business Intelligence, 1993)
20. Jackson, Tony, 'Now It's a Case of Dumbsizing', *Financial Times,* 20 May 1996, p. 10
21. Bidmead, Chris, 'Down to Earth', *Microscope,* 3 July 1996, p. 34-35
22. Handy, Charles, *The Age of Unreason* (London: Arrow Books, 1990)
23. Leavitt, Harold H., Dill, William R. and Eyring, Henry B., *The Organizational World - A Systematic View of Managers and Management* (New York: Harcourt Brace Jovanovich, 1973)
24. Handy, Charles, *Understanding Organisations* (London: Penguin, 1993)
25. *Process Product Watch* available on subscription from Enix Ltd, 3 The Green, Richmond, Surrey, TW9 1PL

4

RECORDS MANAGEMENT AND DOCUMENT MANAGEMENT

*'Ay, thou poor ghost, while memory holds a seat
In this distracted globe. Remember thee?
Yea, from the table of my memory
I'll wipe away all trivial fond records,
All saws of books, all forms, all pressures past,
That youth and observation copied there.'*

Hamlet, Act 1, Scene 5: William Shakespeare

Dealing with the minutiae of managing corporate records such as filing and weeding out ever-expanding, space-hungry filing cabinets is an unglamorous task rendered imperceptibly more acceptable if these records reside in electronic form on a PC's hard disk. Yet business records, be they documents or data, are important to an organisation. At some time or another someone will want to find that particular piece of information, yet it may no longer be in existence, or of it is, it cannot be traced.

This chapter contains an explanation of the key concepts of records and document management and presents a survey and analysis approach to identify, quantify and address records and document management problems.

4.1 WHAT ARE RECORDS?

A dictionary definition of a record is: *'A piece of recorded evidence or information; an account of fact preserved in permanent form'*.

More specifically in the corporate context, a record is created or received by a company in the course of undertaking a business action. The feature that distinguishes a record from any other information is the fact that it provides evidence of the action required, requested, or taken and of the consequences which follow. The continuing business activity of the company is therefore reflected in an integrated series of records.

What constitutes business archives will depend to a large extent on the view of the organisation which holds such records. To the professional archivist they would typically comprise *'records no longer required for the routine administration of the company, but which are nonetheless deemed worthy of permanent preservation on administrative, legal, fiscal, operational or historical grounds'*.[1]

Records may be in any form (e.g. as books, reports, drawings, forms, correspondence), may contain any type of information (e.g. text, numbers, photographs) and may be stored on any media (e.g. microfilm, paper, magnetic disk, optical disk).

Records can be contained in manual or computerised systems which in turn may be concerned, for example, with transaction processing, provision of management information, or decision making.

Records may be active or live when they are in frequent use and physically accessible within a working area, or from that area via, for example, a computer terminal. They may become inactive when less frequently used, and are no longer liable to change.

Certain records are considered vital as without them an organisation would encounter major operational or legal problems.

It should be noted that physical objects such as test samples or models represent records of a different kind which, although seemingly outside the scope of this book, may embody information of importance. Such information could, for example, be captured as a photograph or video recording for use in a document management system.

4.2 THE NEED FOR RECORDS MANAGEMENT

Records are information in tangible form, and as such should be appropriately managed throughout the information life cycle described in section 2.11. Some may question the need for such action, but consider the position of an organisation where:

- ◆ accounting records are destroyed in a fire and details of major creditors are lost

- ◆ 'as-built' engineering drawings cannot be found quickly enough to deal with emergency maintenance on a chemical plant

- ◆ papers vital for the defence in a court action are not to be found in the defending organisation's files

- ◆ records that relate to one another are held on different media such as paper, microfilm and computer hard disk and cannot be effectively integrated to provide the complete picture

◆ reports are produced to no standard format and referencing system, thereby hindering their storage and retrieval

◆ forms are created without due thought as to their intended use and value thereby proliferating rather than saving paperwork

◆ the hard disks on personal workstations are filling up with unorganised word-processed documents and spreadsheets with no thought as to their value for retention

◆ it fails to meet the 'Good Manufacturing Practices' documentation requirements laid down by the US Food and Drug Administration for pharmaceutical plant.

Records management aims to address such issues through the management and control of an organisation's records irrespective of the medium on which they are stored, and of their source.

While records management issues have generally been dealt with comprehensively in the literature,[2,3] many organisations lack a records management strategy, the elements of which are shown in Figure 4.1.

RECORDS MANAGEMENT STRATEGY		
RECORDS SURVEY AND ANALYSIS	RECORDS DESIGN	RECORDS RETENTION SCHEDULING
RECORDS MEDIA AND STORAGE SELECTION	RETRIEVAL SYSTEMS SELECTION	SYSTEMS IMPLEMENTATION
RECORDS ADMINISTRATION AND CONTROL		

Figure 4.1 The elements of records management

The key role that records management can play in improving the management of information is, however, being acknowledged at national levels. Thus the Paperwork Reduction Act in the United States requires government agencies to incorporate records management and archival functions into the design, development and implementation of information systems, to ensure that records can be accessed irrespective of form or medium, and to provide records management training of agency staff. In the UK the Government's Treasury Department promulgated in the past good records management practice through its Records Management Programme and a series of guidance notes. At the time of writing an International Standard on records management is at committee stage – based on the Australian Standard AS4390. It is expected to appear in two parts: Part One - a high level standard concerned with policy and strategy; and Part Two - a technical report covering the detail of the process.

4.2.1 The benefits of records management

The adoption of a records management programme provides the following benefits:

- ◆ Facilitates the efficient transaction of the organisation's business through, for example:
  - faster retrieval of information needed for operational, legal, research or historical reasons
  - reduction in lost or misplaced information
  - minimising space and storage equipment costs
  - managing the creation of new records
  - protection of vital records and reduction in likelihood of lost or misplaced information
  - improved overall control of the records life cycle

- ◆ Discharges the organisation's statutory and regulatory obligations in respect of its records.

4.3 RECORDS MANAGEMENT AND DOCUMENT MANAGEMENT

It is as well to clarify the subtle differences between document management and records management.

With records management the main emphasis is on the organisation and safeguarding of recorded information throughout its life cycle; there are thus strong administrative overtones in the application of this discipline.

Document management as it has emerged, focuses more on the dynamic and transactional nature, and use of recorded information as coherent records of information meaningful to their relevant users. Thus all documents are potentially records, but not all records are documents. A comparison of the two is presented in Table 4.1.

Records management and document management are not

	RECORDS MANAGEMENT	**DOCUMENT MANAGEMENT**
Definitions	*Records* are pieces of recorded information providing evidence relating to business actions.	*Documents* are coherent records of information meaningful to their relevant users
Principal focus of attention	Administrative control	Operational use
	Physical storage	Work flow
	File classification	Indexing
	Retention	Revision and version control
	Statutory and legal requirements	Operational needs
	Storage media	Information content
	Integrated series	Individual items

Table 4.1 A comparison of records and document management

alternative ways to manage information; they are complementary approaches which must be applied in a coherent fashion. It is important to ensure that all the management elements are addressed so that an organisation can capitalise on its available information.

4.4 *INFOBUILD:* AN INFORMATION LIFE CYCLE MANAGEMENT APPROACH

The dual approach of records and document management involves consideration of all the information life cycle stages noted previously in section 2.11. In this section, elements of the *Infobuild* approach are outlined in the form of a programme of work which helps to address these and the broader knowledge management issues.

4.4.1 The strategic framework

In an ideal world, the programme is part of an overall information systems strategy approach (see section 2.7). It should be applied to information irrespective of its medium of storage and should ensure that objectives, responsibilities and policy are defined and that the necessary staff, structure and tools are provided to undertake the records and information management activities.

If the programme is to be confined to a particular function or department, it is still necessary to identify the information and business process interfaces with other parts of the organisation and with those that reside outside the organisation. This will facilitate the design of the interfaces, for example by encouraging suppliers to conform to information interchange standards, and will lay the foundation for any future expansion of the programme beyond its initial scope.

4.4.2 Records and document survey and analysis

Due to the different foci of records and document management, the facts and perceptions gathered for subsequent analysis relate to both the administrative and operational issues that largely differentiate the two management approaches.

In order to ensure that all cradle-to-grave aspects are dealt with, the information gathering should involve surveying existing records and documentation types, collections and associated practices relating to the information life cycle activities:

- ◆ Acquisition
- ◆ Creation
- ◆ Retention
- ◆ Storage
- ◆ Retrieval

- Communication
- Revision
- Utilisation
- Destruction
- Organisation
- Monitoring and control.

Where the magnitude of the investigation is substantial, as measured for example by the size of company and number of functions to be covered, there can be benefit in undertaking a scoping survey to identify key functions and issues prior to the more detailed analysis. If, however, the problem being investigated is at the task level, it tends to be self-contained and localised and so can usually be dealt with at the detailed analytical level.

4.4.3 The scoping survey

The aim here is to recognise the main records and documentation issues that need to be focused upon at the next stage. This can be achieved using a variety of techniques, but should typically include interviews with function heads and key operatives coupled with personal observation of information collections and business processes, with the whole procedure being aided by having initially compiled some form of check list.

The checklist should not, however, be followed slavishly. An imaginative and questioning approach should be adopted since what one is told, for example, may be perceptual rather than factual. Furthermore, just because the functions or individual tasks have 'always been done in this way', does not of itself argue for their continuance. The facts and perceptions gathered should include those of a qualitative and quantitative nature.

One way that has proved of value when undertaking strategic studies is to imagine a two-dimensional matrix (which I call *Infomatrix 1*, Table 4.2). The life cycle activities are along one axis. The other axis of the matrix contains the key elements which together can be considered to make up 'an organisation'. These elements comprise a

LIFE CYCLE	Structure	People	Processes	Tools
Acquisition				
Creation				
Approval				
Retention				
Indexing				
Storage				
Retrieval				
Communication				
Revision				
Utilisation				
Destruction				
Organisation				
Control				

Table 4.2 Infomatrix1 *for obtaining an information management overview*

framework of relatively unchanging policies and standards, the people who work for the organisation, the tasks they undertake and the tools and physical resources they use (see Figure 2.8, page 24).

While pursuing the study, continually assess the merits and deficiencies in these elements against the information activities that are undertaken (possibly applying some subjective numeric ratings in each box). Gain an overview of the flow of work, so that overall an awareness of the business processes is obtained, including any interfaces between manual and computer systems. The aim is not to gather extensive data, but to identify key factors. At the end of the study the completed matrix (albeit in the form of a written report) provides a sound basis for determining areas for future action.

By this means one also avoids blind automation of existing practices. The solution to an organisation's information management problems is rarely achieved by simply purchasing hardware, software or communication systems. More often than not the answer involves non-technical solutions such as changes in procedures and tasks, reorganisation of staff responsibilities, etc.; aspects that should be covered as part of strategic information systems planning of which business re-engineering or business process redesign can be considered to be a part.

4.4.4 Detailed survey and analysis

The time and effort needed to undertake the detailed survey and analysis across an organisation or a major department may be considerable. However, if short cuts are taken there is the likelihood that any existing deficiencies in the manual records system (for example, duplication of records, redundant material, lack of indexes) will be carried over to any computerised system that replaces it; i.e. GIGO - Garbage In, Garbage Out!

The number and range of questions needed to gather the required survey data are extensive. They can, however, be divided into two types. One is concerned with the dynamics of the information life cycle, while the other focuses on physical characteristics, structure and layout of specific types of record.

4.4.5 The activity-oriented survey

In order to ease what might seem a daunting task, a similar approach to that taken for the scoping study can be adopted by basing the survey around the same information activities. These activities represent the answer to the question what information processes are being undertaken. This time the utilisation activity is broken down into sub-activities 'read, add, amend, copy and delete' which can be related to actions undertaken by individuals (or systems) on specific types of document. This level of detail is not usually necessary for a scoping study.

LIFE CYCLE	What?	Why?	Who?	How?	Where?	When?	How many/often?
Acquisition							
Creation							
Approval							
Retention							
Indexing							
Storage							
Retrieval							
Communication							
Revision							
Utilisation							
Destruction							
Organisation							
Control							

Table 4.3 Infomatrix2 *for detailed survey and analysis*

The other axis of *Infomatrix2* (Table 4.3) now contains the questioning words or phrases what, why, who, how, where, when, how many and how often.

To explain this further, each of these words is aimed at gathering particular types of information as explained in Table 4.4

QUESTION	THE INFORMATION TO BE GATHERED
What	Ensures that the specifics are identified, e.g. what documents are acquired, created, etc.
Why	The reason behind the activity. A key question for identifying redundant, inappropriate activities, documents, etc.
Who	Identifies the people involved; ties the activity to individuals or groups of people who may be the source or recipient of the documents
How	Determines the methods used, which may or may not involve the use of information technology
Where	Focuses attention on locations for the activity; locations may need to be specific, e.g. a staff member's PC, or could satisfactorily be identified more generally, e.g. a supplier's name and address
When	Identifies when the activity relating to the document occurs
How many	Gathers quantitative data about numbers and volumes
How often	Ensures that variations with time are identified

Table 4.4 Detailed survey questions

Infomatrix2 is focused on activities and should, as with the scoping study, consider fact, opinions and perceptions.

Identification of the flow of records and documents is particularly important as it will assist in the redesign of business processes which needs to be undertaken if the maximum use is to be made of new information technology. It is important, however, to ensure that logical business functions are not changed to fit the technology; the reverse should be the case. While the overall function such as purchasing will still be required, changes in the way business processes are undertaken to provide that function may well be merited.

The data gathered from the survey will contribute to the task of process redesign. Such an exercise will normally require a multi-disciplinary team offering skills and knowledge in the business of the organisation, in IT, in records management and in the redesign process itself.

Computer-based tools can facilitate the recording, analysis and assimilation of the information. A powerful analysis tool which is well suited to supporting the *Infomatrix* approach, is Hyperknowledge™,[4] which uses a 'what-how-why' paradigm to capture knowledge. The process model view is used to create processes, and organise them into a 'how' and 'why' structure. 'What' lists and knowledge matrices are used to capture the 'what' dimension.

Identification of the various types of document along with their usage patterns provides pointers towards storage and retention requirements as the examples in Table 4.5 show (based on Figure 3.1[5]).

DOCUMENT CATEGORY	EXAMPLES	LIFE CYCLE PATTERNS
Ephemeral correspondence	Sales brochures; unsolicited mail	Acquire, log, temporary store, short retention
Administrative corporate documents	Procedures; quality manuals; standards; board minutes	Create, authorise, index, communicate, revise, retain (legal requirements)
Transaction documents	Cheques; invoices; transmittals; applications	Acquire, create, authorise, index, communicate (workflow)
Reference documents	Articles; data books; reports; directories	Acquire, communicate (loans), subject/full text indexing
Design documents	Drawings; CAD designs/models; parts lists; bill of materials	Create, approve, log/index, communicate (controlled distribution; workflow), revise (annotate; version control)
Maintenance documents	Schedules; manuals; parts lists; procedures; standards	Create, approve, index (hyperlinks to drawings), revise (annotate; version control)

Table 4.5 Document types and usage patterns

4.4.6 The record- and document-oriented survey

In addition to the activity-oriented data, there is the need to gather information concerning the characteristics of documents (be they paper or electronically based) as this will influence decisions regarding, for example, the applicability of document imaging and of particular imaging systems, be they microfilm- or electronically-based for paper-based information. These characteristics principally relate to physical aspects, structure and layout. Examples of the main features to consider and the types of question that arise concerning system selection are summarised in Table 4.6.

CHARACTERISTIC	INFORMATION GATHERED	EXAMPLE BACKGROUND QUESTIONS
Physical characteristics	Dimensions	Can scanner handle size range?
	Number of pages (range and average)	Can imaging system handle the volume throughput? Should the scanning of legacy documents be done in-house or by a bureau?
	Single- or double-sided printing	Is flat-bed or sheet-fed imaging system required?
	Mono or colour printing	Will mono scanning be adequate or is colour important?
	Presence of diagrams and graphics	How detailed are they, what scanning resolution is required?
	Presence of half-tone photographs	Is grey scale capture required?
	Type of paper	Can the thin or thick stock be handled in a sheet-feeder?
	Method of assembly or binding	Is it acceptable to break the binding to create single sheets, or must the document be handled in bound form?
	Condition (tears, fading, folds, dirt, etc)	How much pre-preparation is required prior to scanning or filming (e.g. photocopying creased originals and scanning the copies)?
	Whether handwritten or typed	Will OCR be able to handle the typed script?
	Presence of annotations/ marginal notes	Will marginal notes fit within scanning area?
	Size range of type face	What scanning resolution is necessary to ensure effective OCR?
Structure and layout	Standardisation of layout	Is it a form; is the form structure consistent enough to permit its removal as a separate entity when scanning?
	Logical structure	Is key data in the same location so that it can be automatically captured for indexing?
	Mixing of non-textual with textual information	Will the scanner be able automatically to detect and OCR just the text information?
	Existence of bibliographic data	Is the data e.g. title, author, reference number, summary, publication date in locations which enable it to be captured for indexing during scanning?

Table 4.6 Physical and structural characteristics of paper documents

4.5 RECORDS MANAGEMENT DATA

Much of the data collected via use of *Infomatrix1* and *Infomatrix2* and an analysis of the document characteristics needs to be recorded for records management purposes. A suitably designed form can be used to log the information which will then prove valuable for devising retention schedules.

The kind of information to be logged will include:

- Name of the department or unit whose records are being surveyed
- Person undertaking the survey
- Person interviewed
- Person responsible for the records
- Date of inventory
- Title of the record series (e.g. purchase orders)
- Description of record series
- Earliest and latest dates in the record series (note any gaps)
- Numbers and volumes of records
- Number and rate at which records are accumulated
- Estimates of future numbers (e.g. annual figures over next five years)
- Format of record (e.g. correspondence, drawing, etc)
- Identification of any form work, document or report formats for later analysis; have formats changed with time (see sections 4.7 and 4.8)
- Storage media (e.g. paper, microfilm, optical, magnetic)
- Type of storage equipment (e.g. lateral filing, open shelf)
- Physical space occupied by the records
- Filing arrangements and file classification schemes (e.g. alphabetical, numeric)

- Frequency with which records are accessed (helps identify those records which are active or inactive)

- How vital the records are

- Details of other copies of the same records (reason for making copies; format and media of copy - e.g. printout from microfilm; quantity and location - helps identify unnecessary duplication)

- Details of any policies or procedures which are being followed (or not followed) relating to the record (and its copies), including those for its retention and disposal (helps identify, for example, legal or regulatory requirements).

Any inventory form used is best designed to facilitate incorporation of the collected information into a database, and may simply be created at the outset as an input screen to enable direct input on a notebook computer taken round the organisation.

Consideration can be given to designing the form in such a way that it could be circulated as a questionnaire for completion by staff. Although this may save time, there is the danger that those completing the form may not fully understand what they are being asked to do, despite any prior briefing they may have had. Furthermore they may miss noting some records which are important to the survey. Hence if this route is undertaken, it should only be used selectively, and the information should always be validated in some way, for example by visiting the staff member and their area of responsibility.

4.6 Records system design

This design phase is focused principally on the conceptual and physical organisation of records, or their document counterparts. It also involves consideration of the creation and use of form work and document and report formats. These three elements of records design are considered here.

4.6.1 Hierarchical classification

Irrespective of the media on which records are stored, they should normally be conceptually organised to match the way in which the users of the records work. This applies equally to paper-based and electronic records. Thus project, case and company name record files are likely to satisfy the needs of those concerned with consultancy, litigation and suppliers respectively. Information gathered from the records survey provides the basis for designing the records system to cater for these needs.

Classification is the conceptual and often physical grouping together of records into hierarchies, each limb or level of a hierarchy dealing with the same type of topic. This 'cabinet', 'folder' arrangement is typified by paper-based filing systems which, for example, use codes or titles to determine the filing location and order of the records, and cross-referencing to aid tracing related or synonymous subjects. Such hierarchical classifications direct one to the part of a collection most likely to include the information that is sought.

In many organisations insufficient thought is given to these aspects of records design. In particular there is often no consistency across the organisation or even within individual departments. The arrangement of records may be left to individual staff, and with each staff change, the files are reorganised to suit the new incumbent. Consequently there is a lack of continuity in the records, and access to earlier information is severely impaired if not rendered impossible. Paper records and those held electronically on stand-alone PCs frequently suffer in this way.

Benefits can be gained by adopting a suitably uniform storage hierarchy across an organisation, for example it:

- Enables faster retrieval of records
- Reduces mis-filing
- Facilitates training of those handling records
- Standardises records keeping
- Eases gathering of information on specific subjects from across the organisation
- Provides a basis for assigning retention schedules
- Facilitates computerisation of the records.

Storage hierarchies (or file classifications as referred to by records staff) should be designed to suit the specific needs of each organisation, and hence may benefit from some time and effort spent on formulating them. Nevertheless there are certain general principles that can be applied in the design of such a classification scheme.

Thus it is helpful if the coding for the file classification comprises a subject hierarchy easily remembered by the acronym FAST:

- Function within the business
- Activity within function
- Subject within activity
- Topic within subject.

Generally no more than four subject levels are necessary.

Typical functions might be Personnel, Finance and Accounting or Research and Development. An activity within Personnel might be training. Within this activity the user will have the records groups broken down into subjects such as particular training courses or the names of individual staff. Within each sub-category the records are organised in the most appropriate way, such as alphabetically by name of staff in the latter instance - an example of a self-indexed arrangement.

Note that the business functions chosen for the file classification do not necessarily equate one-to-one with the structural departments in the organisation. The classification system must reflect the business functions undertaken and not the organisational structure. In this way if the organisation restructures, but is still undertaking the same business functions, the file classification remains the same.

The concept of such a hierarchical classification is valid for both manual and computer-based systems and in fact should be suitably consistent across the whole of an organisation's records and documents, irrespective of the storage media used. Document management systems usually provide the ability to organise information into logical hierarchies (cabinets, folders, documents) as well as allowing other (or the same) users to have different logical views (i.e. groupings of documents) to suit the tasks they are undertaking.

4.7 Forms management

Much of the cost and inconvenience in using records systems arises from the creation of unnecessary records and the excessive duplication of others. Forms are one way in which the recording of information can be standardised to ease its capture and subsequent use.

However, form work itself can suffer from poor design and unnecessary proliferation and hence its creation and use needs to be managed along with other records. Good design and consistency in its use is particularly important in relation to electronic imaging and the use of optical character recognition.

In order to address this issue, an inventory of all forms (printed, hand-written and computer-generated) in use should be compiled and maintained with the general aim of increasing productivity and reducing forms production and usage costs. All types of form for use in the organisation should be registered and coded.

Specific aims are to:

- Eliminate unnecessary
  - forms
  - copies of forms and
  - items on forms

◆ Consolidate forms serving similar purposes

◆ Prevent the creation of unnecessary
- new forms and
- revisions to existing forms

◆ Design forms for maximum effectiveness

◆ Ensure, as appropriate, proper reproduction, stocking and distribution

◆ Maximise the appropriate use of computer-based systems for form generation, information capture, distribution and storage.

The existence of a standard form layout can be used to advantage in electronic document imaging systems by saving on storage space and access time. Since the layout of information on a form is standardised, it is not necessary to store the blank form structure along with the information it contains. Forms removal software packages are used to perform this extraction. The information is stored and overlaid on a single copy of the form structure at display time, for example. Alternatively electronic forms creation and management software is available which provides total control over the design and intended use of the form and the information which it contains. This approach provides a more efficient and reliable way of collecting and manipulating the information than relying on paper-based forms which must pass through an inevitably error-prone scanning and image capture process.

The elements of a forms management programme covering analysis and design are given in Table 4.7.

4.8 REPORTS MANAGEMENT

Reports are typically produced to document results, facts, information and action which are of lasting significance and which may have wide distribution within or outside the organisation.

Reports of different format and structure will proliferate if no controls are exercised; hence

STAGE	ACTIVITY
Analysis	Identify the purpose of the form
	Specify how it is used in operation
	Estimate the time taken to complete it
	State the required number of copies and how they are distributed
	Indicate the filing and retention procedures
	Interview or survey the form's recipients
Design	Eliminate redundancy and duplication
	Make them easy to complete
	Make them self-filing
	Ensure they are readily accessed and the contents easily analysed
	Aim to replace paper by electronic versions
	All forms should have: • a title • name of issuing authority • reference code • edition/version/update code and issue date • retention period

Table 4.7 Forms management programme

as in the case of forms, an inventory of all reports (printed, hand-written and computer-generated) in use should be compiled and maintained. Similarly all types of report produced in the organisation should be registered and coded.

Specific aims are to:

- Eliminate unnecessary reports

- Consolidate reports wherever possible

- Redesign the contents of reports to increase their effectiveness

- Limit the number of copies of reports, their frequency and their distribution to that which is needed (rather than that which is wanted)

- Maximise the appropriate use of computer-based systems for report generation, information capture, distribution and storage.

Besides presenting the key information about a report in a compact, easily assimilated way, the availability of a standard report data page also facilitates capture of the data for indexing purposes, whether the report is prepared electronically or captured by scanning the paper page into a document management system. An example is given in Figure 4.2.

ACME COMPANY INC	
Report number:	Security classification:
Publication date:	File reference:
Title:	
Author(s):	
Report summary:	
Keywords:	
Content and listed distribution approved by:	
Internal distribution:	External distribution:
Recipients of this summary page may obtain a copy of the full report from Central Information Services (e-mail ACMEINFO).	

Figure 4.2 A standard data page for reports

The elements of a reports management programme are given in Table 4.8.

STAGE	ACTIVITY
Analysis	Identify the purpose of the report
	Determine originating authority
	Determine frequency
	Determine timing
	Record number of copies distributed
	Identify any standard distribution
	Indicate the filing and retention procedures
	Determine costs for: • research and compilation • clerical preparation • production • distribution
	Interview or survey the report's recipients
Design	Eliminate redundancy and duplication
	Standardise on structure and layout as much as possible
	Include summaries for long reports
	Aim to replace paper by electronic versions which can be seamlessly incorporated in a document management system
	All reports should have: • a title • name of issuing authority • reference code • edition/version/update code and issue date • retention period

Table 4.8 Report management programme

4.9 DEVISING RETENTION SCHEDULES

There is a natural tendency for individuals, and companies, not to destroy information as 'it might come in useful sometime'. On the other hand when forced to think of destroying records, for example because of lack of storage space, destruction is often undertaken without assessing the operational importance of the material or the legal implications. Alternatively, records may be 'dumped' with a commercial records storage firm without proper consideration of retention periods or referencing and indexing requirements to facilitate their subsequent identification.

It is therefore necessary that all records, irrespective of the medium on which they are stored, should have a retention period allocated to them which properly satisfies operational, legal, research or historical requirements.

The retention period for records may be arrived at by considering the purpose behind the information contained in the records and the key retention criteria, as outlined in Table 4.9.

	RETENTION REASON	**COMMENT**
PURPOSE	To provide evidence	Records generated for statutory, regulatory or legal reasons. • Prescribed or implied retention periods may apply
	To provide instructions	Records conveying instruction (e.g. policies and procedures) • Implies long retention periods
	To provide information	Records conveying fact or opinion • Retention period will vary depending on the nature of the information
CRITERIA	Legal	Records covered by statutory or legal provision
	Operational	Records required to undertake the day-to-day business of the organisation
	Research	Records having actual or potential future value for research or development reasons or which are of historical significance.

Table 4.9 Guidelines for determining retention

Applying retention schedules can be facilitated by having the records classified according to the hierarchical arrangements outlined in section 4.6.1. This is because many of the records having the same classification codes will have identical retention periods. In this instance retention schedules are effectively applied to classes of records, i.e. records which form part of an integrated series.

Where it is not possible to identify classes of records, retention can be defined at the file level within the file classification system.

Retention values should be applied to both active and inactive records and are typically assigned in months or years, or by way of codes if it is not possible to know the precise span of the retention period. For example, records may need to be kept permanently, until superseded or after completion of the work involved. In these cases the codes P (permanent), L (latest issue) and FC (following completion) could be used.

The following is the minimum data that should be recorded concerning retention decisions:

♦ Identification of the record (e.g. using the title and/or file classification)

♦ Total retention period according to the convention used

♦ Reason for retention (as per Table 4.9)

Destruction of records must be authorised by a suitably responsible person. This authorisation and the disposal must be recorded in a manner which accords to a documented and auditable procedure. In this way the likelihood is kept to a minimum of there being a challenge in a court of law on the basis that the disposal was not part of a normal business process. The topic of legal admissibility is considered in more detail in Chapter 5.

Retention schedules should be regularly reviewed, typically annually, or when events occur which affect the management of records, for example the creation of new departments, company mergers or acquisitions. The retention schedule can also be used to note the security classification for the records thereby providing a single point of reference when considering both duration of storage and access control issues.

An idea of what an outline retention schedule for the technical department in a petroleum exploration company might look like, is shown in Table 4.10. As an alternative to microfilm, storage on write-once optical media (WORM) may be considered appropriate, for example.

4.10 STORAGE AND RETRIEVAL SYSTEMS

With the ever-decreasing unit cost of storage, and the increasing power and sophistication of search software, the argument that you no longer need to consider disposing of records, or concern oneself with records classification or indexing is at first sight persuasive.

While it may prove to be relatively inexpensive to store vast amounts of information permanently, there are other considerations. For example, if certain records are no longer required, their continued presence in a retrieval system (whether automated or manual) may slow the speed of access to the active records as well as require a larger system to handle the totality of information.

The concepts of retention and hierarchical storage arrangements (records file classifications) are therefore of equal relevance to document management systems as to paper-based records systems.

By itself a hierarchical arrangement may not provide all the necessary mechanisms for finding the information that is sought. What is usually required is the ability to search and retrieve using other criteria related to the records such as titles, dates, authors, drawing numbers, version numbers, project numbers, subject keywords, and possibly full text searching also.

OUTLINE TECHNICAL RECORDS RETENTION SCHEDULE							
RECORDS	\multicolumn{5}{c|}{**YEARS**}		**NOTES**
	1	3	5	10	P	
CONTRACTS						
Bid evaluation records	R	D				Unsuccessful bids
Evaluation committee	R		D			After project completion
Contract documents	L		D			After project completion
Post award letters, etc.	L		D			After project completion
PROCUREMENT						
Requisitions	L	R	D			After project completion
Indents	L	R	D			After project completion
Purchase orders	L	R	D			After project completion
Invoices	L	R	D			After project completion
Correspondence	L	R	D			After project completion
ENGINEERING						
Drawings						
◆ pre 'as-built'	R		D			
◆ 'as-built'	DN				PM	
Specifications, procedures		D			PM	For design/construction
Data sheets		D			PM	
Calculations					PC	Computer-based
Inspection reports		D			PM	
PETROLEUM ENGINEERING						
Well files					P	Vital records
Seismic tapes					P	Vital records
Technical reports					P	Vital records
GENERAL						
Personnel files	L	R	D			After termination
Library journals	L	L	R	D	S	Depends on relevance and availability from external sources
Publications	DS	DS	DS	DS	S	Depends on relevance and availability from external sources

D   Destroy/dispose
DS Destroy when superseded
DN Destroy original 'N' years after microfilming and superseded
L   Local storage
PC Computerised storage
PM Permanent on microfilm then destroy original
R   Remote storage
S   Selective

Table 4.10 Typical retention schedule for engineering function

This ability, achieved by indexing the information in the records, is a particularly crucial ingredient of any information storage and retrieval system where the records cannot be read by the human eye. If a paper-based system is poorly indexed, the searcher can at least physically and visually scan through the contents of a filing cabinet, for example. This approach is also possible, if more tedious, when the information is stored on microfilm. However, in an electronic document imaging system (or any system where the information is stored digitally) such a mode of searching is not possible. If insufficient attention has been given to indexing, the records and hence the information they contain are effectively lost for ever.

The concepts of information indexing and retrieval are considered further in Chapter 6.

4.11 Implementation, administration and control

The records management programme should ideally be implemented as part of an overall information systems strategy plan for the business. Implementation will involve consideration of issues relating to organisational structure, information technology, staffing and work activities concerned with managing and exploiting records.

The results of the programme and the encompassing records management strategy and policies can be documented in a records manual to provide a reference point for current standards and procedures. A records manual should form part of an organisation's quality management system. Typical contents of a records manual are:

1. Introduction

    ◆ Purpose of the manual

    ◆ Scope and definition of records management

2. Records Management Policy Overview

    ◆ Objectives (including its place in the overall IS strategy)

    ◆ Responsibilities of key personnel

    ◆ Statutory, legal and confidentiality issues

3. Records Operations

    ◆ The records function (e.g. descriptions of the records centre services and procedures)

    ◆ Records creation (covering, for example, general principles, forms and reports management and electronic records)

    ◆ Acquisition of records

- Retention and vital records
- File classification
- Storage
- Access and retrieval.

The overall administration and control of records management is facilitated by exploiting database and information retrieval software coupled with an appropriate choice of storage systems which will allow, for example, less active records to be transferred between online magnetic storage to near-line optical storage media. Thus hierarchical classifications, retention schedules and details of authorised destruction can be incorporated in the indexing and retrieval tools used to search and find individual records, or the information they contain. Document management systems should therefore be capable of providing automated records control.

Although focused on the legal admissibility of information stored on write-once media (such as WORM optical disks and CD-ROM), the code of practice DISC PD0008 and its associated compliance workbook produced by BIS provide valuable guidance for those reviewing or preparing management procedures for records and documents.[6,7]

REFERENCES IN CHAPTER 4

1. Stockford, Bridget, 'Getting Started' in Alison Turton (ed.), *Managing Business Archives*, published in association with the Business Archives Council (Oxford: Butterworth-Heinemann, 1991)
2. Emmerson, P. (ed.), *How to Manage Your Records: A Guide to Effective Practice* (Cambridge: ICSA Publishing, 1989)
3. Penn, I.A., Pennix, G. and Coulson, J., *Records Management Handbook* (Aldershot: Gower Publishing Company, 1994)
4. *Hyperknowledge* (Cambridge: Logical Water Ltd, http://www.hyperknowledge.com)
5. *Document Management Guide and Yearbook* (St Albans: Cimtech, 1996)
6. *Code of Practice for Legal Admissibility of Information Stored on Electronic Document Management Systems*, DISC PD0008, British Standards Institution, 1996
7. *Compliance Workbook: Legal Admissibility of Information Stored on Electronic Document Management Systems*, DISC PD0009, British Standards Institution, 1996

PART 2

TECHNOLOGY AND RETRIEVAL

5

TECHNOLOGY – PROMISES FULFILLED AND UNFULFILLED

'In our popular culture today, the discussions of computers and information is awash with commercially motivated exaggerations and the opportunistic mystifications of the computer science establishment. The hucksters and the hackers have polluted our understanding of information technology with loose metaphors, facile comparisons, and a good deal of out-and-out obfuscation.'

The Cult of Information - The Folklore of Computers
and the True Art of Thinking: Theodore Roszak

Considerable hype continues to surround many of the IT industry's offerings. Artificial intelligence, CASE (computer-aided systems engineering) tools, and executive information systems are examples of developments which were promised by some to be the ultimate, all-pervading solution to deploying the knowledge of experts, dealing with system development backlogs and providing top management with ready access to critical business data. Although much has been achieved in these areas, the sobering light of experience in applying the technologies has helped define more clearly the narrower boundaries within which benefits can be achieved.

The range of information technologies available to support the information life cycle can be equally daunting as it is wide in scope and often leading edge (see Figure 5.1). The technologies range from applications such as optical character recognition for converting text images to editable form or providing additional indexing terms, to broader-based integrative approaches as exemplified by workflow software which incorporates a range of technologies to support information-centric business processes.

The matching of technology to the life cycle activities is a key part of the *Infobuild* approach for identifying and analysing records and document management needs, as described in the previous chapter. This chapter contains an overview of key information technologies. The topic of databases and information retrieval software is covered in detail in Chapter 6.

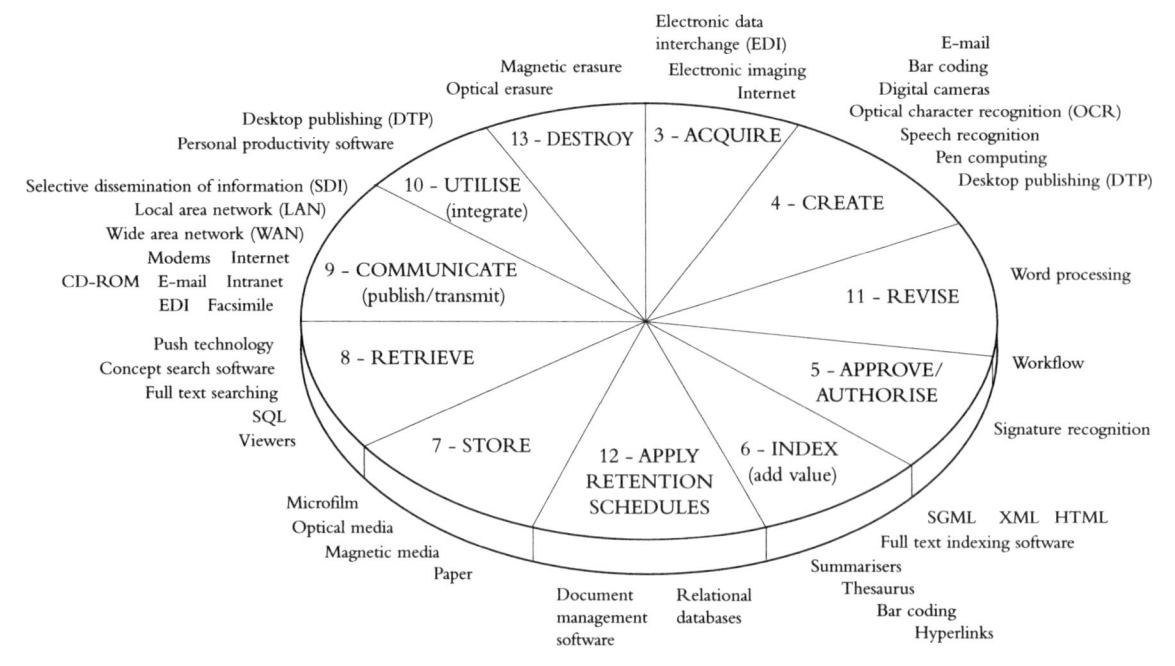

Figure 5.1 Technologies and the information life cycle

5.1 CLIENT/SERVER TECHNOLOGY

An 'integrated document management system' implies the use of computers connectable by some form of network. Arguably the main driving force in the development of networked computing is 'client/server' technology.

As with many other buzzwords, the technology is open to different interpretations. In essence it involves one or more networked computers employed by users – these computers are termed 'clients' or 'client stations'. The resources required by users and accessed via these clients are provided by other, usually more powerful computers on the network, known as servers. These can be high-speed microcomputers, minicomputers or even mainframes. They are usually categorised according to the type of resource they provide, for example:

- ◆ file servers (providing central disk storage and access controls for each user's files)

- ◆ database servers (holding data centrally, accessed from the client)

- ◆ transaction servers (providing rapid access to usually mission-critical databases)

- ◆ print servers (providing common access to networked printers)

♦ fax servers (networked fax services which reduce reliance on paper)

♦ web servers (utilising Internet-type web technologies for accessing information and interactive services).

5.1.1 Fat and thin clients

Depending on requirements, document management applications, such as image storage and retrieval can be client-based - used by the one workstation on which the application resides - or server-based, whereby the application is located on a server and is available to more than one user with suitable access control. The former is an example of a 'fat' client, because most of the application runs at the client end. The latter instance involves a 'fat' server holding the application.

In general the move is towards fat servers, especially for mission-critical systems. They have the advantage that management of services and their deployment are less demanding on technical support staff as staff resources can be concentrated on this one server. If the application is client-based, then support staff have to spend more time managing all the client workstations connected to the server. This can be a time-consuming exercise, especially when software upgrades or bug fixes have to be installed. Note that having a fat server does not automatically mean that only 'thin' clients are attached to it. Fat clients may still be required for those users needing applications for specialist or personal use.

In recent times a challenger to the traditional PC-based technology emerged in the form of the network computer (NC). The NC is designed as a low-cost thin client for use with Internet and Intranet technology. It derives its functionality by connection to a network from which it acquires the necessary software and documents with which to work. It was originally championed by Larry Ellison, the founder of Oracle. A subsidiary company, Network Computer Inc, established a set of guidelines, known as the Network Computer Reference Profile. NC technology has not at the time of writing had the impact on the PC market hoped for by its proponents. This is partly due to the fact that it is designed to operate with applications written using Java, a programming language still in its infancy as regards large-scale acceptance and deployment.

One company that has influenced the move to server-based computing solutions is Citrix Systems. Its Winframe software enables a Windows NT server to act as a timesharing central computer with Windows applications running on the server and only screen changes being sent to the attached PCs, NCs or Windows terminals. MetaFrame is Citrix's server component that allows non-Windows clients, such as DOS, Mac and UNIX clients, to run Windows applications on the server.

5.1.2 Two- and three-tier architectures

It is rare that technical literature concerned with client/server technology fails to make reference at some time to two-tier or three-tier architecture. Although it has been interpreted in different ways over the years, it has much the same meaning as fat and thin clients in that it relates to the way the main functional elements (typically user interface, application logic and shared data) are split between the client and server. Thus two-tier architecture is one in which the user interface is stored in the client, the data is stored in the server and the application logic is located either in the client or in the server. With three-tier client/server architecture the user interface is in the client, the business application logic is stored in one or more servers, and the data is stored in a database server. This form is considered to be more flexible and scalable than two-tier and is seen to be the growth area for client/server systems.

5.1.3 Middleware

Software for client/server has three components:

- front-end software (for users to connect to servers, submit requests and receive information)

- middleware software (the set of software residing between the client and server)

- server software (to interpret requests and provide secure access to services - for example, printing, faxing, communication or database access and processing).

Middleware encompasses all distributed software that functions as a conversion or translation layer between clients and servers. It facilitates communication and provides application program interfaces - APIs - for developers. APIs are important elements when implementing an application such as document management. They enable the application program to communicate with the operating system or other system programs such as a database management system (DBMS).

Examples of software that comes under the middleware banner are shown in Table 5.1.

5.2 COMMUNICATION NETWORKS

Distributed processing needs effective and efficient communication network systems to link computers and associated resources. The two main categories of network are:

- local area networks (LANs)
  - operate within a limited geographical area, for example a single building, or campus

- wide area networks (WANs)
  - which involve connecting geographically dispersed facilities by high-speed lines, satellites or public telephone lines, for example.

MIDDLEWARE ACRONYM	MEANING	USAGE
TCP/IP	Transmission Control Protocol/Internet Protocol	A communications protocol that enables dissimilar systems to be networked together. TCP/IP is the protocol of the Internet
ODBC	Open Database Connectivity	A database programming interface from Microsoft that provides a common language for Windows applications to access databases on a network
CORBA	Common Object Request Broker Architecture	Software that handles the communication of messages to and from objects in a distributed, multi-platform environment
OLE	Object Linking and Embedding	Allows an object such as a spreadsheet or video clip to be embedded into a document, called the client application or OLE container
MAPI	Mail Application Program Interface	Enables an application to send and receive mail over the Microsoft Mail messaging system
HTTP	HyperText Transport Protocol	Used to access and retrieve resources on servers on the World Wide Web. Web site addresses begin with an http:// prefix

Table 5.1 Software that comes under the middleware banner

Interconnection between LANs, and between LANs and WANs is not necessarily straightforward due to the different systems on the market and the different types of data that are handled. Several devices - variously termed bridges, routers, gateways and hubs - exist to facilitate interconnection and have developed to the point that in some cases the distinction between them is somewhat blurred.

In general terms connection between small LANs of like design can be accomplished by a **bridge** which effectively creates one large LAN for the user. Bridges are targeted at inter-connecting LANS where the protocols do not support inter-networking. **Protocols** are the agreed procedures or physical characteristics that permit different types of equipment to communicate effectively.

Interconnection of several, larger networks is better effected using **routers.** These provide protocol-dependent intelligent routing should linkage failures occur. They can also connect LANs having different topologies.

Gateways are another way to connect dissimilar networks. They are focused on reconciling the different network protocols by translating 'foreign' protocols into the one protocol used by the backbone. A backbone is the part of the network through which the major network traffic passes. Hence it often provides the highest speed transmission paths in the network and runs the longest distance. Smaller networks are attached to the backbone.

Hubs have emerged as a means of combining bridges, routers and gateways into a central 'intelligent' box thereby simplifying network management.

Generally large corporations are better able to ensure the availability of high bandwidth services via LANs and WANs than can individuals or small businesses, who need to connect to such high speed networks via standard telephone lines.

5.2.1 Transmission speed and bandwidth

Information is transmitted either in digital or analogue form. **Digital** transmission is fundamental to computing technology and involves the use of discrete signals or pulses, having one of two states, variously known as on/off, high/low or 1/0. The basic element is the binary digit, or **bit**.

Analogue transmission uses a continuous wave form. Digital information is more readily controlled and has greater accuracy than its analogue equivalent. The digital watch and the analogue variant with moving hands exemplify the difference.

Information such as text, sound, video or images is encoded using the binary numbering system. Characters are usually represented as a **byte** which comprises 8 bits, and thereby provides 256 possible combinations to symbolise letters, numbers and punctuation symbols as well as control codes.

The increase in collaborative computing driven by the adoption of technologies such as workflow, e-mail, conferencing, groupware and document management has highlighted the need for high capacity networks capable of carrying the burgeoning data and image traffic. The demand is for increased **bandwidth**, which is the transmission capacity of an electronic line such as a communications network. It is expressed in **bits per second** (bps) or in **Hertz** (Hz - cycles per second). It should be noted that two communication lines operating at the same bits per second rate may not be transmitting characters at the same rate due to the fact that one line is asynchronous and the other is synchronous (see section 5.2.3).

Transmission speeds may also be expressed in terms of the **baud** which is often used synonymously and erroneously for 'bits per second'. The two are, however, only equivalent where the communication line signal is in one of two states to represent a single binary digit (bit). In other circumstances it is possible that 1,200 bps are sent at 600 baud, for example. It is therefore important to clarify the meanings behind the terms used. Most users will encounter the term baud applied to the speed of modems.

Transmission speed and bandwidth are key factors in the design of networks for imaging applications. Images created by scanning are large due to the amount of digital data they contain. To improve their speed of transmission through a network it is necessary either to increase the network's bandwidth or create a smaller image. The latter can be achieved by lowering the scanning resolution, adopting a different mode of scanning if acceptable, or compressing the image, a topic dealt with later in section 5.8.2.

5.2.2 Baseband and broadband

Baseband communication involves the passing of digital information through the network cabling. Digital communication networks are therefore baseband networks. Most personal computer networks and electronic imaging systems are of this type. The networks are relatively simple in make-up, and certain versions use inexpensive twisted pair cabling rather than the dearer coaxial medium. However, baseband networks can only carry one signal at a time and operate over a geographically limited area.

A **broadband** network uses analogue transmission, and hence requires conversion (modulation) of the signal from digital to analogue as it enters the cable, and demodulation from analogue to digital form at the recipient's end. The conversion is undertaken by devices similar to the ubiquitous modem (**mo**dulator-**dem**odulator). Broadband networks can operate at higher transmission speeds and allow communication over greater distances than are achieved by baseband systems. Since they can also carry several signals at a time, broadband systems are able to carry integrated data, voice and video signals. Such high bandwidth networks can, for example, provide remote access to imaging systems when it is necessary to use the analogue telephone system.

5.2.3 Synchronous and asynchronous communication

High speed transmission is vital within the workings of a computer and in electronic imaging systems, because of the large amount of data that has to be communicated between the various system components. This need is satisfied by using **synchronous** communication whereby the data (i.e. characters) are transmitted at a fixed rate between the transmitter and receiver whose operations are synchronised by electronic clock signals.

Asynchronous communication does not rely on having equal time intervals between characters, but instead uses a 'start' bit and 'stop' bit either side of each character. Due to the fact that asynchronous communication involves transmitting additional bits with each character, such a communication line offers a slower character transmission rate than does a synchronous line operating at the same bit per second rate.

Both these modes of synchronising the flow of data may be associated with the serial transmission of data.

5.2.4 Parallel and serial communication

The eight bits which make up a character code (byte) can travel from the transmitter to the receiver in one of two ways: either in parallel where each bit passes along a separate channel, or serially with each bit being sent in turn along a single channel.

Parallel communication provides high-speed transmission over short distances, typically up to about 15 feet. Over longer distances the data being transmitted may be corrupted. Its most common manifestation is the parallel interface used to connect printers or storage devices to personal computers, for example. As such the interface is an extension of the computer's internal high-speed bus.

Serial communication is not restricted by distance. However, prior to transmission along a communication line, the parallel stream of data from the computer's bus must be converted into a serial stream of bits. The reverse process takes place at the receiver. Synchronous or asynchronous communication is employed to ensure that the characters (bytes) within the data stream are recognised as such.

5.2.5 LAN technologies

LAN technologies are typically categorised by the type of access method as listed in Table 5.2. Most of these technologies allocate bandwidth by a process of contention whereby each user is competing with every other user for use of the maximum bandwidth. Access is obtained either by acquiring a token (in the case of the Token Ring LAN) which provides the permission to broadcast, or by starting to broadcast and being prepared to stop to avoid a collision. This latter approach, called Carrier Sense Multiple Access/Collision Detection (CSMA/CD), is the access method used in Ethernet.

LAN TYPE	SPEED	COMMENT
Ethernet	10 Mbps	The most widely deployed technology. Uses CSMS/CD to resolve contention
Switched Ethernet	10 Mbps	No contention
Fast Ethernet	100 Mbps	Uses CSMS/CD with some modifications
Gigabit Ethernet	1000 Mbps	E.g. optical fibre backbone
Token Ring	4 or 16 Mbps	Developed originally by IBM
FDDI	100 Mbps	Uses optical fibre as the cabling
ATM	25 Mbps – 2.4 Gbps	Highly scalable

Table 5.2 LAN technologies

Other LAN technologies use switches to eliminate contention. Thus switched Ethernet provides a dedicated 10 Mbps for each client by means of its own LAN segment. FDDI (Fiber Distributed Data Interface) is a token passing network that uses optical fibre cabling and is capable of transmitting at 100 Mbps up to two kilometres.

ATM (Asynchronous Transfer Mode) arguably offers the greatest hope for those with insatiable demands for bandwidth. It is a high-speed switching network technology suitable for both LANs and WANs and handles data, real-time voice and video. It combines the high efficiency of packet switching used in data networks, with the guaranteed bandwidth of circuit switching used in voice networks.

ATM involves dividing all network traffic into 53-byte packets. Very fast switches are used, and this, together with the small packet size allows voice and video frames to be inserted into the data stream sufficiently frequently to provide real-time transmission. In addition, ATM establishes a connection between sender and receiver that is maintained throughout the session. Although its market share compared with other network technologies is still small, due mainly to its high (but falling) costs, it is being increasingly deployed. This is aided by the backing of the ATM Forum set up in 1991 to promote ATM networking technology.

5.2.6 WAN technologies

The major limiting factor on bandwidth across a dispersed network is rarely in the LAN, but in the WAN where there is reliance on having fast switches and suitable cabling to handle the demand for high speed transmission.

There is a wide range of physical line types or services used as the backbone for WANS. They offer a range of speeds, with the focus increasingly being on SONET standard services. SONET (Synchronous Optical Network) is a fibre optic transmission system for high-speed digital traffic. It is an intelligent system providing advanced network management and more flexibility than the commonly encountered T1 and T3 lines which SONET is expected to replace over time. The range of WAN technologies is shown in Table 5.3.

WAN operation is based on packet-switching technology for sending packets of data, each with a header address for the packet's destination. Hence individual packets do not have

LINE TYPE/ SERVICE	SPEED (Mbps)	COMMENTS
DS0	0.064	North American standard
DS1 (T1)	1.54	North American standard
E1	2.05	European CCITT standard
DS1C (T1C)	3.15	North American standard
DS2 (T2)	6.31	North American standard
E2	8.45	European CCITT standard
E3	34.37	European CCITT standard
DS3 (T3)	44.74	North American standard
STS-1 (OC1)	51.84	SONET service
E4	139.26	European CCITT standard
STS3 (OC3)	155.52	SONET service
DS4 (T4)	274.18	North American standard
E5	565.15	European CCITT standard
STS-12 (OC12)	622.08	SONET service
STS-24 (OC24)	1244	SONET service
STS-48 (OC48)	2488	SONET service

Table 5.3 WAN technologies

to follow the same path to their destination. There are four main such packet-based technologies as detailed in Table 5.4.

For those users wishing to utilise higher bandwidth services such as those offered by the Internet, and who do not have the luxury of corporate LANs and WANs, there are various means of connection, for example dial-up modems and the Integrated Services Digital Network (ISDN). Keeping pace with advances in modem speed is facilitated by those modems that have flash memory chips into which new software can be loaded. The main features of these and other connection technologies are shown in Table 5.5 opposite.

PACKET SWITCH TECHNOLOGY	SPEED	COMMENTS
X.25	64 Kbps	The oldest packet switching standard
Frame Relay	1 to 2 Mbps on T1/E1	Popular variable length packet technology, developed from X.25 for digital circuits for data traffic
SMDS (Switched Multimegabit Data Service)	45 Mbps on T3	Variable length packets, divisible into smaller fixed length cells. Suitable for data traffic
ATM (Asynchronous Transfer Mode)	2.4 Gbps	Uses 53 byte cells

Table 5.4 Packet-switching technologies for WANs

5.2.7 Communication channels – cabling, wireless and satellite

Communication channels for LANs are currently based almost exclusively on physical cabling of which there are three main types - twisted pair, coaxial and fibre optic. A simplified categorisation of cabling based on their transmission capacity is shown in Table 5.6.

Twisted pair comprises two insulated wires covered by a sleeve and is typically used for telephone wires. In this unshielded form (UTP) it is cheap to use for wiring LANs, but the signals carried are not well protected against electromagnetic interference. A shielded version (STP), incorporating an insulating sleeve around the two wires, provides greater protection against interference and offers higher transmission speeds.

CATEGORY	CABLE TYPE	APPLICATION
1	UTP	Analogue voice
2	UTP	Digital voice, 1 Mbps data
3	UTP, STP	16 Mbps data
4	UTP, STP	20 Mbps data
5	UTP, STP	100 Mbps data
6	Coaxial	100 Mbps+ data
7	Fibre optic	100 Mbps+ data

Table 5.6 Simplified categorisation of cabling

Coaxial cable is a well-established communication medium for cable television and comprises a wire core encased in insulating material which is itself encircled by a

CONNECTION TECHNOLOGY	SPEED (Kbps)	COMMENTS
V.32bis	14.4	For asynchronous and synchronous 4800, 7200, 9600, 12000 and 14400 bps analogue modems. Allows modems to change speeds as required.
V.34	33.6	For 28800, 31200 and 33600 bps analogue modems.
V.90	56	An analogue modem that communicates at 56 Kbps downstream and 33.6 Kbps upstream. Intended for use with Information Service Providers and online services.
ISDN BRI	128	Dial-up digital modem. ISDN's Basic Rate Interface (BRI) service. Comprises two 64 Kbps 'B' channels for data or voice and one 16 Kbps 'D' channel for signalling and placing calls. Can be 'bonded' to form one channel.
ISDN PRI	1544	Digital modem, High-speed Primary Rate Interface (PRI) service with up to 30 'B' channels and one 'D' channel which can be bonded to achieve high data transmission rates. Also known as ISDN30 by BT.
T1 etc E1 etc	1544; 2055	See Table 5.3.
HDSL	1544	High bit rate Digital Subscriber Line (HDSL) using existing telephone cable (two twisted pair).
ADSL	6000 (in) 640 (out)	Asymmetrical Digital Subscriber Line (ADSL) provides greater bandwidth going into a property than leaving it. Uses a single twisted pair.
Cable modem	10,000	A modem connection between a computer and a cable TV service for Internet access. Most domestic cable systems are uni-directional, thus a 'standard' modem is still required for replying or sending information outwards.
B-ISDN	100,000 upwards	Broadband ISDN that uses fibre optic cables. Uses ATM/SONET.

Table 5.5 Connection technologies

conducting shield. An insulating sleeve covers the complete assembly. The design reduces electrical interference and is suitable for high speed transmission over long distances. Understandably it is more expensive than twisted pair, but it has a higher bandwidth thereby allowing it to transmit a large amount of information.

Fibre optic cable comprises flexible glass tubing through which the data is transmitted as light impulses. The cable is not prone to electrical interference, it permits very high transmission rates, is lighter and less bulky than conventional wiring and can carry much more communication traffic due to its very high bandwidth.

98   *Technology and Retrieval*

Cabling a LAN can be expensive in terms of the cost of the physical media, its installation in the building structure and any subsequent reconfiguration or expansion. **Wireless networks** would appear to offer a solution to these problems. However with speeds of transmission in the 10s of Kbps they fall short of those achieved with Ethernet or Token Ring systems, for example. Although the technology will develop, and products are already on the market, this transmission speed gap between wired and wireless systems is likely to persist.

With the increasing globalisation of business and the availability of cheaper skilled labour in other countries, there is increasing use of satellite communication. Tasks such as high volume data entry of litigation support documents and insurance forms can be cost-effectively undertaken by transmitting images of the documents and forms to the remote location from the client's site. Typically data is keyed from the transmitted image. Those supplying such services claim, for example, that up to 30,000 forms or documents can be transmitted and processed within 24 hours. The completed and verified data can be returned to the client in a variety of formats including SGML/CALS databases (see section 5.8.36).

5.3 BUSES AND INTERFACES

High speed communication of data is essential within the workings of a computer and is achieved via an internal signal path called a **bus**. In IBM-PC and compatible machines, bus design has progressed from the original ISA, to EISA, VL-bus and PCI bus, each development offering advances in speed and throughput. Details are summarised in Table 5.7.

The Industry Standard Architecture (ISA), originally developed for IBM's AT (Advanced Technology) computers, provides a 16-bit data bus. With increasing speed of the microprocessors, and particularly with the introduction of the 80386 chip, the ISA bus proved inadequate for the more demanding applications. IBM therefore developed a 32-bit bus, Micro Channel Architecture (MCA) for its top-end computers. MCA is incompatible with ISA and although some manufacturers licensed the technology, a large group developed the Enhanced (or Extended) Industry Standard Architecture (EISA) which is backward compatible with ISA. VL-bus (VESA Local-BUS) is a peripheral bus from VESA that was used mainly in 80486 processor-based PCs. None of these designs is able to make the most of the computer microprocessor's inherent speed and the current standard offering is the Peripheral Component Interconnect (PCI), a local bus design promoted by Intel and supporting 32- and 64-bit data paths and bus mastering.

BUS TYPE	SIZE	SPEED
ISA	16 bit	8 MHz
Micro Channel	32 bit	5-20 MHz
EISA	32 bit	8 MHz
VL-bus	32 bit	Up to 40 MHz
PCI	32 and 64 bit	33 MHz
AGP	32 bit	66 to 132 MHz

Table 5.7 Bus types

PCI is supported by over 100 manufacturers. AGP (Accelerated Graphics Port) is Intel's high-speed graphics port that directly connects the display adapter and memory. The PCI bus design is of particular importance to imaging systems as it speeds up dramatically the working of displays and mass storage systems.

Speed of data transfer between a computer and peripherals such as printers, hard disk drives and optical storage, is a key consideration in the design of systems that involve the movement of large quantities of data. The Small Computer System Interface (SCSI) represents the most common choice for such applications, but although widely used it is not fully standardised across all manufacturers. Most SCSI boards enable several peripheral devices to be daisy-chained off the one board.

Beyond SCSI there is the prospect of fibre-channel-based interfaces according to the IEEE 1394 standard. This high-speed serial bus, also known as FireWire allows up to 63 devices to be connected and will provide an ideal means for attaching video peripherals.

A summary of SCSI and IEEE 1394 specifications is provided in Table 5.8.

TYPE	TRANSFER RATE Mbps	MAXIMUM NO. OF DEVICES
SCSI-1	5	8
SCSI-2	5	8
Fast SCSI-2	10	8
Wide SCSI-2	10	16
Fast Wide SCSI-2	20	16
8-bit Ultra SCSI-2	20	8
16-bit Ultra SCSI-3	20-40	16
8-bit Ultra2 SCSI-3	40	8
16-bit Ultra2 SCSI-3	40-80	16
IEEE 1394	100, 200, 400	63

Table 5.8 SCSI specifications

A further interface of particular importance for mobile computing, is the 16-bit PC Card standard formulated by the Personal Computer Memory Card International Association (PCMCIA). It enables credit-card size units – for example disk drives, modems, SCSI cards – to be incorporated in laptop computers and attached to desktop computers using an accessory. There are currently three main varieties, the original Type I slot used mainly to hold memory cards, Type II cards which are thicker and used for a wide variety of networkable devices, and a Type III slot for incorporating larger cards or holding two Type II cards. The PCMCIA subsequently formulated the 32-bit CardBus standard. It can use cards operating at different voltages and offers power management features to increase the battery life of the portable computer in which it is incorporated.

5.4 THE INTERNET AND THE WORLD WIDE WEB

The Internet is made up of thousands of inter-connected academic, commercial, government and military networks in over 70 countries, millions of hosts and tens if not hundreds of millions of users. A host is a mainframe, mini or workstation that directly supports the Internet Protocol (the IP in TCP/IP). Users have access to unpublished data, journals and bulletin board systems. It is also widely used as a world-wide electronic mail network. E-mail connection to the Internet is available through many online services such as AOL, Freeserve and Compuserve.

The Internet Society (ISOC) was established in June 1991 to maintain and extend the development and availability of the Internet and its associated technologies. In June 1992 the Internet Activities Board (the governing body for the Internet) proposed to associate its activities with the society and was renamed the Internet Architecture Board (IAB). The IAB is considered a technical advisory group of the ISOC.

The Internet Engineering Task Force (IETF) is the protocol engineering and development arm of the Internet. The IETF is a large open international community of network designers, operators, vendors, and researchers concerned with the evolution of the Internet architecture and the smooth operation of the Internet. It is open to any interested individual and works on the specifications of new standards.

The Internet Corporation for Assigned Names and Numbers (ICANN), established in 1999, administers Internet numbers and domain names.

5.4.1 The World Wide Web

The precursor of the World Wide Web (WWW) was a small, home-brewed personal hypertext system developed between 1989 and 1990 at CERN, Geneva's European Laboratory for Particle Physics. Early access to hypertext files and Internet news articles was demonstrated with the line-mode and graphical NeXTStep browsers. Before the end of 1991, CERN announced the Web to the world. The number of registered Web servers grew from 62 in April 1993 to 1,248 by May 1994. By July 1994 the Web had outgrown CERN's capability to deal with it, such that now the development venture comprises a collection of organisations and expertise called the World Wide Web Consortium (W3C).

The Web was originally conceived as a convenient way to disseminate information within an organisation. It behaves like a networked repository of information that pools together useful knowledge, allowing collaborators at remote sites to share their ideas, as well as information on all aspects of a common project. Information residing on the Web can be smoothly reshaped by alterations in hypertext links to represent the state of new knowledge in a constantly changing environment. Furthermore, the highly scaleable design of the Web requires no centralised administration of information. These properties have helped the Web to expand rapidly from its origins in CERN to the Internet, irrespective of boundaries between nations and disciplines.

Innovative uses for the Web have grown substantially so that it has become a place of communication and learning, a new marketplace, and a showground for new information technologies. However, success brings its own problems because the ever-increasing use of the Internet is highlighting the inadequacy of its performance for many users, and particularly for the pioneers of the technology – government, academic and research workers and institutions. For this reason these communities are developing Internet2, a high-speed network for the exchange of real-time, multimedia information. This network is not intended for commercial use, but it is likely that the technological developments will eventually be adopted by the global Internet.

5.4.2 Architecture of the WWW

The WWW organises, transmits and retrieves information of all types by using a combination of hypertext, graphics and multimedia technologies, unified in a set of naming conventions, network protocols, and document formats, and using a highly scaleable client/server architecture.

Besides the Web there are other information systems like Gopher and WAIS that use similar client/server architecture but have different purposes and roles. Gopher is like a web but without full hypertext capability. It uses a menu system that allows information to be organised in a hierarchy of directories. WAIS (Wide Area Information Server) provides no navigation facilities and uses indexing exclusively to transport users into the desired location of documents on the Internet. Text files can be searched by keyword using the Z39.50 query language similar to SQL (Structured Query Language).

Using the analogy of a book as information space, Gopher can be described as its table of contents, WAIS the index pages, and the WWW the hypertext body where the bulk of the contents reside.

The software architecture of the Web comprises the following inter-operating components:

- ◆ clients that allow users to navigate the Web or even interact with the server (an example of such a client is the browser Netscape Navigator)

- ◆ servers that allow Internet sites to publish information or export data to the world

♦ proxies that facilitate communications and provide access control for sites that must rely on an intermediary host for communication with the Internet (e.g. sites behind a firewall - a security barrier between the larger Internet and a smaller local area network within an organisation).

Despite the numerous different protocols in existence, the WWW utilises a universal addressing system called universal resource locators (URLs). A list of Internet protocols using URLs is shown in Table 5.9.

The primary and native network protocol used between the WWW clients and servers is HyperText Transfer Protocol (HTTP). This enables the WWW clients and servers to communicate efficiently, providing performance and features not otherwise available.

WWW also defines a HyperText Markup Language (HTML) which is an SGML-compatible document format that every WWW client is required to understand. It is used for the transmission and representation of basic items such as text, lists and menus as well as various styles of inputs in a fill-out form. Further information on HTML and SGML is provided in section 5.8.3.2.

PREFIX	SERVICE ACCESSED
http://	World Wide Web server
ftp://	FTP server (for file transfer)
news://	Usenet newsgroups
mailto://	e-mail
wais://	Wide Area Information Server
gopher://	Gopher server
file://	file on a local system
telnet://	applications on a network server
rlogin://	applications on a network server
tn3270://	applications on a mainframe

Table 5.9 Standardised URL prefixes for the Internet

A form is in essence a dialogue box with check boxes, radio buttons, pull-down menus and fields for editing. Radio buttons are on-screen buttons that allow only one selection to be made at a time from the button set offered. The author designs a form with the desired buttons, menus, etc. A program is written called a common gateway interface (CGI) application to handle the input, e.g. filling a request, looking up information, adding a reader's name to a mailing list. This becomes an interactive publication as the subscriber reads the pages and fills out the form. The CGI acts on the form in the way its program was designed and a new page can be created for the subscriber based on that data. CGI scripts provided the first means for Web sites to interact with databases and other programs. Java and JavaScript programs and ActiveX components are increasingly being adopted and are likely to predominate for such requirements.

5.4.3 Hardware for the Internet - Web clients and servers

Servers for making information available on the Internet (or on an Intranet) are typically based on Unix, Windows NT or, more recently, Open Source Software, such as Linux (see section 5.10). Planning a Web server needs to take into consideration the peak request load and the peak connection rate rather than the total numbers of requests serviced. Furthermore the speed of the outgoing network ports for the clients may be more of a constraining factor than how fast the disk and processor are.

In general the four principal factors to consider are:

- ◆ the size and performance of the network connection

- ◆ the surfing habits of the clients (do they undertake a great deal of indexing and server processing which will be stressful to the server's processor)

- ◆ storage requirements (SCSI disks will be required where many gigabytes are involved; IDE-based disks if data is limited to a few hundreds of megabytes)

- ◆ access patterns of the clients (more primary memory is required for HTML and WAIS users).

On the client side there is an ongoing debate as to whether the PC is dead in the world of the Internet. Low-cost access devices (see network computers - section 5.1.1) are envisaged which provide ready access while drawing their functionality from the Internet itself by downloading their operating system and applications when turned on.

5.4.4 Intranets

While public (and most professional and media) attention has been focused on the explosive development of the Internet, the in-house use of the same technology (Intranet) in a client/server environment may now exceed its usage on the World Wide Web. The World Wide Web was originally targeted at information dissemination inside an organisation. With the coming of the Intranet, the WWW has returned to its roots.

People have been quick to recognise that what is being done externally on the Internet can also be done internally, with the same benefits of speed, immediacy, simplicity and low cost. The sheer ease of the solution has meant it is one everyone can buy into, and it can be up and running in hours, not months - running before, or even in grey parallel with, 'official' systems. The Intranet has the additional benefit of scaleability - it works for a team of ten or ten million and offers tools for groups to work together while being apart.

A word of caution, however: the rapid take-up of Internet technology in-house has often been pursued without due consideration of its relationship and co-ordination with other information system developments within the business, such as document management and groupware. The merits and drawbacks of the various technologies are often not appreciated. This can lead to such systems being viewed as alternatives to one another rather than as means to build a coherent information and knowledge management infrastructure. Project management issues concerning system selection and design are considered further in Chapter 7.

5.5 INPUT DEVICES

Most of the information handled in organisations is not immediately amenable to computer processing as it is not in electronic form. To capitalise on the benefits of technology there needs to be effective means of inputting information into computers at the time it is created, and of capturing and converting information that has been previously recorded in some other way.

The electronic keyboard with its roots in mechanical typewriting is still the main input device for text. Variations have been devised to help avoid the occurrence of repetitive strain injury, including Microsoft's 'The Natural' keyboard, and rearrangement of the keys as in the Dvorak keyboard design which departs from the normal QWERTY layout. More radical approaches have included the Microwriter keyboard which used five keys, plus two control keys usable by the fingers of the right hand to enable rapid text input coupled with printer control and communication abilities. These departures from the ubiquitous QWERTY keyboard are rarely to be seen in use and no major design advances, or replacement for the QWERTY keyboard, can be foreseen for manual input.

The following sections cover alternative input devices to the traditional keyboard.

5.5.1 Speech recognition

Speech recognition has three main uses:

- command and control
  - e.g. navigation of graphical user interfaces
- data entry
  - e.g. physicians and nurses entering data into forms while examining patients
- dictation
  - creation of free-form or structured documents.

Speech recognition systems generally have three components:

- a vocabulary or dictionary (which is often customisable to include specialist and additional words)
- language model (to identify spoken words from the context)
- speaker model (which is trained to the individual speaker).

Early systems used discrete-word input where users pause between words. The move is towards continuous-speech recognition (i.e. chunks of meaning) rather than individual words. All systems have large vocabularies and complex language components for free-form dictation. For structured report generation the language module will be simpler.

Extraneous noises can distort communication, and different dialects can confuse the speech recognition device. Some applications have a recognition accuracy approaching 100%, but such a success rate is generally only achieved where the vocabulary employed is limited so that the recognition circuitry can be tuned accordingly. This approach is exemplified by interactive voice response systems as used to access a bank's central computer via the telephone.

There is little doubt that speech recognition will become an integral part of commercial office software with the wider availability of systems based on continuous-speech input, and the benefits that will come from neural-net technology to reduce influence of extraneous noise and create more flexible, speaker-independent models.

There is also the reverse application where the recorded text is converted into synthesised speech. This can be used to read faxes and e-mails through a voice messaging service. The technology is a valuable facility for visually impaired users.

All this functionality requires suitably powerful hardware for the speech-recognition software. For discrete speech systems it may be possible to run them on 66MHz 486 machines. Continuous speech software, however, will require a Pentium of at least 166MHz and 32MB RAM if acceptable response times are to be achieved.

An interesting variation on traditional voice dictation to tape is the use of open network dictation: dictation is stored on a network where it can be managed as part of a normal workflow, then retrieved and transcribed by typists no matter in which office they happen to be located.

5.5.2 Pen-based computing and hand-held computers

Handwriting or drawing directly onto a computer screen is largely the basis of so-called pen computing. Recognition of what is entered generally relies either on the position at which the entry is made if some kind of structured form is displayed (digitising tablets can be used in this way), or requires the use of in-built handwriting recognition software.

The initial euphoria which greeted the launch of Apple's Newton in 1992 was tempered by awareness of the limitations in the technology, particularly relating to handwriting recognition software. The more recent developments in the palmtop computer market as exemplified by the Psion Series 5, 3Com's Palm Pilot and those running Microsoft's CE operating system, have been accompanied by a renewed interest in software for recognising handwriting rather than simple printed characters. However, apart from limited use, or specialist applications, such data entry techniques will not entirely replace the keyboard.

Success in the marketplace for hand-helds is more likely to be achieved by offering a combination of input means (e.g. keyboard, pen and voice) coupled with seamless communication abilities for mobile computing. In this regard the investment by Nokia, Ericsson and Motorola in Psion's EPOC software via the Symbian joint company was a significant event and places them squarely in competition with Microsoft.

5.5.3 Bar coding

Bar coding is a two-step input technology as it first requires a code to be generated and printed out for subsequent reading and hence conversion into computer-processable form. Bar codes are familiar patterns on supermarket goods, but have a wider range of applications in areas such as stock control, version control for drawings and manuals, library lending and archive storage of company records as part of a records retention programme. Basic reference and indexing details of documents can be encoded and used to speed up index capture during document imaging and help manage the flow of batches of work.

A range of international bar code standards exists and hence code generation software and bar code readers (both fixed and mobile) must be properly matched. Bar code images can be incorporated in, for example Visual Basic, C, C++ and OLE-2 applications using a third-party OLE developer's kit.

The commonly encountered bar codes are one dimensional, in that they are read by passing a reading wand across their width. A two-dimensional code, PDF417, from Symbol Technology holds up to 1.1 KB of data on a single symbol. PDF417 is the de facto standard 2-D symbology and is likely to gain wider acceptance given that the American National Standards Institute (ANSI) has published a new 2-D standard, ANSI MH 10.8.3M unit loads and transport packages for two-dimensional symbols. It recommends the use of PDF417 for all shipping, receiving and supporting EDI documentation. It is anticipated that this ANSI standard will form the basis for industry-specific application specifications.

5.5.4 Digital cameras

Until recently the incorporation of photographic film-based images into digital documents required the use of a scanner. Although relatively inexpensive scanners for film and slide material are available for the domestic market, this intermediary stage can now often be omitted by using digital camera technology that records the image in a form which can be loaded directly into a computer. While not suitable for capturing text-based information, such cameras are useful where photographic images need to be incorporated with text in documents, for example estate agent brochures and publicity leaflets. They are also proving invaluable for engineers on site undertaking maintenance or survey work who require instantly available records of the assets under investigation.

The cameras are available from a range of suppliers both from the computing and traditional film camera industries. Prices are dropping month by month with the lower-priced cameras offering lower image resolutions than their higher cost professional counterparts. To transfer the captured image to a computer, the cameras may incorporate links for direct uploading to a PC, or some form of intermediary storage ranging from floppy disks to flash memory disks which offer considerably greater storage space.

5.5.5 Optical and intelligent character recognition

Optical character recognition (OCR) is a means to convert printed or bit-image representations of documents into editable form for a computer.

The earliest technology used matrix matching by comparing the shape of a scanned alphanumeric character with a database of letter shapes. Provided the shapes were in the database and a single font was used throughout the document, recognition could usually be guaranteed. Multiple font documents, however, could not reliably be converted.

Feature extraction followed and involved analysing how a letter was formed rather than its complete shape. The effectiveness of this approach was improved by 'noise elimination' whereby the software concentrated on the reliable fragments of a character and ignored extraneous marks or blemishes.

The later incarnations of OCR have true learning ability. Usually referred to as intelligent character recognition (ICR) products, they enable a user to enter via the keyboard the identity of characters or punctuation marks which the ICR software has failed to recognise. At subsequent encounters with the same symbol, the ICR software generates the appropriate ASCII code without the need for further human intervention. ICR products are available which can be operated selectively in either standard or learning modes. Additional facilities may include spelling dictionaries, analysis of word position to increase the accuracy of the recognition and ability to retain the page layout including columns and graphics around the OCR'd text.

Clearly defined text printed on paper can usually be reliably recognised provided the point size of the characters is not too small. Where an electronic raster image, such as a received fax, is subjected to OCR, the resolution at which the source document was scanned can be a major factor in determining the success or otherwise of the conversion. Increasingly technology such as neural-network based recognition engines are being applied to improve the accuracy of converting bit-map images into editable text.

For normal size text, i.e. 10 point or above, scanning resolutions down to 200 dot per inch (dpi) may be adequate. For smaller points sizes, however, low resolutions will not provide the necessary precision, hence scanning at 400 dpi will be more reliable.

OCR/ICR technology can be used to facilitate speedier indexing of documents. Such indexing may involve applying OCR to the complete text, or to particular areas of the document where indexing information will be found. Forms or summary pages of reports are typical examples of the latter case. Data input by capturing information using specialised form-work software can equate to approaching 100,000 keystrokes per hour. This compares with the average data entry operator speed of just over 11,000 keystrokes per hour.

Reliable recognition of hand-written documents is still some way off, although some success has been achieved with applications such as form-filling where the character set or vocabulary are limited and greater care is taken to ensure uniformity when entering the characters. Despite these difficulties, commercial deployment of recognition technology based on neural network modelling is already evident in the finance industry to process cheques involving the recognition of dot-matrix printed and hand-written information.

Even with the best endeavours, an OCR/ICR system is very unlikely to operate at 100% recognition across what will usually be variable sizes font and quality of original. This may not be important if the recognition is to extract indexing words from the free text of a report, or correspondence. The fact that most words for the index will have been recognised accurately will usually still allow the document to be retrieved even if a certain number are not correctly translated.

Where maximum recognition accuracy is vital, the complete OCR systems should be optimised for the types of document that are to be handled. For example, if OCR is to be undertaken on form work, then it can be beneficial to employ form removal software first. This removes the form structure leaving a smaller data file whose textual information can therefore be more rapidly dealt with by the OCR software.

While the focus of most OCR products is on converting the images of the characters to ASCII-editable text that can be indexed and searched, the patented Adaptive Pattern Recognition Processing (APRP) approach of Excalibur is based on the binary patterns in the data itself. Thus the data to be indexed and searched is not limited to words, but may also be pictures or a video clip. This approach is claimed to be particularly suited to dealing with large volumes of legacy paper documents that need to be converted into text searchable form.

While more OCR products will enter this growing market it is likely that there will be further consolidation amongst the suppliers. OCR software is increasingly bundled with compact scanners, some being an integral part of a keyboard. Soon OCR will be just part of standard office productivity software.

5.5.6 Pointing devices

Working with a computer requires the user to make selections, be they to initiate action or respond to options that are presented on the screen. Although speech recognition as described above can be used, these actions normally require the use of externally operating pointing devices such as a mouse or tracker-ball, or of essentially in-built facilities as provided by a touch screen.

A mouse requires a level surface across which it can be moved. Where space is at a premium, and this particularly applies when using lap portables or notebook computers on the move, the tracker-ball, or some similar in-built design, provides a practical alternative.

A simple way to interact with a computer is to use a screen that is sensitive to touch. Palmtop computers are usually fitted with such screens and are commonly used in conjunction with a stylus. Different designs of touch screen technology are available, based, for example, on capacitive techniques, some of which can operate behind thick protective glass screens where proof against vandalism is required. Resistive membrane products can be used with gloved hands as may be necessary in medical or industrial environments.

5.5.7 Electronic imaging

Electronic imaging involves the use of a scanner to convert the image of human-readable documents, be they on paper or microfilm, into a binary digital representation suitable for computerised storage, retrieval and transmission. Unlike a microfilm image, an electronic image is not in itself human-readable, but first has to be processed for output to a display or hard-copy device.

The bulk of business documents are still in paper form, and much of this will not have readily accessible electronic equivalents, if they exist at all. Electronic imaging is a key technology which has contributed to the success of integrated document management projects that require the incorporation of existing or newly received paper documents.

5.5.7.1 Scanning for image capture

Two main, but overlapping, markets exist for scanners. The first, and longer established is that relating to desk-top publishing (DTP) where scanners in conjunction with image editing software are used to capture and as necessary edit such features as line artwork, photographs and text. These scanners range from relatively inexpensive hand-held units, affordable for home use and capable of capturing images in black and white or colour, to sophisticated flat-bed colour units aimed more at the commercial printer. In these instances the focus is on incorporating the images, or any OCR-converted text in publications.

The second market relates to document imaging. Here the emphasis is on the information content of the material that is imaged, rather than its aesthetic appearance. Hence requirements will arise for such facilities as full text indexing, long-term high-capacity storage, back-log conversion and high bandwidth communication networks.

The capture stage is the most critical, as what can be achieved during any subsequent processing depends on the quality and type of image information initially secured. While this statement can be applied to micrographics applications, electronic imaging is a more complex process and differs from microfilming in that scanning time (as opposed to microfilm exposure time) is affected by such factors as resolution and the presence of continuous tone or colour in the documents. This demands that greater attention be taken during the scanning stage of the make-up of the document. This attention is needed otherwise it may not be possible to make optimum use of the document's information in a computerised environment.

Documents can be rich in terms of the variety of information objects they contain. This richness can include, for example, text in various typefaces and sizes, line drawings, graphics, spreadsheets, tables, photographs and form work, some or all of which may be in colour rather than black and white. For the purposes of the scanning process images can be categorised under the headings:

- bitonal images
  - these require only two levels of intensity, as in line art work such as black and white engineering drawings, or pages of typed alphanumeric text.

- continuous tone images
  - these exhibit indivisible transitions from dark to light (shades of grey) as in a black and white photograph.

- colour images
  - these incorporate the three primary colours and shades of grey to register brightness. A colour photograph is such an image.

The output format for the resulting image is usually the Tagged Image File Format (TIFF).

5.5.7.2 Scanner control software

For many scanners, there is more than one choice of scanner control software, the principal ones being TWAIN and ISIS.

TWAIN (Toolkit Without An Important Name) is a *de facto* interface standard that lets applications communicate with scanner software to scan and acquire bitmap images. It was originally defined by a working group of scanner manufacturers and software publishers including Aldus, Caere, Eastman Kodak, Hewlett-Packard and Logitech, and was principally aimed at addressing the needs of desktop publishing.

ISIS (Image and Scanner Interface Standard) was developed by Pixel Translations to target high-volume document image capture and processing systems. ISIS is the basis for the AIIM/ANSI MS61 API standard for scanners in the document imaging environment.

A comparison of the two is provided in Table 5.10.

FEATURE	ISIS	TWAIN
Architecture		
API for image acquisition	Yes	No
Image viewer	Yes	No
Print modules	Yes	No
Image data format conversion	Yes	No
Image data compression & data types	12	None
File read/write	Yes	No
Pipes★	Yes	No
Packet streaming architecture	Yes	No
Optimised to run scanners at rated speed	Yes	No
Platforms supported		
Windows (16-bit and 32-bit)	Yes	Yes
Macintosh	Yes	Yes
OS/2	Limited	No
UNIX	Yes	No
Market and Support Issues		
Primary application	Production imaging	Desktop publishing
Scanners supported	125+	125+
Applications supported	100+	100+
Standard	AIIM/ANSI MS61	*De facto*
Technical support	Paid	Volunteer
Module testing/certification	All modules	Sometimes
Licence fees	Yes	No
Availability of commercial-quality tools	Yes	No

★ ISIS provides a mechanism to use ISIS modules in combination to perform specific imaging functions. Two or more ISIS modules linked together in this fashion are called an ISIS pipe.

Table 5.10 Comparison of ISIS and TWAIN[1].

5.5.7.3 Resolution in electronic imaging

Scanner resolution is normally expressed in terms of linear dots (i.e. pixels) per inch (dpi). The number of pixels in a line, and the number of lines used to create the bit map, indicate the resolution employed. The resolution chosen must be at least equal to that required for any subsequent processing and output. However, opting for too high a resolution may increase the size of the digitised documents to a level where storage space demands, or data transfer speeds over networks, or both, become unacceptable. It also increases scanning time.

The resolution chosen depends on the particular application (Table 5.11). For bitonal images, the binary digital signals (bits) produced from scanning have only to represent black (bit 1) or white (bit 0), and not shades of grey, to create the required bit map. Thus

112   Technology and Retrieval

SCANNING RESOLUTION (DPI)

	200	300	400	800	1200	2400
36		Commercial colour				
24		DTP colour				
12		Commercial continuous tone				
8	DTP continuous tone					
1	Line art		DTP line art		Commercial line art	

BITS PER PIXEL

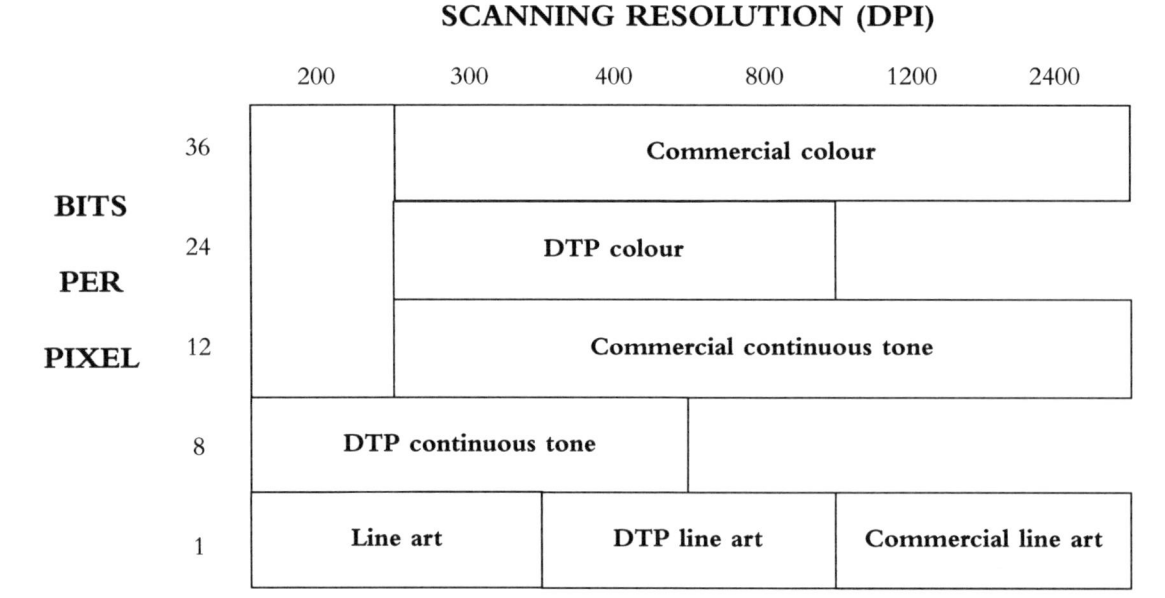

Table 5.11 Typical scanning resolutions for different applications

1 bit per pixel is sufficient information to record bitonal images.

Photographs and specialised images, such as X-rays, achieve their rich visual effect by the continuous range of tones they exhibit. The scanning process must ensure that any needed subtleties are not lost. It is, in fact, unnecessary fully to capture and process the huge amount of data which this subtlety represents. For visual interpretation, 8 bits per pixel, which provide 256 levels of grey, is perfectly adequate for most applications. Use of grey scale does, however, increase the storage requirements (Table 5.12).

A scanning resolution of 200 dpi is typically adopted for line art work such as engineering drawings. For most office applications 300 dpi range is acceptable as it is well

DOCUMENT (compression)	RASTER (scanning resolution)			VECTOR	ASCII
	200 dpi	300 dpi	400 dpi		
A0 Drawing bitonal (uncompressed)	7.74	17.43	31.00	0.40	
A0 Drawing bitonal (25:1)	0.31	0.70	1.24	0.40	
A4 bitonal (uncompressed)	0.48	1.09	1.93		
A4 bitonal (10:1)	0.05	0.11	0.19		0.005 - 0.001
A4 256 grey scale 8 bits per pixel (uncompressed)	3.87	8.70	15.47		0.005 - 0.001
A4 colour 32 bits per pixel (uncompressed)	15.47	34.80	61.87		

Table 5.12 Typical file sizes (megabytes) for raster images, vector and ASCII text

matched to the 300 dpi output of laser printers. Scanning at 400 dpi is usually only necessary where smaller typefaces (10 point or less) are encountered which need to be legible on the image, or subjected to OCR.

5.5.7.4 Contrast in electronic imaging

Most scanners capture information in a multi-bit per pixel, grey scale format, and this information would be retained for photographic or colour applications. However, to cater for line art, or to enable the grey scales of photographic material to be simulated on bitonal laser printers, the grey scale data must be processed to produce single bit per pixel images. This is effected by 'thresholding' and 'dithering' respectively.

The text or lines on a bitonal original may not be uniform in intensity. Hence a threshold, or contrast level, must be set to distinguish between black and white. This distinction can be made automatically by a scanner based on such factors as the average density of the document's background and data from scanning the region surrounding individual pixels. Dynamic thresholding, available in some units, automatically adjusts the threshold level in relation to the quality of the document being scanned.

Dithering in scanning technology is akin to half-tone photographic reproduction in newspaper printing, in that both use accumulations of solid printed dots to give the overall illusion of shades of grey. In dithering the pixels, or printer dots, are arranged in groups, or half-tone dots. The printer dots making up each half-tone dot are an appropriate mix of black or white to simulate the shade for that point on the original. Thus to cater for 256 grey scale levels, each half-tone dot comprises 16 x 16 (256) printer dots (pixels).

There is, however, a trade-off to be made between resolution and grey scale. For output on a 300 dpi laser printer, the 16 x 16 printer dot would produce an effective half-tone dot pitch of 18.75 lines per inch (300/16), and hence an unacceptably granular image.

Depending on the scanner design, thresholding and dithering can be undertaken concurrently, if necessary on appropriate areas of the same page so that bitonal areas are subjected to thresholding and photographic areas are dithered.

5.5.7.5 Source document scanning in electronic imaging

Optical scanners provide the means to capture the images of paper or microfilm documents. Such units are available in flat-bed and rotary designs and are operated in conjunction with a computer or microprocessor unit which processes the digitised product and prepares it for storage on suitable media. Scanners for electronic document imaging generally need to cater for higher-volume throughputs, and a greater range of document sizes and formats than are met in desktop publishing. In this context hand-held scanners are not suitable. Nevertheless, relatively inexpensive A4 flatbed monochrome scanners primarily intended for DTP are available for small-scale, low-volume electronic document imaging applications. There is also a move to marketing hybrid systems, that is scanners that can photocopy and printers that can scan and fax documents.

In general terms, a scanner incorporates a light source which illuminates the document page. Black areas on the page absorb most of the light, while white areas reflect it. For grey areas, light is reflected in proportion to shades of grey. During line-by-line scanning of the page, the light reflected from the document is detected by a charged coupled device (CCD) comprising a single, linear arrangement of individual photo-sensitive cells. The light falling on each cell during a line scan is converted into an electrical charge whose magnitude corresponds to the intensity of the light received. These analogue charges are then converted into digital signals for further processing. The image of the document page has thereby been captured as a two-dimensional grid of individual picture elements ('pixels') or raster image – a process termed 'bit-mapping'.

For colour scanning, the light beam can be split into its red, green and blue (RGB) components which are each captured along with their associated grey scales by individual CCD arrays. The RGB elements may subsequently be converted into cyan, magenta, yellow and black (CMYB), a format usually employed for colour reproduction.

The throughput speed attained using a particular scanner depends on the scanning resolution which is chosen and whether colour scanning is adopted when coloured documents are encountered. Scanning at higher resolutions and for colour require more information to be captured in digital form. Throughput speeds quoted for different scanners may be misleading in that they are not necessarily directly comparable from one model to another due to key factors being included in some instances but ignored in others. For example, scanning speeds are often based purely on the speed of transport of documents through a sheet feeder mechanism. However, in live systems the actual throughput speed must take the whole scanning process into consideration. Thus the speed with which documents can be processed includes not only other inescapable time elements associated with each scan, such as those relating to indexing, image quality checking and image compression but also *ad hoc* occurrences such as removing that unexpected paper clip or re-scanning necessitated by document feeder jams or failures to meet quality control targets.

The mechanics of achieving relative movement between the document and the scanning light depend on the design of the scanner, each being suited to particular applications. Some scanners are produced by suppliers already established in micrographics, hence designs often draw on those used for flat-bed or rotary cameras, although a precise distinction is not always possible as regards scanners. Generally scanners can be divided into flat-bed or sheet-fed designs.

In flat-bed units, documents are handled as if being used with a photocopier in that the documents are placed individually and usually face-downwards on a glass surface from beneath which they are illuminated. Relatively low throughput rates are achievable as they are not simply dependent on the speed of scanning, but also on the time taken to manually remove a scanned document and replace it with its successor.

Depending on the particular scanner model, automatic sheet feeding devices may be fitted to enable stacks of documents to be fed to, and ejected from the scanning surface with minimum operator intervention. This design resembles in many ways that found in facsimile equipment on whose technology scanners are based. As throughput speeds increase there is always the danger of mis-feeds leading to the capture of a skewed image. This can reduce the accuracy or render impossible the use of optical character recognition (OCR).

As with any mechanical paper-handling system, its smooth and continuous operation may be disrupted, for example by encountering staples, tears or creases. It is therefore important that documents are checked prior to scanning to take the necessary remedial action. Many of the defects that adversely affect mechanical handling also influence the quality and accuracy of the captured image as compared with the original, and hence their rectification is equally important when using flat-bed scanners.

Small hand-held scanners have become popular, but their use is mainly directed towards desktop publishing where there is the frequent requirement to incorporate portions of text or graphics from an existing document into one which is being word-processed. The scanners are generally narrower than standard page widths and to capture a whole page requires several passes to be made. The fact that relative movement between page and scanner is achieved by hand can lead to unevenness in image capture and complications when using OCR software or joining the individual image segments. Nevertheless compact hand-held scanners are available which not only undertake OCR, but have in-built language software to provide 'instant' translation between different foreign languages.

5.5.8 Microfilming and microfilm scanning

Micrographics is the term generally applied to cover the creation and use of miniaturised, human-readable images of original documents which are held on film material. With its origins in photographic technology, microfilm is a long-established, well-proven medium for long-term storage of inactive records.

A microform image may be captured directly either from the original paper document, or from an electronic original as held on a computer. The former method is called source document microfilming, and the latter computer output microfilming.

The common storage formats for microfilmed images are:

- aperture cards (holding a single 35 mm film frame)

- microfiche (sheets of film with images recorded in a grid pattern)

- microfilm jackets (rectangular flexible carriers with channels into which pieces of imaged microfilm are slid)

- 16 mm roll film.

Unlike scanning times for electronic imaging, exposure time for microfilming is not altered by variations in page size or by filming coloured material or documents containing shades of grey as in a black and white photograph.

A range of camera designs are available including those which not only microfilm the documents but also digitally scan them so that, for example, the film versions of originals can be stored as back-up security copies and the digital versions are available for day-to-day business use and communication.

Although the market for microfilm continues to decline, the desire to integrate and make accessible recorded information within organisations has seen an increase in the use of scanners to digitise microfilmed documents. The equipment ranges from microfilm reader-printers with in-built digitising capability to production microfilm and aperture card scanners.[2]

5.6 STORAGE TECHNOLOGIES

The computer's main memory - random access memory (RAM) - provides an area for virtually instant access and high speed processing. It can also be configured to provide a portion of its storage capacity as cache memory for holding frequently accessed data or program instructions so that they are readily available as and when required. It is, however, a volatile storage medium so any data it contains is lost should the computer be switched off. Non-volatile storage is provided by magnetic and optical media.

Storage systems have traditionally been considered as online or off-line, but these terms are open to differing shades of interpretation. In broad terms, online indicates that some form of direct connection has been established between a computer and a system, device or service, while off-line indicates the lack of such a connection.

However, while a hard disk and hence the data it stores are usually permanently connected and available as and when required, a disk drive uses removable media - individual storage disks - and these may not be physically in the drive at the desired time. Hence, disks that are not loaded in the drive can be considered as being off-line and only become on-line once they have been loaded manually or by some automated mechanical means. This latter approach is exemplified by auto-loaders for CD-ROMs and jukeboxes for optical storage disks. Due to their automated nature, these devices provide a half-way house between the traditional online magnetic hard disk and conventional magnetic disk and tape drives and have been referred to as near-line storage systems. As commonly interpreted, 'off-line' describes storage media such as magnetic tapes or back-up disks which are infrequently accessed and are stored on racks or shelves.

As should be apparent, a hierarchy of storage systems exists, and labelling them simply in terms of online versus off-line, or magnetic versus optical technology does not provide the necessary precision when formulating a storage strategy for a particular application such as document imaging. Factors such as data volumes, speeds and frequency of access, data transfer rates, storage capacity and life expectancy of the storage media need to be assessed. For electronic imaging systems the ability automatically to optimise the use of different storage media within the hierarchy is a key consideration.

It is important to point out that many of the storage technologies, particularly some of the smaller removable magnetic and optical media systems aimed at the consumer rather than the business market, do not fully conform to *de jure* standards even if such standards exist at all. As with any fast moving technology, designers and developers have been ahead of the standards bodies (noteworthy here is the decision of the International Electrotechnical Commission – IEC – to launch its Industry Technical Agreements, a high-speed process aimed at delivering industry specifications in months rather than years). Meanwhile one mainly has to rely now on *de facto* standards pertaining to those products that are gaining the lion's share of the market. Nevertheless, when investing in storage technology, be aware that the particular format or drive system chosen may be obsolete in just a few years and render the stored data inaccessible should the media or the drive fail. It is therefore important to have a storage management and data migration policy to protect one's information.

The growing demands for larger storage capacities generated by the increasing use of electronic images and multimedia information has largely been satisfied by developments in both magnetic and optical storage media and drive units.

5.6.1 Magnetic storage

Digital information is stored by using read/write heads to orientate magnetic material on the storage device so that it corresponds to the information's data bits. The read/write heads read the data by sensing magnetic polarities.

Magnetic tape has long been the main vehicle for back-up and archival storage ranging from a handful of small tape cartridges to high-capacity tape libraries for storing, retrieving, reading and writing multiple magnetic tape cartridges. Since data can only be found by sequential searching of the linear tape, access times to reach the required information is usually measured in several seconds or even minutes.

Hard disk drives, now with capacities well into the gigabyte range are important components of imaging systems. They provide a fast-response image processing storage medium and the initial location for holding the bit-mapped images resulting from scanning. Developments in drive media, such as the use of magnetoresistive (MR) technology for read/write heads on a magnetic disk, have dramatically increased areal densities - the amount of data bits in a given area – so that storage capacity is estimated to be doubling every year, while the cost per gigabit is halving. Overall it is unlikely that newer technologies such as optical storage will overtake the performance and capacity of fixed magnetic devices in the immediate future.

As regards removable magnetic storage media, the long-established 3.5-inch 'floppy' with a capacity of 1.44 MB has limited use in image storage applications being barely able to hold a single page of A4 text scanned at a resolution of 300 dpi. This limitation has been addressed in recent times by a diverse range of new media and drive units few, if any, compatible with one another or conforming to existing standards. This makes decision making difficult, particularly in the business context where the requirement is for long-term, secure and accessible storage.

Competing removable medium technologies aiming to replace the standard 'floppy' disk have arrived in the marketplace from companies such as Syquest, Iomega and Sony, each offering capacities of over 100 MB per disk. However, these are not compatible with the floppy. Since most users have information stored on the ubiquitous 3.5-inch floppies, some developments in larger capacity storage media and associated drive technology allow this existing format to be read and written to, for example the LS-120 and the more recently launched HiFD disk. The bewildering choice of removable storage technologies makes it equally difficult for computer manufacturers and users to decide which type to adopt. Do they opt for backwards compatibility with floppies or choose an incompatible format offering larger storage capacity, and risk the consequences of technology obsolescence or the developer going out of business, as happened to Syquest?

Solid state storage is exemplified by flash memory. This is a read-write storage chip that holds its content without the need for power. It is the basis of 'flash cards', the solid state storage disks used in hand-held computers and digital cameras and available in PC card slot format. The CompactFlash flash memory format from SanDisk Corporation is one with which other peripherals, such as mini magnetic disk drives conform, enabling them to fit into a standard Type II PC card slot with the aid of an adapter.

At the other end of the storage spectrum is RAID technology which was built on developments aimed at improving fault tolerance and performance. RAID (redundant array of inexpensive disks) involves mounting many small disk drives in a single cabinet to provide overall storage capacities of many gigabytes to rival optical storage levels. RAID is available at different levels of sophistication as noted in Table 5.13.

Similar technologies to RAID are being applied to provide faster back-up times and improved fault tolerance for tap drive arrays (RAIT).

5.6.2 Optical storage

Optical storage media are direct-access disks on which the information is written and read by laser light. Although they do not yet have the speed of access and retrieval of magnetic media devices, they do not suffer corruption from stray magnetic fields, are less vulner-

LEVEL	CONFIGURATION
0	Single disk only or multiple disks using disk striping only (which interleaves data across multiple disks for better performance. It does not provide safeguards against failure).
1	Data is read from, and written to, a pair of identical 'mirrored' drives. If one of the RAID 1 mirrored drives fails, the other takes over. It offers highest reliability, but doubles storage cost.
2	Bits (rather than bytes or groups of bytes) are interleaved across multiple disks. It uses error detection and correction.
3	Bits are striped across three or more drives, together with error-checking data. Used to achieve the highest data transfer, because all drives operate in parallel. Parity bits are stored on separate, dedicated drives. Highest performance. If any one drive fails, its data can be inferred from the others.
4	Similar to Level 3, but manages disks independently rather than in unison. Uses dedicated drive for parity. It is not in common use.
5	Data is striped across three or more drives for performance, and parity bits are used for fault tolerance. It is the most widely-used form of RAID.
6	Similar to RAID 5, but does two different parity computations. Highest reliability, but not widely used.

Table 5.13 Available RAID levels

able to extremes of temperature and, although only proved by laboratory tests rather than real life, have a claimed life extending to 30 years or more.

Optical media have proved to be popular for archival storage, for publishing and information distribution and latterly and increasingly in a re-writable form as direct competitors for magnetic disks. The technology can be broadly divided into supplier recorded non-erasable, user recorded non-erasable and re-writable categories.

Supplier recorded non-erasable media are those where the information is implanted on the disk at the time of manufacture and include CD, CD-ROM and more recently DVD-ROM and DVD-Video disks.

The success of CD-ROM technology with its 650MB capacity, is due to the fact that its development has largely been based on widely agreed and adopted standards, a fact that has not applied generally to other optical disc formats. While its main application has been for educational and professional publishing often involving multimedia, the inclusion of CD-ROM drives as standard equipment in PCs has meant that CD-ROM is now widely used instead of 3.5-inch floppies for software program and documentation distribution.

The DVD format has the same overall dimensions of a CD, but considerably larger storage capacities. Originally focused on the market for pre-recorded film, DVD stood for 'Digital Video Disk'. However, the development of the technology is positioning it in the same market segment as CD-ROM and its variants and it is seen as the eventual replacement for analogue Laser Disks and the ubiquitous VHS recording tape.

WORM (Write-Once-Read-Many), CD-R and DVD-R disks are recorded in the user's environment, but the recorded information cannot be erased. The popularity of CD-ROM in the home and at work has created the tendency for the name to be used as a catch-all for optical storage media, and write-once technology in particular. This, coupled with the still competing standards for DVD technology, can lead to confusion when choosing optical storage and may lead to inappropriate media being selected.

Erasable, or re-writable, optical disks, like magnetic disks, can be rewritten over and over again. Rewritable disks use either magneto-optic (MO) or phase change technology. MO drives use a combination of magnetic and laser technology to record and erase the date. The disks are robust and are aimed at high capacity business applications. Phase change disks (CD-RW, DVD-RAM and PD – the latter from Panasonic) are lower cost consumer-oriented products based purely on optical technology.

A summary of DVD media is provided in Table 5.14.

DVD VARIANT	FORMAT	CAPACITY GB	COMMENTS
DVD-ROM	Single or double-sided; single or double layer	4.7; 8.5; 9.4; 17	Read-only
DVD-R	Single and double-sided	3.95; 7.90	Write-once medium for creating masters
DVD-R/W	Single or double-sided	3.95	Pioneers's own specification; effectively an extension of DVD-R. Not intended as an end user product, but for content developers.
DVD-RAM	Single or double-sided	2.6 or 5.2	Re-writable format sanctioned by the DVD Forum and supported by Matsushita (Panasonic), Hitachi, JVC and Toshiba. Uses a cartridge. Panasonic's reads/writes to PD disks
DVD+RW	Single or double-sided	3.0 or 6.0	Re-writable from break-away group Sony, Philips, Hewlett Packard, Ricoh, Yamaha and Mitsubishi. Competes with DVD-RAM. Does not need a cartridge. Incompatible with DVD-RAM and DVD-R/W, but more compatible with CD-R and CD-RW.
MMVF	Single or double-sided	5.2; 10.4	(MultiMedia Video File) Rewritable DVD format. Currently only available in Japan

Table 5.14 DVD variants

5.6.3 Future storage technologies

Arguably the future rests with holographic storage as it will avoid the use of rotating storage media and offers virtually instant access to highly very high capacity storage. It employs two laser beams simultaneously to change the state of particles in a crystal. These are then read by another laser beam and interpreted as data. Although years away from commercial exploitation, researchers have already been able to store 12 GB of feature film in a crystal the size of a sugar cube. The PRISM (Photorefractive Information Storage Materials Consortium) project is funded by the US Government's Advanced Research Projects Agency with consortium members including IBM and Stanford University.

Closer to commercial deployment are new technologies, Near Field Recording (NFR) from Terastor and Optically Assisted Winchester (OAW) from the Quinta Division of Seagate. Similar to magneto-optic in concept, the technologies greatly increase storage capacity; Quinta claims an increase factor of 10 to 20 times over current designs.

5.6.4 Life expectancy

When statements are made about the life expectancy of optical storage media, there are three major issues that need to be considered to assess the validity or otherwise of the claims:

- life expectancy is not based on actual experience

- the technology (e.g. drive units) associated with the media has also to be assessed

- standardisation may be lacking.

Microfilm has the advantage of having been in use for a sufficient number of years to prove its ability to retain information in a readable and accessible form. Optical media generally have their life expectancy estimated based on the results of accelerated testing, much of this having been undertaken only by the manufacturers themselves. In overall terms, erasable media have a shorter claimed life expectancy than write-once media, with the former ranging from around 10 to 40 years, while the latter is estimated to reach 100 years.

Failure to live out the claimed lifespan can be due to a number of factors, some of which do not have such a harmful effect in the case of microfilm. Thus dust particles have been shown to be a more important factor than was at first realised. They adversely affect not simply the integrity of the data on the disk, but also the workings of the various systems and sub-systems; hence the developments by vendors to prevent the formation and entry of dust by improving component design and construction and to extract it where it might arise by controlling air flow and introducing filters.

These problems highlight the second major issue noted above, namely that one cannot simply focus on the life expectancy of the disk media. Images on a microfilm are readable by the human eye, given relatively unsophisticated mechanical aids. Simple observation can confirm the continued existence of the stored images in a readable form. With optical media, however, the information stored on a disk needs technology to render the same outcome. Highly engineered disk drives are required operating in conjunction with sophisticated sub-systems and software. The life expectancy of this associated technology is in most cases going to be less than that of the storage media, particularly if the amount of data that comes to be handled by the system accelerates usage of the system beyond its rated capacity.

When looking to replace ageing technology to support existing optical storage the third issue comes to light, that is the lack of standardisation. The media themselves, the physical formats and the logical file structures are present in a variety of incarnations with few *de facto* and *de jure* standards to support them. While manufacturers might like to retain their existing customer bases by providing backward compatibility should the customer upgrade to the latest systems on offer, such compatibility cannot be assured. Market forces coupled with the irresistible advance of technology tend to stay in advance of standardisation. Without proper planning, therefore, the unwary customer can find that their archived optically stored information cannot be read on the equipment they have just acquired.

The 'proper planning' referred to must include giving due attention to records management considerations as described at length in Chapter 4. Thus, if the retention schedules devised for business records show that certain records need to be kept for 'the life of the company', for example, then the records management strategy must deal with such factors as media choice and conversion. This means choosing the storage media that provides the proper balance between such factors as the need for and frequency of access to the records and their retention periods. The strategy may well adopt a dual media approach with some records being placed on microfilm for longer term retention, but having them on optical media for ready access.

An important change in the terminology of life expectancy was taken by ANSI in its specification ANSI IT9.1 relating to microfilm. It dropped any reference to the word 'archival' and replaced it with the concept of 'life expectancy' and LE designation. The number following the LE symbol is a prediction of the minimum life expectancy in years for which information can be retrieved without significant loss when properly stored under extended-term storage conditions.

To take account of the estimated life expectancy of any optical media that the business uses at present, and the changes in technology over time, the strategy should include plans and time-scales for transferring the existing optically stored information onto new (not necessarily different) media. This is no more than data processing departments have done for many years with data stored on magnetic tape.

5.6.5 Legal admissibility

Having the originals of documents would seem to be the surest way of guaranteeing the legal acceptability of such records and the information they contain. For most people the word 'original' implies a paper-based document. However, with the advent of computers and associated software such as that used for word-processing, computer-aided-design (CAD) and electronic trading, the 'original' is usually created in electronic form and may, in fact, never be printed out. The use of such technologies can therefore lead to a blurring of the distinction between originals and their surrogates. Although in the end it is up to the court to decide what is, or is not admissible, gaining legal acceptance for a particular record is more likely to be the norm if suitable care and attention have been taken over the operational procedures that have lead to its creation, and the management policies that have been applied to monitor, control, audit and document such procedures.

5.6.5.1 Legal aspects of microfilm

The use of microfilm in business can be traced back to the 1920s, well before the development of computers. Initially applied to the filming of cheques, micrographics is a well-established means for long-term storage of records across government, commerce and industry. Despite this long history, and the fact that there are many examples where microfilmed records have been accepted as evidence in court, problems can still be encountered in gaining such acceptability. These problems are not so much related to the film media *per se*, but rather to deficiencies in the aforementioned procedures and policies that lead, for example, to doubts about the authenticity or accuracy of the filmed records and their information content.

These issues continue to be addressed on two main fronts. Thus various national and local governments have laws and regulations relevant to the use of records as evidence, as exemplified by the Federal Rules of Evidence, Uniform Rules of Evidence and Uniform Photographic Copies of Business and Public Records As Evidence Act in the US, and the Police and Criminal Evidence Act in the UK.

Alongside the regulatory approach there are micrographic-related standards and guidelines relevant to legal acceptability. In the UK, for example, there are several standards and guides produced or adopted by the British Standards Institution covering, for example, legal admissibility,[3] requirements for evidence,[4] authorised signatures[5] and processed film for archival records.[6] The first referenced publication outlines a properly controlled and planned programme for microfilming source documents to facilitate the acceptance of microfilm copies as substitutes for the originals.

Computer-output-on microfilm (COM) presents its own problems. Although the product is a set of microform images, the images emanate from computer-stored data and not from paper-based source documents. Hence the issue of admissibility is very much focused on the computer system rather than the storage medium. The aspect of quality control is, however, covered in a BS ISO standard.[7]

5.6.5.2 Legal aspects of optical storage

Some of the general issues pertaining to legal admissibility of microfilm discussed above can apply equally to electronic imaging and optical storage. Electronic imaging has the additional handicap, however, of being a newer technology where standards are lacking or incomplete in such areas as media, formats and disk drive units. There is thus a lack of industry and user experience based on stable and well-understood equipment. Furthermore, electronic images are readily amended given the appropriate software, and the changes are likely to be 'seamless'. It is therefore more taxing to police electronic imaging activities than those associated with micrographics.

Apart from the concerns of individual businesses, there are national issues. For example the transfer of geographical information to Poland was seen as being hampered by the lack of acceptance of digital information on magnetic or optical media by the administration and judiciary.[8]

With increasing computerisation of businesses, there is the need to ensure proper authorisation of activities ranging from electronic payments to modification of engineering drawings. Systems to recognise signatures and enable them to be transferred to documents held on a computer are available. While they avoid the non-computerised stage often employed of printing onto paper and signing manually, they may introduce questions as to the acceptability of the electronically transferred signature if the document is subsequently placed onto optical disk or microfilm, for example.

The same BS committee concerned with the legal admissibility of microforms, also considered electronic images of documents. The result was the issue of a standard for managing write-once optical media.[9] It should be noted, however, that adherence to such recommendations is in itself no guarantee that the image will be automatically admissible (such a proviso can equally be applied to microfilming).

5.6.5.3 Guidance on legal admissibility

To help address the issue of admissibility it is important that a sufficiently comprehensive policy and set of authorised procedures are in place and are monitored and controlled throughout the life cycle of the document.

The BSI DISC code of practice PD0008,[10] now in its second edition, describes the implementation and operation of systems that store information electronically and addresses the issues of authenticity, legal admissibility and evidential weight irrespective of the storage media involved, be they optical or magnetic, re-writable or write-once. The code covers all types and combinations of electronic file that may contain data, for example, sound, coded characters, formatted text, moving or still images and computer-aided design (CAD).

A companion workbook, PD0009,[11] assists users in evaluating their systems for compliance with PD0008 by providing step-by-step guidance and a set of quantitative parameters for determining conformance. Completion of PD0009 for each system provides an auditable trail of such compliance.

In essence, to maximise the chances of legal acceptability:

- ensure the electronic records provide the best evidence available

- ensure the electronic records have been created and used in the normal course of business activities

- have a comprehensive and documented records management strategy with accompanying policies, procedures and retention schedules that are in operation, are being monitored and controlled and are auditable.

The recommendations and guidelines outlined and referenced in this section are no more than what should already be part of an organisation's information management and information systems strategies, its quality and project management ethic and the associated policies and procedures. Although somewhat narrow in its view of information management, a DISC guide concerned with this topic[12] provides a useful complement to the aforementioned code of practice.

The Association for Information and Image Management – AIIM (which recently merged with the Information Management Congress - IMC) publishes a Legal Admissibility Series[13] which contains all four parts of the industry guidelines.

5.7 Display technologies

The choice of display should be determined by the type and pattern of the work that is undertaken. Key factors in making a choice are screen size, resolution, number of colours and refresh rate. The ability to deliver the required combination of these is determined by the display adapter. Display adapters, which are also referred to by other names such as graphics boards and video display cards, provide the interface between the computer and the display screen (monitor) and use high speed memory (VRAM - video random access memory) to deliver the performance required. The more colours and the higher the resolution, the greater the memory that is required on the display adapter.

Resolution is the degree of sharpness of the displayed text or image, and is expressed in terms of a matrix of dots (pixels); for example, 1024 x 768 means 1024 columns and 768 rows of pixels are displayed on the screen. For display monitors the main resolutions have been standardised by the Video Electronics Standards Association (VESA), the most common ones being 640 x 480, 800 x 600, 1024 x 768 and 1280 x 1024.

Having a high resolution display and a powerful video controller on the adapter board may not in itself provide the display speed required if the PC's bus is not fast enough. For image intensive applications a high speed bus design is preferable as it permits speedy transfer of data from the microprocessor to the graphics board.

The number of colours that can be displayed is related to the bit depth – the number of bits required to represent a pixel in storage. Thus for black and white (monochrome) displays, a pixel is represented by a single bit. For grey scale where shades from black to white are represented, and for colour, the bit depth required will range from 4 to 24 bits per pixel. The common colour designations for displays are summarised in Table 5.15.

NAME	NUMBER OF COLOURS	BIT DEPTH
Standard VGA	16	4
Super VGA	256	8
High Colour	32,000	15
High Colour	65,000	16
True Colour	16,000,000	24

Table 5.15 Colour and bit depth

Refresh rate measures the rate at which an image is refreshed on the screen. Too low a refresh rate is likely to show itself as screen flicker, hence aim for a rate of at least 75Hz.

The more demanding the application, the greater the number of colours required. Thus while 16 or 256 colours will suffice for normal office word-processing applications, full-motion video and photo-realistic images will demand up to 16 million colours.

Generally for document imaging applications the greater the screen resolution the better. This is not necessarily always the case. For example, if an image is composed of a fixed number of dots, as it would be from scanning, then it will appear smaller on a screen that has a higher resolution. However, if the character size is scaleable (as are Truetype and PostScript fonts) the character size can remain the same, while legibility will improve. Where documents are to be viewed, a 'portrait'- rather than a 'landscape'-shaped screen is preferable, sized to display a full page.

For high-end applications, for example involving computer-aided design, multimedia and complex windowing, the displays tend to be of proprietary design. UNIX workstations generally use high-resolution colour graphics and large screens. Cheaper monitors capable of running the X-Windows graphical user interface are available for network operation.

5.7.1 CRT and LCD screens

The foregoing considerations do not take account of the type of display monitor. The two main strands of development for display have been screens based on the well-established cathode ray tube (CRT) and those using the liquid crystal display (LCD) technology.

Display technology remains one of the least satisfactory aspects of a PC. The images may have improved markedly in the last five years – high resolution 17-inch CRT monitors showing millions of colours are increasingly affordable - but the devices themselves have a history traceable back to the thermionic valve. CRTs remain large, fragile, heavy and difficult to control.

Developments in CRT technology such as flat square tubes and shadow masking to improve image quality for high resolution use are maintaining the dominance of this type of display. However, the falling costs of its main competitor the LCD (liquid crystal display) is likely to see the latter the dominant display technology by 2004, according to US research.[14]

LCDs for computer displays comprise passive display (super twisted nematic - STN) used extensively on laptops for mono and colour displays, and active display - also called thin film transistor (TFT) used for laptop colour screens.

Dual Scan improves STN display by dividing the conducting matrix of the screen into two sections, each being scanned simultaneously. This design reduces the time required to refresh the complete screen. Passive displays are not as sharp as active matrix designs and offer a narrower viewing angle.

Active display (TFT) has a matrix of individual transistors in place of the conducting strip grid. Although this design is more expensive and requires more power than a passive display, it does provide a larger viewing angle and a faster refresh rate.

An existing limitation of LCD as compared with CRT designs is its lower screen resolution, though this too is being addressed by researchers. Alternative display technologies on the horizon are plasma display panels and, more futuristically, light emitting polymers, the latter operating like CRTs but having minimal depth, thereby avoiding the bulkiness of current CRT monitors.

5.8 INFORMATION AND DOCUMENT STORAGE AND INTERCHANGE STANDARDS

For document management technology to be successfully deployed within and between organisations, due attention must be given to the range of standard ways in which the various elements of a document life cycle are supported. This topic is too broad to cover in detail here (for more information see, for example, reference 15 at the end of the chapter) and is limited to those issues most likely to be encountered in the document management arena.

5.8.1 Graphics formats

Graphic images can be created by a variety of software products variously named drawing packages, business graphics, paint programs, CAD and scanning software. Due to the fact that these products have emerged over the years from different developers, different file formats exist to describe the structure of the digital data representation of the image as held on computer storage. More disturbingly, different implementations of the same format are often found. Knowledge of the file formats created and accepted by an imaging (or any other) product are important factors in determining the ease with which it can be integrated with current and planned systems.

A file format comprises the data itself and a header section which typically includes the resolution, mode of compression and the image's dimensions, which are required to ensure that the image can subsequently be recreated accurately. Even if one format is acceptable for a particular application, it may not be suitable for another, and hence the need for conversion arises. For any pair of different image file formats, software may be available for effecting a direct conversion between the two. If a large quantity of image data exists in the one format, and this is to be translated into a single target format, then these direct converters provide an effective and efficient solution. Where a variety of formats exist this method of conversion becomes cumbersome because of the need to utilise different direct converters for each unique combination of source and target formats. The alternative is to have a two-stage process where the source formats are first converted into a basic common format, edited (if necessary) and then output in the target format.

Where conversion to one's own software application is not possible, document viewers may be employed which allow the information to be displayed, normally for read-only access (see section 5.13 for more information on viewing technology).

5.8.1.1 Raster and vector formats

The bit-mapped, raster image of a bitonal document, such as an engineering line drawing or a page of text, is produced by optical scanning. It is relatively simple in concept as in visual terms it is formed of black dots arranged on a white background. The commonly encountered format for raster images is TIFF (Tagged Image File Format) which can deal with monochrome, grey scale, 8- and 24-bit colour. Although widely accepted as a *de facto* standard, variants exist across different system vendors. Nevertheless the fact that it is ubiquitous makes it the first choice for many users as a transfer format.

GIF (Graphic Interchange Format) is a format developed by Compuserve for images. It supports 8-bit (256) colour, and is widely used on the Web. However, it is likely to be replaced by PNG (Portable Network Graphics), a new bitmapped graphics file format endorsed by the World Wide Web Consortium. PNG provides a range of new and advanced features including 48-bit colour and the ability to display at one resolution and print at another.

Vector-based images, which form the basis of computer-aided design (CAD), are created using software which relies on mathematical representations of shapes such as curves and lines. The image is effectively created by drawing. The format is quite different to that for raster images and this prevents traditional CAD vector editors from operating on documents that have been scanned in. Similarly raster editors are incapable of handling CAD images.

An important standard for vector data is IGES (Initial Graphics Exchange Specification) which caters for exchanging three-dimensional images. For two-dimensional images, the DXF format derived from the AUTOCAD software is widely adopted as a *de facto* standard. An international standard for storing and exchanging two-dimensional graphical (vector) data is the Computer Graphics Metafile (CGM).

To enable the two formats to be worked on in an integrated fashion requires that either one format is converted to the other, or specialised software is utilised which allows them to coexist. Depending on the sophistication of the software, the complete raster image or selected parts of it can be converted, i.e. 'vectorised' by commercially available or bespoke software, or manually by using digitising tablets. For vectorisation, scanning at 400 dpi rather than the more usual 200 dpi is recommended, otherwise diagonal lines may have a staircase-like appearance known as 'jaggies' or 'aliasing'. Storage sizes for vector images may be less than their raster equivalent, but as the information content, and hence complexity of the drawing increases, the greater compactness of the compressed raster image becomes apparent.

Developments in raster image processing, and the advantages raster images offer in improved integration with other information in organisations, including easy distribution for viewing, is changing the focus of attention away from CAD systems. Software is available to convert CAD files to raster without the need for scanners. A common approach is to convert CAD files to the well-established Hewlett-Packard Graphics Language (HP-GL) vector format, and use the rasterisation software to create CCITT Group 4 compressed images (see next section).

Note that to print out a vector graphic on the ubiquitous laser or ink jet printer, it is first necessary to rasterise all text and graphics into a bitmap.

5.8.2 Compression standards

Although higher capacity and lower cost-per-Megabyte storage systems will continue to emerge, the storage requirements for images should not be underestimated. To mitigate this various compression techniques are available which can be categorised broadly into two types, 'lossless' and 'lossy'. As the name suggests, a lossless technique does not lose any of the information that is contained in the original. This is particularly important if the information to be compressed is computer programs or data which must remain unaltered. Examples of formats which provide such compression are ZIP and ARC (often used by software companies to distribute their programs) and GIF. However, with the need to be able to reconstitute the original exactly, the compressions achieved will generally be less than 8 to 1 and often nearer 2 to 1. Such limited compression ratios are not really adequate for the needs of document imaging, and are certainly unacceptable where there is the requirement to deal with information-intensive material such as colour photographs or moving video.

The mainstream applications for electronic imaging relate mainly to bitonal (black and white) text and line art, and the rasterised bitonal images are normally stored in compressed form using CCITT (International Telegraph and Telephone Consultative Committee) Group 3 or 4 standard compression algorithms as devised for facsimile technology (see Table 5.12). These lossless compression techniques employ run-length encoding whereby short codes are substituted for successive groups of identical pixels. Group 4 is suited to high speed transmission of images. The actual file size reduction achieved will depend on the characteristics of each document. Thus a drawing containing large areas of white background will compress to a smaller file size than one filled with line work.

A commonly encountered compression method is LZW (Lempel-Ziv-Welch). It offers compression ratios from around 1.5:1 to 2:1, and is employed widely for modems, GIF and TIFF files and PostScript Level 2.

Lossy techniques provide orders of magnitude with greater compression ratios. This is possible by relying on the fact that much of the information humans deal with does not require to be reproduced exactly as the original. Even though some detail is lost, this may not be noticeable to the human eye and brain, or if it is it does not necessarily impair recognition.

As in other areas of technology, proprietary and research developments in compression run ahead of agreement on standards. Thus artificial intelligence is applied to recognise standard form layouts and treat this structure independently of the variable data on the forms. This reduces processing and storage needs. Of particular significance is the development of fractal technology which offers increases in image compression ratios far greater than that which is currently commonly achieved.

The Joint Photographic Experts Group (JPEG) is an international committee concerned with the digital compression and coding of continuous-tone (grey-scale and colour) still digital images. The JPEG standard is applicable in such areas as electronic mail, multimedia products and imaging devices including printers and scanners. A technical guide to JPEG picture compression is available from BSI.[16]

5.8.3 Compound documents and document architecture

Documents are complex entities which need to be defined in standard ways and from various viewpoints if they are to be reliably transferred between different computerised information and still retain the ability to process them according to the user's desires. The concept of a compound document (one which contains a variety of data types such as text, tables, spreadsheets, graphics, sound and video) is important and is one around which standards are developing.

Compound documents may be in revisable form so that they can be edited by one's own word processing package. They can also be formatted to provide the desired appearance on the page. They may be required to be in revisable formatted form.

To help manage this complexity there has emerged the concept of objects and components with a *containing* component managing the outer document structure and *object-managing* components, one for each object type.

5.8.3.1 Object technology approaches

The size and complexity of most applications in a networked environment creates problems when users attempt to inter-work with data and documents. Componentware aims to address this problem by providing prefabricated parts of applications that a developer can bind together. Three key component technologies are:

- OLE (Object Linking and Embedding - from Microsoft)

- JavaBeans (from Sun Microsystems)

- CORBA (Common Object Request Broker Architecture from the Object Management Group - OMG).

OLE is based on Microsoft's Distributed Component Object Model (DCOM). An OLE object such as a spreadsheet can be embedded in a document, termed the container application. If it is required to update the object, the application that created it, for example Microsoft Excel, is launched by double clicking the object. The application in this instance is called the server application.

Rather than being physically embedded in the container applications, the object can be linked to it. A pointer provides the logical connection between the container and the object. If the content of the linked object is changed, then every document that has the same link is automatically updated when it is next opened.

Microsoft's ActiveX is a more recent extension of DCOM and enables a web browser to view any type of document, whether or not it forms part of a web page.

DCOM is a compiled language standard and hence differs from other object models, such as JavaBeans. This can make it impossible to distribute the components over a heterogeneous network of operating systems and hardware.

JavaBeans is a component software architecture from Sun Microsystems that runs in the Java object-oriented program environment. Its development drew on lessons learned from COM, OpenDoc and Borland's VCL. Since it is not a compiled language it is fully portable and JavaBeans components are able to be run in a distributed, mixed vendor computing environment using Sun's Remote Method Invocation (RMI) or the OMG's CORBA.

The Object Management Group (OMG) is the world's largest software development consortium with a membership drawn from software vendors, software developers and end users. Established in 1989, its mission is to promote the theory and practice of object technology for the development of distributed computing systems. CORBA is part of the Object Management Architecture (OMA) from the OMG. It is a widely supported form of middleware that handles the communication of messages between objects in a distributed, multi-platform environment by way of a standard CORBA interface definition language. Many enterprises already have CORBA implementations in use and CORBA compliant components that can inter-operate with CORBA services. To further protect investment in new technologies such as Java, CORBA suppliers are addressing the need for bridges between CORBA, Java and ActiveX.

A fourth and promising object-oriented architecture was OpenDoc, whose development was driven by the Component Integration Laboratories (CLI) established with support from Apple and IBM. Its aim was to allow multiple data structures (text, graphics, sound, etc.) to be stored in a single document. It supported small software modules, called 'part handlers' in addition to linking to full applications. Its main drawback as compared with OLE was that substantive products did not appear, and it is unlikely that further development will now take place given that CLI was dissolved in June 1997 with assets being returned to the sponsors.

5.8.3.2 Mark-up languages – SGML, HTML and XML

The first document architecture standards initiative emerged in 1986 from the publishing industry as the Standard Generalised Markup Language (SGML), and covered both the logical structure and content. The main aim was to facilitate document design and layout and to provide a method of coding documents that rendered them independent of any particular system. SGML is an ISO standard[17] and is the most widespread means of encoding and exchanging structured documents, being used extensively in the publishing industry (e.g. CD-ROM and electronic books) and by the US Department of Defense's CALS initiative (see section 5.8.3.6).

SGML incorporates the concept of a hierarchical document structure (e.g. book, chapters, section) with the main structural elements encoded, between which the content resides. In order to decipher format commands in an SGML document, SGML uses format definitions in a separately-created Document Type Definition (DTD) file. SGML is thus a kind of meta-language, because it describes another language to create the DTDs each of which is a descriptive programme defining the structure of a particular class of documents. SGML is a comprehensive language that can be used to define hypertext links.

HTML (HyperText Markup Language) is a subset of SGML and is a standard for defining hypertext links between documents. HTML is arguably the most important development in standards since ASCII. HTML files on the World Wide Web probably represent the largest set of SGML encoded files. A major problem is the lack of standardisation for HTML despite its links to SGML. Because of the explosion of interest in the World Wide Web, browser developers, such as Microsoft and Netscape, push ahead of existing standards with extensions for dealing with new requirements. This creates problems as pages that display properly on the latest version of one vendor's browser may look quite wrong, or not display at all on the other vendor's product. The acquisition of Netscape by AOL (America-On-Line) and the outcome of the US Federal action against Microsoft will have a bearing on the way browser technology and the commercialisation of the Web develop.

A drawback of HTML is that it is focused more on the creation of hyperlinks (a predefined linkage between one object and another) and on the way a document appears, rather than dealing with content of the document. XML (Extensible Markup Language) enables developers to make the data within a document accessible. This is achieved by using tags to define virtually any data item within the document, for example customer, order reference and product code. This allows Web pages to serve as active databases, and will provide a major boost for electronic commerce.

The World Wide Web Consortium (W3C) is supporting the standardisation of XML and of the Document Object Model (DOM) which provides the interface for Dynamic HTML whereby HTML tags can be changed dynamically via a language script.

5.8.3.3 PostScript

PostScript is a page description language from Adobe Systems that is used extensively across microcomputers, workstations, minis and mainframes. It is the *de facto* standard in commercial typesetting and printing houses. It comprises PostScript commands as language statements in ASCII text that are translated into the printer's machine language by a PostScript interpreter built into the printer. Fonts are scaled to size by the interpreter, thus eliminating the need to store a variety of font sizes on disk.

Encapsulated PostScript (EPS) is a file format for transferring a graphic image between applications, for example for importing into a page layout program. EPS files are larger than most other graphics file formats, but are readily compressed to around a quarter of their size as they are text files.

An international standard[18] for a Standard Page Description Language (SPDL) is based on work largely undertaken by Adobe and Xerox. It covers the interchange of documents or parts of documents in formatted, non-revisable final form ready for printing; there is no information about the logical structure of the document.

5.8.3.4 Open Document Architecture (ODA) and Open Document Interchange Format (ODIF)

In 1985 the European Computer Manufacturer's Association (ECMA), who were particularly concerned with such aspects as document transfer between different systems, formulated the Office Document Architecture (ODA) which was subsequently adopted by the ISO and then the CCITT (now the ITU-T).[19] ODA broadened the coverage of content data types to include raster and vector, and introduced a description for layout structure. In May 1990 ISO decided to change the name of Office Document Architecture to Open Document Architecture to emphasise the applicability of the standard beyond the office.

ODA provides for the representation of documents in processable form, which allows revision by a recipient, and in formatted form, which allows the precise specification of the document layout. ODA also supports the transfer of documents in formatted processable form. Compliance with the standard is defined by document application profiles (DAPs).

The main difference between ODA and SGML is that SGML does not provide the physical views of a document that enable ODA to facilitate interactive editing. Unlike OLE, ODA deals with paginated documents and hence prescribes particular classes of document. While this might restrict developers in their design of document classes, adherence to ODA does help guarantee the portability of documents.

For transfer between different systems, ODA documents are transmitted in an Open Document Interchange Format (ODIF) either using Abstract Syntax Notation One (ASN.1), which is employed by the ISO X.400 electronic mail standard, or the SGML notation, Open Document Language (ODL).

ODA, like many standards, lags behind advances in technology. Although ODA is supported by major companies, and a toolkit is available to help develop ODA applications, few such products have arrived on the market.

The differences between SGML, SPDL and ODA[20] are that :

- ◆ SGML is a standard for the logical structure of documents and their interchange in revisable format

- ◆ ODA deals with documents in revisable and formatted form

- ◆ SPDL covers the interchange of documents or parts of documents in formatted, non-revisable final form ready for printing; there is no information about the logical structure of the document.

5.8.3.5 STEP The Standard for the Exchange of Product Model Data

Information concerning products needs to be linked to the product throughout its life cycle from conception and design, to production, operation and maintenance. The STEP project was initiated in 1984 with the following objectives:[21]

- ◆ creation of a single international standard, covering all aspects of computer-aided-design (CAD) and computer-aided-manufacture (CAM) data exchange

- implementation and acceptance of this standard in industry, superseding various national and *de facto* standards and specifications

- standardisation of a mechanism for describing product data throughout the product's life cycle, independent of any particular system

- separation of the description of product data from its implementation thereby facilitating neutral file exchange, sharing product databases and long term archiving.

The standard embracing these concepts was published in 1994.[22]

5.8.3.6 CALS

An example of user pressure in forcing the pace on standardisation was the Computer-aided Acquisition and Logistic Support (CALS) initiative from the US Department of Defense. This developed from the recognition by the DoD that as a major buyer of products and services, considerable savings in time and cost could be made by enforcing, and providing guidance to their suppliers on standards in the area of data interchange, data management and data access.

CALS became mandatory for all DoD contracts let since January 1990 and its philosophy has gained acceptance around the world in major manufacturing and contracting enterprises to the point that its acronym is generally referred to now as meaning Continuous Acquisition and Life Cycle Support. While its initial focus may have been on international standards such as those relating to SGML, CGM, and IGES, it has had a major influence on making organisations look more closely at their business processes and their methods of inter-working between engineers, functions and organisations.

The move towards information-rich computerisation using such initiatives as CALS is depicted in Figure 5.2.

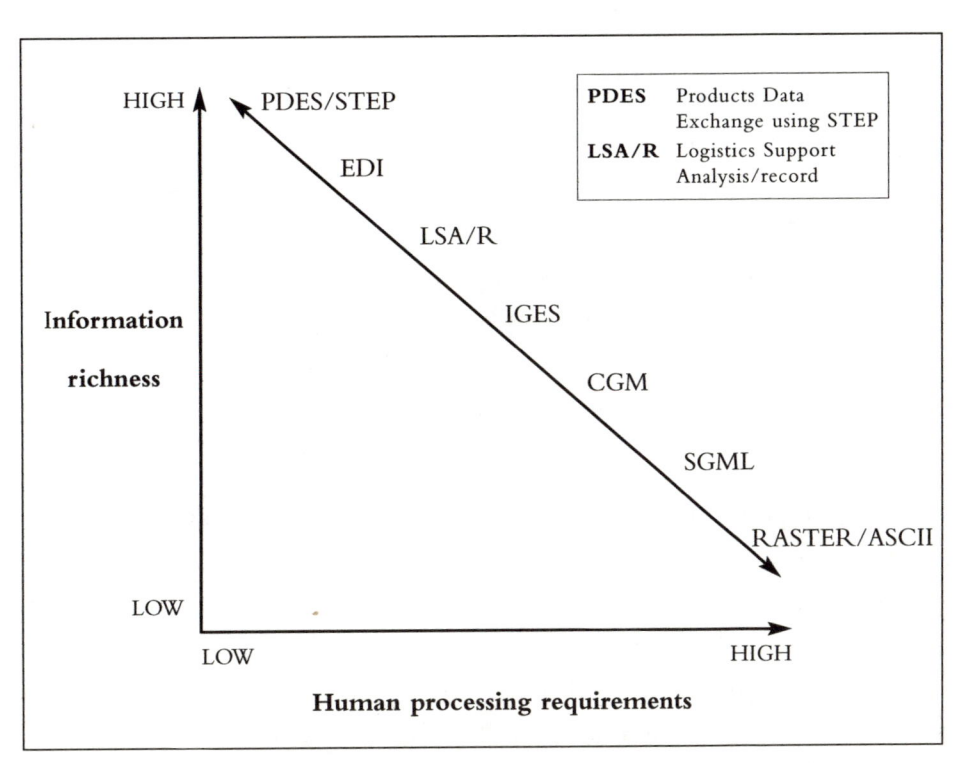

Figure 5.2 The hierarchy of information management standards

5.9 DOCUMENT MANAGEMENT STANDARDS

The diversity of document management products and of the technologies on which they are based may have provided the users with an extensive pool of solutions from which to pick, but it also introduced problems associated with inter-operability between the different offerings.

Typical of the problems faced by users within organisations are:

1 Access to documents across the organisation

2 Integration with desk-top applications

3 Inter-operability between repositories of documents managed by different systems.

5.9.1 Islands of information

The first problem is usually more to do with functional organisation within an enterprise, rather than technology *per se*. The various corporate functions, such as accounts, procurement, research and human resources will usually organise their information according to local needs, procedures and available technology. This leads to the creation of islands of information that are not readily accessed by other functions.

There is no 'quick technology fix' for this problem, as it needs to be addressed first at the business level. This will involve analysis of the business processes and of the supporting data (in this context - indexing information for documents and their content) to provide suitably consistent and coherent process and data models which, following their adoption, can facilitate management of information, and communication across the organisation. It is only when the 'business' is understood, that technology can sensibly be applied in support.

5.9.2 Links to desktop applications

The second problem relates to the ease with which a document management system can be integrated into the user's normal way of working with their computer. The relevant standard here is ODMA (Open Document Management Application Program Interface), the most recent version of which is v.2.0. This was approved by the ODMA Task Force comprising a coalition of suppliers to the document management market.

ODMA enables desktop applications such as word processors and spreadsheets to be tightly integrated with document management systems, and hence with search and retrieval functions and other document control facilities. Users can then manage documents irrespective of their file format or physical location. Furthermore they can request and retrieve different renditions of the same document, be they the native form (e.g. Microsoft Word), HTML or Adobe Acrobat PDF. ODMA also supports compound documents, for example a spreadsheet linked to a word processing file.

ODMA permits systems to identify documents by specifying a document's format, such as by MIME type or file extension, and by other attribute information (e.g. author, owner, version information, check in and check out information, keywords, subject and URL links). These additional means of identification enable those seeking information to be more specific when searching a document collection, thereby improving the precision of the retrieval process.

5.9.3 Inter-operability for DM

Compliance to the Document Management Alliance (DMA) specification, DMA 1.0, addresses the third problem by enabling document management products from different vendors to inter-operate. In particular DMA 1.0 provides for:

- means to automatically locate repositories

- capability to map common document attributes across repositories, even when those attributes have different names on different repositories

- support for versioning documents

- support for the concept of file folders

- ability to browse across DM systems using Explorer or Internet browsers

- ability to manage multiple renditions of a document, e.g. PDF

- automatic discovery of document classes, properties and search operators

- the ability to search across multiple repositories simultaneously, and merge the search results

- full international support

- more methods for delivery of documents to clients.

The DMA standard is approved by leading document management suppliers. Its development by the DMA Task Force was actively supported by large organisations such as Boeing and the US Department of Justice who have already invested heavily in various document management technologies, and hence are keen to see improvements in interoperability. The first DMA-compliant products from suppliers were announced to appear during 1998! The extent to which these products comply with the elements of the standard does, however, require clarification from each of the vendors.

ODMA, as differentiated from DMA, is a many-to-one client-side standard that enables desktop packages to talk to a single document management system; DMA is a many-to-many client and server standard which enables multiple clients to talk to multiple document management systems. Having a unified look-and-feel for the end user avoids the need to learn the idiosyncrasies of different document management system interfaces.

A further important standards initiative is Web Distributed Authoring and Versioning (WebDAV). This defines extensions to the Internet HTTP protocol allowing Web pages created with one web authoring tool to be revised using a different web authoring tool. Although WebDAV may offer some document management functionality such as 'checking out' or 'tracking' a Web page, the standard is seen to be complementary with DMA, and both organisations are collaborating to avoid duplication and confusion.

5.9.4 Inter-operability for workflow

A second major standards initiative arises from the WorkFlow Management Coalition (WfMC). Its purpose is to provide inter-operability between workflow software products, these being employed to provide support for electronic-based document-centric business processes, such as document review and approval. The DMA and WfMC standards are complementary and may be used in combination.

Areas of standardisation in which the WfMC is working include process definition interchange, client application interface, applications interoperability, and administration and monitoring. The latter involves the means to facilitate workflow event recording within the OMG object services architecture.

The ability to combine document management and workflow standards to make a virtual supply chain was demonstrated in the Standards Pavilion at the AIIM '98 conference in Anaheim, California. In this multi-process scenario, six different workflow vendors accessed three different vendor's document management repositories, integrated with DMA middleware, into a single virtual information store.

5.9.5 Other standards

There are many other standards of relevance to document management, too numerous to detail here. A valuable source is the previously mentioned Association of Information and Image Management (AIIM). It publishes books, guides, technical reports and standards amongst which are ones dealing with the preparation of documents for scanning[23] and test objects for ongoing quality control for scanning.[24]

Before leaving this topic it is worth noting the Web-based Enterprise Management (WBEM) initiative to unify the numerous standards used to manage networks, PCs, peripherals and software applications. This initiative, now being pursued by the Desktop Management Task Force (DMTF) is aimed at exploiting the benefits of emerging technologies such as the Common Interface Model (CIM) and XML.[25]

5.10 Operating system software

The internal activities of a computer, including input and output of data and its processing, are controlled by programs that also provide facilities for the user to interact with the system. Certain designs of computer have proprietary operating systems (OS) which will generally only run on their hardware; examples are MVS and VM for IBM mainframes and minicomputers, VMS for Digital Equipment VAX minicomputers and VME for ICL's mainframes.

Other OS software is more portable in that it will run on a variety of manufacturers' machines. Unix is an example as it runs on hardware ranging from personal computers to mainframes. It was developed from the ground up as a multi-user and multi-tasking OS (multi-tasking is the ability to run two or more programs in one computer at the same time). As such UNIX is ideal for multi-user applications such as enterprise-wide document management. However, variants exist which are not fully compatible and the industry is still not organised and committed to standardising Unix. The main flavours of UNIX are Sun Microsystem's Solaris, Hewlett-Packard's HP-UX, IBM's AIX, Santa Cruz Operation's (SCO) Unixware and Digital Unix.. Industry analysts believe that in the long term no more than three of these can survive, with the current betting favouring the first three, despite the undoubted muscle of Compaq who may support the product of its major corporate acquisition, Digital.

Unix is under increasing threat from Microsoft Windows NT which offers the same look and feel as Windows95/98 and promises to provide organisations with a single operating system design from desktop to enterprise servers. Microsoft has, however, found it difficult to deliver its promises and its long awaited NT5.0 – the multi-user version of NT, now called Windows 2000 – has taken a long time and considerable effort to develop, there being serious concerns about its robustness and scalability, features which represent UNIX's great strength.

A literally 'home-grown' operating system that is gaining increasing credibility is Linux. Developed in 1990 by a Finnish student Linus Torvalds, it is a version of UNIX that runs on x86, Alpha and PowerPC processor. Linux is free and the complete source code is available on CD-ROM, together with a range of programming tools and utilities. It is estimated to be installed on up to 10 million computers worldwide, and is gaining credibility with major players such as ORACLE enabling their software to run on Linux and Intel, the leader microprocessor developer, investing in a Linux distributor.

Linux is the prime example of open source software (OSS), which is seen by some observers to be a significant threat to the dominance of Microsoft. Thus while Linux challenges Windows NT, another OSS product, Apache Web Server is aimed at Microsoft's Internet Information Server.

Network operating systems (NOS) are required to manage resources on a network. They allow remote drives on a server to be accessed as if they were local to the user. They also handle requests from the client for file sharing, access to applications and for the use of networked peripherals such as printers and faxes.

The main NOS contenders are Novell with NetWare and Microsoft with NT Server. Novell has the largest installed base of the two products, but Microsoft is making inroads into its market. This is largely because it can offer a full range of network services as well as full functionality at the client end all under the Microsoft banner. Novell has no desktop operating system or desktop applications (since it divested itself of WordPerfect) and hence has to concentrate on networking and providing effective and efficient linkages to Microsoft's Windows environment.

5.11 PROGRAMMING AND SOFTWARE DEVELOPMENT LANGUAGES

Computers are instructed to undertake tasks using the artificial language of a computer program. Low-level languages are the most efficient, but require considerable expertise to learn and use. High-level languages are more accessible to the computer user and include languages such as C, Pascal, Basic, Fortran and Cobol.

High-level languages must be translated to be comprehended by the computer. This may be undertaken by a compiler which undertakes the necessary conversion to create a machine program that can be operative as and when required. Some high-level languages, such as Java, are not compiled at the outset, but are either interpreted when required or are pre-compiled into an intermediate form. Compiled programs run more quickly than those that are interpreted. However, the strength of interpreted languages like Java is that they are readily portable across different operating systems and hardware platforms.

An object-oriented programming (OOP) language focuses on manipulating concepts that are more familiar to the user and is more flexible than standard programming. It is an evolutionary form of modular programming with more formal rules that allow pieces of software to be reused and interchanged between programs. Major concepts are encapsulation, inheritance and polymorphism.

Encapsulation is the creation of self-sufficient modules that contain the data and the processing (data structure and functions that manipulate that data). These user-defined, or abstract, data types are called classes. One instance of a class is called an object.

Classes are created in hierarchies, and inheritance allows the knowledge in one class to be passed down the hierarchy. New objects can be created by inheriting characteristics from existing classes. For example, the object MACINTOSH could be one instance of the class PERSONAL COMPUTER, which could inherit properties from the class COMPUTER SYSTEMS. Adding a new computer requires entering only what makes it different from other computers, while the general characteristics of personal computers can be inherited. This structuring is similar in concept to the hierarchical structure of a thesaurus used for indexing and information retrieval.

Polymorphism (meaning many shapes) provides the ability of a generalised request (message) to produce different results based on the object that it is sent to. In the world of documents, for example, tax forms can be considered as objects to be associated with a set of claims procedures as part of a work flow process. Such objects are typically found as icons on graphical user interfaces, and it is for this environment that object-oriented programming languages are particularly suited.

C++ is a mainstay OOP language, because it combines traditional C programming with object-oriented features. However its leadership is being threatened by Java which aims to overcome what some view as the inherently confusing, and rarely used features of C++.

5.12 Authoring software

Many technologies are available to assist with the creation of text-based documents. The choice depends on a variety of factors including:

- objectives in creating the document

- size and complexity of the document

- the need to include other media (e.g. pictures, sound, video for multimedia)

- the intended audience.

The technologies can be broadly divided into two main categories - word-processors and desktop publishing (DTP) - the former being associated more with the general office environment, the latter with electronic publishing and long-document creation.

Developed largely from stand-alone software packages under the PC DOS operating system environment, today's Microsoft Windows-based word-processing products now form part of so-called 'office suites' which include spreadsheet, database and drawing software. The dominant player is Microsoft, who arguably are infecting users with upgrade- and feature-fatigue as they include ever more functionality with each release and move increasingly to a web-based environment.

While word-processing software has been enhanced to address the needs for more sophisticated output publishing, the greater demands that arise when dealing with long complex documents or with electronic, multimedia publishing usually requires the use of more powerful and often enterprise-wide software. Examples of such heavy-weight products are Framemaker, Pagemaker and QuarkXPress.

In order to place information on the WWW, it must be structured with HTML tags which tell the browser how to display each element (be it images, paragraphs of text, size, centring, etc). Although it is possible to type in the coding (all tags comprise symmetric pairs commencing with '<' and ending with '>'), HTML authoring tools simplify the process of generating HTML-encoded documents. These tools range from relatively basic HTML editors which catalogue all HTML tags and common structures in menus and provide some error checking, to Web authoring software for creating Web pages automatically from the source document files. Most current word-processing and DTP software is able to generate HTML pages as an alternative output file.

Authoring for online documentation is a complex process involving multiple activities. The whole process may be capable of being done by one program. However, separate programs may be required for each activity, elements of which are shown in Figure 5.3.[26]

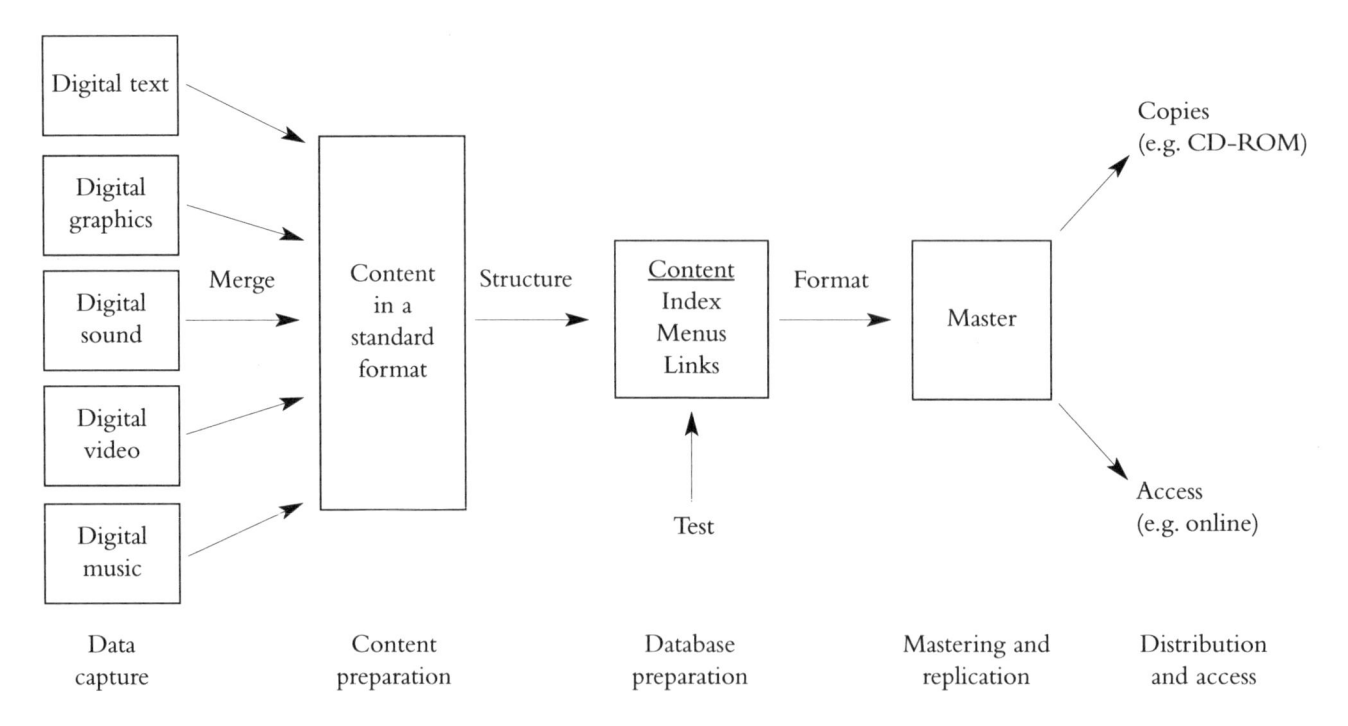

Figure 5.3 Authoring activities for online documentation

5.13 DOCUMENT VIEWERS

One of the main problems facing recipients and users of computer-generated information is the ability to view and read that information if it has been generated using application software which the recipient does not possess. Despite the fact that Microsoft software is the *de facto* standard on the desktop PC, it can be difficult or impossible to ensure that a document that has been created on one type of platform (PC, Apple or UNIX) using one type of application software will be viewable and appear exactly the same when received by someone using a different platform who lacks the same application software. When it comes to reading information stored in spreadsheet, database or graphic formats, and the user only has word-processing applications, the problem is compounded further.

Software products usually have in-built conversion utilities, and third party software is also available to address this specific problem. However, 100% conversion accuracy cannot necessarily be assured, hence the popularity of viewing software.

Two main categories of viewers are:

- file format recognition viewers (e.g. QuickView Plus)
- viewers for documents converted into a single format (e.g. Adobe Acrobat).

The former approach has the advantage that given the viewing software, the user can quickly display information which has been created with other application software even though he or she does not possess the original application. The drawback is that the producer of the viewer has usually to re-program the software to deal with any new applications or upgrades to existing applications. Depending on the particular viewing software, features such as text searching, preservation of display formats (WYSIWYG) and application launching are available.

The latter approach, used by Adobe for its Acrobat product, is aimed at a somewhat different market with a particular focus on document distribution. The Adobe Acrobat family of software provides facilities for converting most computer-generated documents and file formats to a Portable Document Format (PDF) in which format the document retains all the look and feel of the original. Adobe provides a royalty-free reader (also available for down-loading from the World Wide Web) which allows recipients of PDF document to view and undertake limited searching of the text. Annotations and hyperlinks can be added to PDF documents which are fully compatible for use on the Internet or Intranet systems.

Paper documents can be scanned using the Acrobat Capture software to create a PDF file, thereby providing means to integrate paper and existing electronic documents. During the capture process the document undergoes a major transformation with text being subjected to optical character recognition and any unrecognised text along with graphics, logos, etc. being held in raster image format, all within a common PDF.

A further piece of software allows a PDF document to be provided with sophisticated search facilities which are based on an in-built third party product Topic from Verity. The file size of a PDF document is normally less than that of the equivalent TIFF image, thereby saving storage space and reducing traffic on networks.

5.14 CO-OPERATIVE WORKING TECHNOLOGIES

With the trend towards outsourcing services and production, contracting-in expertise as and when required, and globalisation of business, work forces are increasingly becoming fragmented both in terms of space and time. In this context technologies such as Groupware, Workflow and Electronic Data Interchange (EDI) that facilitate communication and inter-working have gained greater prominence and significance.

5.14.1 Groupware and workflow

Virtually every major player these days either has, or is about to release, a product that purports to be everything user organisations could want, when it comes to desktop communications and co-operative working. Differentiating the various products is not helped by the confusion that still reigns as to what is groupware and what is Workflow. The Delphi Consulting Group defines groupware as that which focuses on the information being processed and enabling users to share it. Workflow on the other hand emphasises the process, which acts as a container for the information. Thus groupware is 'information centred' while workflow is 'process centred.' Lotus's view of groupware is based on three central functions:

- communication using rich electronic messaging

- collaboration through use of a rich, shared virtual workspace

- co-ordination by adding business processes to communication and collaboration in order to meet the objectives of a business.

Lotus Notes is seen by most observers as being the front runner in groupware technology. Microsoft with its Exchange product and Novell with groupware are other contenders in this field.

Although its rise to prominence with the coming of document image processing led to the term 'workflow software' featuring increasingly in promotional literature for imaging, workflow management products have a much longer history that predates scanning technology.

There are two main approaches to the implementation of workflow systems. The *ad hoc* casual workflow tools use e-mail, forms and messages as the system infrastructure where information and work is sent out to people whether they need it or not. The higher-end workflow systems are concerned with the proactive management of the flow of work between co-operating individuals and groups of people based on defined procedures and tasks. These systems are usually referred to as engine-based, where the workflow engine handles the management of the actual process and calls other applications and facilities as and when required. They provide significant advantages where close integration is needed and where more sophisticated models of work matching are appropriate.

According to an earlier report from Ovum[27] there are five conditions which need to be satisfied before one can be confident in gaining benefit from implementing the technology:

- processes should have explicit component tasks

- rules should be applied to determine the logic of transition between tasks

- digital information resources should be provided to support the processing of tasks

- tasks should be communicable to workers

- the process should be controllable.

The coming of the Web and the increasing use being made by business of the Internet and Intranets has added another dimension to considerations when planning to adopt groupware or workflow. Many of the new workflow products are entirely Web-based. While offering rapid and less-expensive deployment than non Web-based services, other issues emerge. These include security and the need for improved document management to ensure the underlying document base is up-to-date, approved and has appropriate access controls.

5.14.2 Electronic data exchange (EDI)

EDI is one of the two main messaging services, the other being e-mail. Developed in the late 1970s, it provides savings for business transactions by transmitting orders, invoices and payments electronically. Third parties provide the necessary network services. The service is 'hub' driven in that dominant companies choose a network supplier and other members of the industry (suppliers and dealers) have to comply and use the same EDI services and rules (or protocols) for transmitting and receiving data. Unlike e-mail messages which are free format, EDI message formats are defined and standardised to meet the needs of individual industry groups (e.g. SWIFT for banking and ODETTE for automotive industry).

While EDI undoubtedly reduces the cost of commercial transactions as compared with paper-based systems, an EDI system is costly to set up and operate. These costs can be prohibitive for small and medium-sized companies who are increasingly moving towards Web-based approaches in the form of Extranets. These are Internets which are extended via the Internet to a company's customers or suppliers.

The introduction of XML as a Web-standard (see section 5.8.3.2) is significant. It has been given a boost by the Information Society Standardization System (ISSS) of the European Committee for Standardization (CEN) which approved a project to study and promote XML for EDI. One aim is to map the EDI X12 standard for North America to XML.

5.15 INFORMATION SECURITY

Users of computer-based systems are likely to be mostly aware of user names and passwords for controlling access. This is the tip of the security iceberg, for below that most visible appendage lies a more formidable structure whose size and shape has yet to be fathomed. Beyond the familiar security issues of access restrictions at network, database, record, data item/field and index levels and restriction of the ability to view, amend, add to or delete information, there are new threats. These are posed, for example, by the opening of Internets to the world and the globalisation of network communication.

Controlling access to computerised, networked information has become a major area of concern, particularly with the advent of Internet connectivity. Information security is defined as:[27]

- ◆ confidentiality
  - protecting sensitive information from unauthorised disclosure or intelligible interception
- ◆ integrity
  - safeguarding the accuracy and completeness of information and computer software
- ◆ availability
  - ensuring that information and vital services are available to users when required.

Firewalls are ways of preventing unwanted access or traffic flow, or both, between two networks or parts of a network. Different types of control can be exercised, usually in combination; the common techniques are summarised in Table 5.16.

TECHNIQUE	COMMENT
Packet filter	Preventing or allowing the passage of a packet of data depending on the source address, destination address and the port number.
Network Address Translation (NAT)	Packets leaving the network are given the single port address of the firewall's WAN as the source address rather than that of the internal client machine. The firewall provides the necessary translation when a response is received.
Proxy servers	An application which effectively breaks the connection between the sender and receiver. For example if a client requests a Web page, the application receives the request, fetches the page and passes it back to the client. Hence the client does not have an end-to-end connection out of the LAN.

Table 5.16 Firewall techniques

In addition to these physical devices, recourse can be made to data encryption, an area in which governments are taking a keen interest as they wish to ensure that they can gain access to data for reasons of security or criminal investigation. The use of cryptography is essential for the growth of electronic commerce. There is concern that new laws currently under consideration, and the banning by some governments of the export of strong encryption, will stifle this growth, and also increase the risk of the 'electronic keys' falling into the wrong hands.

The Data Protection Act 1998 is a further example of impending key legislation. Under that Act the UK government's security standard BS7799[28] is a minimum requirement with which to comply. The certification scheme for BS7799 is called c:cure and is accredited by the United Kingdom Accreditation Service (UKAS). The act also bans the export of data (which includes e-mail) to countries that do not have European-style data protection rules including the United States. As a consequence, it is seen that companies will have to ensure that no data ends up on a server in such countries. If it does, measures will have to be taken by the companies to prevent the data from being used in that country in a way that would breach the act.[29]

Apart from securing one's data, there is the need to safeguard the software which manages the data. Escrow involves storing the source code away from the clutches of the software developer to protect the interests of the customer should the developer go out of business. There are moves by the European Committee for Standardisation to develop escrow guidelines, including the process for the users to gain access to the software.

REFERENCES IN CHAPTER 5

1. http://www.pixtran.com
2. Laflin, J., 'Microfilm Scanners', *Information Management & Technology*, Vol.31, No.2, March 1998, pp. 65-70
3. *ISO/TR 10200: 1990* (Equivalent to DD 199 : 1991), *Legal Admissibility of Microforms* - Provides a survey of the status of microfilmed documents in various countries
4. *BS 6498: 1991, Guide to the Preparation of Microfilm and other Microforms that may be required as Evidence*
5. *BS 6321: 1982, Specification for Authorized Signature Lists and their Representation on Microfiche for Bank Operations*
6. *BS 5699: 1979 (in 2 Parts), Processed Photographic Film for Archival Records*
7. *BS IS 8514: 1992 (in 2 Parts), Micrographics. Alphanumeric Computer Output Microforms. Quality Control*
8. Kupiszewski, M., 'Transfer of Geographical Information Systems to Poland as an Example of the Transfer of Information Technology', *International Journal of Information Management*, 13 (1) (February 1993), pp. 41-50
9. *BS 7768: 1994, Recommendations for Management of Optical Disk (WORM) systems for the Recording of Document that may be Required as Evidence*
10. *DISC PD 0008: 1999, A Code of Practice for Legal Admissibility and Evidential Weight of Information Stored Electronically*
11. *DISC PD 0009: 1999, Compliance workbook for Legal Admissibility and Evidential Weight of Information Stored Electronically*
12. *DISC PD 0010: 1997, The guide to good practice in information management*
13. *The Legal Admissibility Series*, Catalog No. TR100. From the Association of Information and Image Management, Silver Spring, USA. (Comprises ANSI/AIIM TR31-Part 1, Evidence; ANSI/AIIM TR31-Part 2, Acceptance by Government

Agencies; ANSI/AIIM TR31-Part 3, Implementation; ANSI/AIIM TR31-Part 4, Model Act and Rule)

14   'Guide to Display Technologies', Supplement to December 1998 issue of *PC Magazine*, Ziff-Davis UK Ltd

15   Tucker, H.A. (ed.), *The Open Information Exchange Technology Handbook* (Twickenham: Technology Appraisals, 1996)

16   *DISC PD 0006:1995, Technical guide to JPEG*

17   *ISO 8879: 1986, Specification for Standardized Generalized Markup Language (SGML) for Text and Office Systems*

18   *ISO/IEC 10180: 1995, Information Technology - Processing Languages - Standard Page Description Language (SPDL)*

19   *ISO 8613* (various parts), *Information processing. Text and office systems. Office document architecture (ODA) and interchange format* BS ISO/IEC 8613

20   Francis, A., 'Page Description Languages' in Hugh A. Tucker (ed.), *The Open Information Exchange Technology Handbook* (Twickenham: Technology Appraisals, 1996), pp. 141-152

21   Fowler, J., 'STEP for Data Management, Exchange and Sharing' in Hugh A. Tucker (ed.) *The Open Information Exchange Technology Handbook* (Twickenham: Technology Appraisals, 1996), pp. 223-238

22   *ISO 10303* (various parts), *Industrial Automation Systems and Integration. Product Data Representation and Exchange*

23   *Planning Considerations, Addressing Preparation of Documents for Image Capture*, Catalog No. TR15. ANSI/AIIM TR15-1997 (Silver Spring, USA: Association for Information and Image Management)

24   *Scanner Test Target Set* Catalog No. X440 (Silver Spring, USA: Association for Information and Image Management)

25   http://www.dmtf.org

26   Horton, W., *Designing and Writing Online Documentation* (Chichester: John Wiley, 1994)

27   Stark, H. and Lachal, L., *Ovum Evaluates Workflow* (London: Ovum Ltd, 1995)

28   *BS 7799: 1995, Code of Practice for Information Security Management*

29   'Data Protect to Survive' *Computing* (London: VNU Publications, 10 September 1998), p. 22

GENERAL REFERENCES

Glossary of Document Technologies, Technical Report ANSI/AIIM TR2-1198, Association for Information and Image Management, ISBN 0-89258-343-6

Computer Desktop Encyclopedia, available on CD-ROM with updates from The Computer Language Company, Point Pleasant, PA 18950 (http://www.computerlanguage.com)

6

INFORMATION AND KNOWLEDGE RETRIEVAL

'A man should keep his little brain attic stocked with all the furniture that he is likely to use, and the rest he can put away in the lumber-room of his library, where he can get it if he wants to.'

The Five Orange Pips, The Adventures of Sherlock Holmes: Sir Arthur Conan Doyle

It is long past the time when information problems could be tackled by one man and his private library. However, Sherlock Holmes recognised the essentials of management as regards sources of information, namely that an information seeker who has not the required knowledge has recourse to recorded knowledge, i.e. information. The indirect method of transferring information between originator and user via permanent records, such as published literature and internal documentation, is invaluable because it ensures continuity and permanency of knowledge independent of people and time.

An overview of the types of information source is provided in Figure 6.1. Although the diagram was drawn up some years ago, the general categorisation still holds true. Note that the information may be stored on any media (e.g. paper, electronic, microfilm) and the user may access it via any suitable mechanism (e.g. physically on a library shelf, or via the Internet or an Intranet).

In this chapter the concepts surrounding information indexing and retrieval are outlined and its relevance to the world of documents is described. Armed with this guidance one will be in a better position to evaluate requirements for particular applications and thereby to make intelligent decisions concerning candidate solutions offered by vendors.

6.1 THE INFORMATION-SEEKING PROBLEM

In general, there are various stages (Table 6.1) in dealing with the problem of finding information. Firstly, there is the realisation of an information need, possibly arising from the lack of information in immediately available personal sources. Secondly, there is the need to know where to go for that information. The necessary referral to a library or a particular filing system, for example, may come from a colleague or an information

150 *Technology and Retrieval*

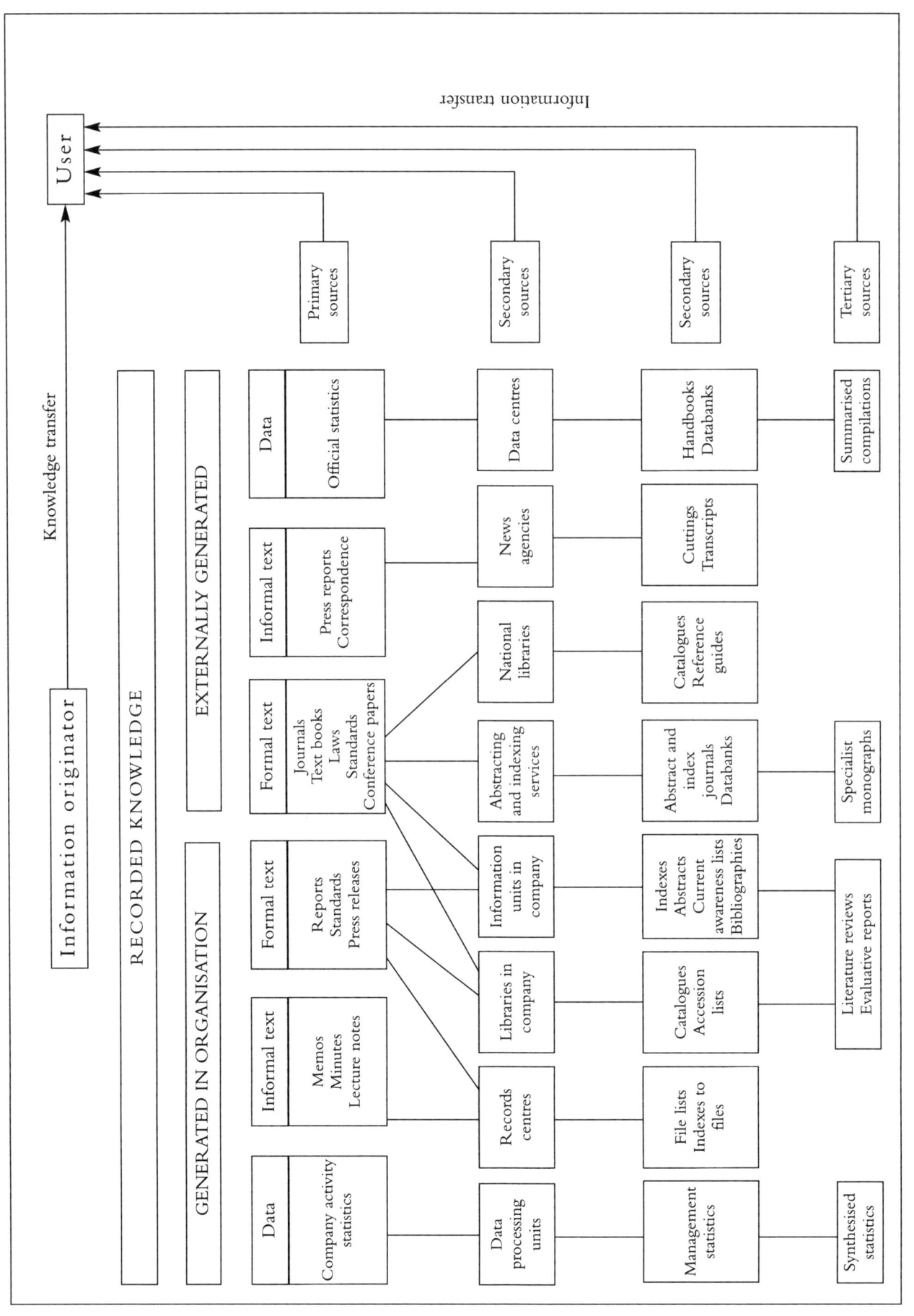

Figure 6.1 Sources of information – a general outline

professional such as a librarian. Thirdly, the required information may be contained in certain documents, so there is the need to identify the references to them. Fourthly, these documents must be provided so that finally the required information can be extracted from them.

INFORMATION PROBLEM	TYPE OF SOLUTION
Information need	Sources to hand
Where located?	Referral service
What document, etc?	Reference service
Where obtained?	Document provision service
What does it contain?	Information retrieval

Table 6.1 Generalised information-seeking problem

These various stages are, of course, not always applicable, neither are they necessarily followed in the order shown. The information seeker, for example, may be searching a company database containing structured data and does not require access to document images, even though they are retrievable via the database. Nevertheless, in considering the design of a retrieval system, the information contained in it will be of no value to the potential user if they do not know of its existence, have no knowledge of its content or are not provided with adequate tools and indexes to search the system.

6.2 THE VALUE OF INFORMATION

Satisfying information needs is complicated by two key factors:

◆ the same information may be of different value to different people

◆ information has different values at different times.

Thus a service report from a maintenance engineer is unlikely to be of interest to those in the legal department. However, if it transpires that as a result of the service, equipment has severely malfunctioned, then the company lawyers may well become involved in litigation and have need to see that report along with other documents such as time sheets and appointment records.

A procurement department will typically organise purchase orders by order numbers which provide the main means for departmental reference and access. Those responsible for paying the suppliers' invoices, however, are more likely to organise their files by the suppliers' names and addresses than by order number.

It should be clear from just these two examples that knowledge of the types of query that information seekers may pose is vital in the design of an information retrieval (IR) system. More than that, the IR system may need to cater for the *ad hoc* query that departs from the planned and expected approach, for example finding that elusive piece of correspondence needed to defend a lawsuit.

6.3 SPEED OF RETRIEVAL

Apart from the ability to find information, speed of retrieval is an important consideration. In a transaction-oriented system or one where it is necessary to obtain vital records to deal with an emergency, speed of retrieval is of paramount importance. In contrast a delay of hours or even days may be acceptable for retrieval from inactive, archived records. The need for fast access, and the likelihood of that need arising, are key factors in determining the effort that should be expended on indexing. It may well be that the cost benefits of limited indexing coupled with longer retrieval times, and hence higher retrieval costs, are determined to be greater than those arising from expending increased effort on indexing to minimise retrieval effort.

Searching and retrieving information from paper-based systems may be time-consuming, but any deficiencies in the indexing or organisation of the documents can be alleviated somewhat by the fact that the information (even if held on microfilm) is at least readable by a human being. If the documents and the information they contain are held on a computer's magnetic disk or on optical storage for example, the information seeker is totally reliant on the efficiency and effectiveness of the index and retrieval mechanism.

6.4 DOCUMENT OR INFORMATION RETRIEVAL?

Two broad categories of document can be identified in organisations:

- ◆ transaction documents

- ◆ non-transaction documents.

While there is often a need to retrieve information across both categories of document, there are important distinctions between them as regards the design of indexes and the requirements for retrieval.

6.4.1 Transaction documents

Transaction documents, for example purchase orders, invoices, credit notes, deeds, cheques, insurance policies and certified as-built engineering construction drawings, provide a record of a business event, such as the placing of an order. Such documents are intimately associated with transaction processing applications. Transaction processing systems represent the longest-established type of computer-based information system. Transaction documents provide evidence of the business event having occurred. As part of an integrated series of records, they show the consequences that followed. They contain prescribed types of information usually arranged in a structured format.

Because of their evidentiary nature and their inherent association with business events, it may be important that transaction documents are retained. Retention may be as originals (in paper or electronic form depending on the initial method of creation), or as facsimiles such as images or photocopies - provided there are no problems over legal acceptability. The emphasis with transaction documents is therefore more on retrieval of the document, at least in the first instance, than retrieval of the information within it.

Since they contain structured data, transaction documents do not usually pose major indexing problems. Thus an index for purchase orders might be adequately based on the order number and name of supplier. A more comprehensive index may be required, however, if an order tracking system is required. In this case the date of the order, the required date of delivery and the name of the requesting department might have to be recorded, for example. For an engineering drawing register, the drawing number, revision number, date and drawing location may be perfectly sufficient for retrieval.

With the increased use of Intranets and Extranets for electronic commerce, and the adoption of XML mark-up language, transaction documents are becoming more dynamic objects and their data content more accessible for further processing.

6.4.2 Non-transaction documents

This second category of document is more problematical as regards indexing because it relates to administrative and reference-type material. Such material is generally less structured and less uniform in make-up than transaction documents. Furthermore they often originate from outside the organisation in the form of publications over which the organisation usually has no control as regards content and structure.

Documents in this category will include policies and procedures, standards and specifications, operating and maintenance manuals, minutes of meetings, research reports, consultancy reports, trade literature, press cuttings, journal articles and books.

While transaction documents are an integral part of day-to-day business processes usually dealt with by staff dedicated to such tasks, non-transactional documents have a broader and more diffuse set of users. Concerns here focus on such issues as management and control, business strategy, research and development, project management, design and production, sales and marketing, and public and press relations. These are the functions peopled by 'knowledge workers'. They are more interested in the information content of documents.

The emphasis here then is on subject-based information-retrieval rather than document-retrieval. Such a requirement is far more demanding of the indexing system since there may be little, or no prior knowledge as to the type of query that a user will pose. Also, there is frequently a need to integrate information across a range of possible sources be they collections of documents or databases containing structured information, or sources internal or external to the organisation. Natural language or controlled language subject indexing (see section 6.6.3) forms the basis of many of the ways to cater for this requirement.

6.5 Document or information storage?

The preceding section was concerned with retrieval rather than storage. This distinction is important because the retrieval process, involving as it does the indexing of information, is essentially an intellectual process. Storage is a separate physical activity.

In the design of the overall computer-based information storage and retrieval system the decision has to be made as to whether complete documents, document surrogates (such as abstracts), pure data independent of any documents or any combination of these, are to be stored. This possible range of information types is shown in Table 6.2.

INFORMATION STORED	EXAMPLE OF DATABASE	INFORMATION RETRIEVED
FULL DOCUMENT with text, tables, figures, etc	Court cases	Case rulings
DOCUMENT SURROGATE e.g. abstract	Article summaries on crime	Relevant references
DATA	Crime statistics	Required facts

Table 6.2 Basic range of information types to be handled

Despite this range of options, there is usually certain basic, and mostly structured, retrieval data to be found in an index to documents, for example:

- document type (e.g. report, correspondence)
- originating organisation
- reference number of document
- security classification
- publication date
- file reference/classification code
- title
- author(s) names
- summary/abstract of document
- keywords (e.g. from controlled vocabulary)

- names of recipients

- retention date (from records retention schedules)

- destruction date

- name of person authorising destruction.

Note that the last three items arise from records management considerations (see Chapter 4). Much of this information may appear on a standard data page in the document as shown in Figure 4.2. This data, or selected parts of it, might be captured electronically by having links between the document's word-processing template and the indexing engine of the document management system, or by digitally scanning pre-defined areas of the page where the document is paper based.

Further guidance on determining index fields is available from two sources: the US Department of Defense and ANSI/AIIM. The DoD defined a minimum set of document profile data[1] and AIIM has a list of suggested index fields for imaged documents.[2]

Where whole documents are to be stored other than on paper, a further decision is required as to the form and media of storage. This may consist of machine-readable text (either from a word-processor or created by optical character recognition of a digital image), microfilm image, digital image (compressed or uncompressed), a vector representation, a drawing or a rendition of the document, for example as HTML or PDF. Deciding which of these options to adopt, either singly or in combination, depends on a number of factors. These include the needs of users for access to the document rather than the data it holds and any constraints imposed by available technology such as storage capacity and response times over a network. The totality of documents and the information they contain must be indexed in a suitably coherent and consistent fashion irrespective of the storage media strategy that is adopted.

6.6 Indexing - the key to retrieval

Indexing at first thought may seem to be a straightforward process. However on further consideration various choices usually need to be made. These concern such factors as the need for simple listing of the documents as against more detailed indexing, the requirements for conceptual organisation of the information rather than random arrangement, and the use of natural language as against a controlled vocabulary. Many of the duties concerned with document handling are of a basic clerical nature, or are at least easily taught, such as use of a microfilm camera or optical scanner. Indexing, however, requires some familiarity with the types of documents being handled and, for in-depth indexing, a knowledge of the subjects to which they relate. The pertinent concepts described here are cataloguing, subject classification and indexing.

6.6.1 Cataloguing

Substantive information such as books, research reports, manuals and engineering drawings are typically recorded as discrete pieces of information, in some form of descriptive catalogue or register. Such an approach is encountered in a company library for example. For published material, standard library cataloguing rules, such as those of the US Library of Congress, are widely employed. These record details of author(s), title, publisher, publication date, subject classification code and the internationally recognised reference code, ISBN (International Standard Book Number) or, in the case of periodicals, the ISSN (International Standard Serial Number). This catalogue information is usually reproduced in the early pages of publications, and available in machine-readable form (MARC- Machine Readable Catalogue) for incorporation in a company's computer-based library system. Such automation avoids the need for separately filed library catalogue cards covering authors(s), title and classification number, for example.

Although such cataloguing rules are aimed principally at published material, the principles should be adopted for registering any substantive information irrespective of the media on which it is stored. Catalogue information, as exemplified above, provides the basic data for lists of substantive documents and for indexes to them: for example, useful subject search terms may appear in the titles.

6.6.2 Classification

While a catalogue records the base descriptive information of individual items, which may be all that is required to deal with enquiries on the information collection, there is usually the need for deeper, structural information content analysis. One approach is to use a classification scheme.

Classification involves the conceptual, and often physical, grouping together of items within a hierarchical (tree-like) subject-based structure. One has in effect to determine to which conceptual pigeon hole a piece of information is assigned. A file classification devised as part of a records management programme (see Chapter 4) is an example of such a method of organisation.

The file classification and retention schedules are important factors when determining indexing requirements. There is thus little point in indexing a document if it is not worthy of retention. Where retention is required, it may only be necessary to index at the level of the file or folder which contains the documents. Some typical options are outlined in Table 6.3.

EPHEMERA NOT FILED OR INDEXED
MERITS FILING BUT NOT INDEXING *File/folder is indexed*
MERITS FILING AND INDEXING *File/folder and item are indexed*
MERITS FULL TEXT STORAGE *File/folder is indexed* *Text of item may be fully searchable*

Table 6.3 Key retention and indexing criteria

Note that with the implementation of document imaging, additional decisions would need to be made, such as:

- should the paper be scanned and converted to a digital image?

- if so, should the original paper be kept along with the image, or should only the image be retained?

- should the image be subjected to OCR?

- should the OCR'd versions be retained along with its associated image?

- should a rendition of the document be made, for example, the image might be converted to a PDF such as Adobe Acrobat?

Many types of document within organisations fall naturally into conceptual groupings which are to a degree self-indexing. Thus invoices and purchase orders will usually be referenced by their respective invoice and order numbers, and can therefore be arranged accordingly. If the queries posed on such collections are only based on these numbers, then a self-indexing arrangement is sufficient. However, that is rarely the case as information such as the supplier's name may be sought. In such cases additional indexes need to be created, since for all but the smallest collection of documents, searching through the complete collection for these names is not a realistic option.

Despite the availability of updated, and widely accepted standard subject classification schemes, such as the Dewey Classification (DC) and the Universal Decimal Classification (UDC) in the library field, the principles are difficult to apply consistently. This problem will be appreciated by anyone who has tried to decide into which single file a piece of correspondence should be placed which deals with a variety of topics.

Such classification schemes assign codes to subjects, and these codes are typically used to determine the filing order for the information, particularly in paper-based systems. More than one classification code can be applied to a document to reflect different subject viewpoints. In filing terms this is similar to copying one paper document onto the several different files with which it is concerned, or providing cross-references to the item from the related files.

Although these standard classification schemes can be used for file classification, and hence for pigeon-holing records by subject, their use for information retrieval where more detailed indexing is required is less successful than other approaches which are outlined in the following sections.

An example of a classification is to be found in the directory services provided by the Internet-based portal companies such as Yahoo. Although they usually provide Web searching (a topic covered later in section 6.7), a major benefit of portal companies is the ease with which users can navigate to sites and services of interest to them via a directory structure.

6.6.3 Natural language and controlled language indexing

The subject classification approach described above will normally direct one to the part of a collection most likely to include the information that is sought, rather than pinpoint the required information precisely. Indexes, however, will indicate specific and likely relevant items of information within that collection. Indexes exist in many forms and may be produced manually, or with the aid of computers, or by a combination of the two. They appear in books, in card indexes and provide conceptual access to computer-stored information.

In creating an index for computer-based retrieval, there are two basic approaches which may be used, either alone or in combination. Thus index terms may be 'natural language' terms, such as those appearing in the original text of the title, abstract or body of the document. Alternatively the terms are determined by the indexer, possibly drawing on a pre-determined, 'controlled language' vocabulary such as a subject classification, a list of subject headings, or a thesaurus.

A thesaurus is a vocabulary of controlled indexing language, formally organised so that *a priori* relationships between concepts are made explicit. The difference between a classification scheme and a thesaurus is exemplified in the field of standards. Here the International Standards Organisation (ISO) has an International Classification for Standards which consists of around 40 subject groupings of terms each with a decimal-type notation. It is intended as an aid to placing standing orders, arranging catalogue information and producing bibliographies for example. It is not designed to be used as a detailed indexing tool for which one might look towards the ROOT thesaurus from the British Standards Institute.

In devising such a controlled language, it needs to be matched to the subject content of the particular information collection that is to be indexed, to the type and detail of the questions that will be posed, and to the relative experience of the users of the retrieval system. While there may be existing controlled languages that are suitable as the basis for devising a new scheme, considerable intellectual effort and time may still have to be expended to create the desired thesaurus. It is therefore important to ensure that such effort is commensurate with the associated benefits. Guidance on thesaurus construction is provided in references 3 and 4.

The use of controlled languages is well-established and predates the computer era. However, natural language only became a realistic option with the advent of the computer and machine-readable text as generated by word-processors or optical character recognition software operating on digitally-scanned documents. In general terms, natural language indexing saves effort at the input (indexing) stage, but places an increased burden on the searcher. Controlled languages incur higher indexing costs, but facilitate searching. Comparative features of these languages are presented in Table 6.4.

NATURAL LANGUAGE	CONTROLLED LANGUAGE
Strengths: • Words of author used, hence quality not dependent on having an indexer • Provides an exhaustive index when all the document text is employed, thereby offers potential for high recall • Use of actual individual words from text ensures highly specific indexing and precision • Up-to-date, as any new terms in text are immediately available in index • Searcher uses natural language words and phrases • Minimal effort and hence low input costs to apply as process is automated • Easier exchange of information between databases as there is no controlled language to translate	**Disadvantages:** • Words of author may be misconstrued • Difficult and costly to index exhaustively • Searching limited to use of the language's terms which may not be sufficiently specific • Liable to be out-of-date; time lag while terms added to thesaurus • Artificial language has to be learned by the searcher • Index terms may inadvertently be omitted by indexers • Costly in effort to apply at indexing time • Exchange of information between databases difficult if controlled languages differ

Disadvantages:
• Effectively limited to machine-readable text
• Intellectual effort placed on searcher to think of e.g. synonyms and hierarchically related terms, to avoid missing relevant information
• Syntax problems involving incorrect association of search terms which leads to erroneous information being retrieved
	Advantages:
	• Applicable to both manual and machine-readable information
	• Helps searching by e.g.:
	  • controlling synonyms
	  • providing a hierarchical structure of broader, narrower and related terms
	  • providing scope notes
	  • qualifying homographs
	  • expresses concepts elusive in free text
	• Minimises syntax problems by use of e.g. compound terms
	• Helpful for numerical databases and multi-lingual systems

Table 6.4 Comparative features of natural and controlled language[3]

There are proponents for both approaches, and in fact it is possible to combine them in various ways to enhance performance for specific applications. A generalised flow diagram for indexing documents in an information retrieval system is shown in Figure 6.2. The controlled vocabulary, if used at all, could be applied at the input or output stages or in both cases.

While the need for information is normally on textual material, identifying, searching and retrieving images, whether of physical objects, photographs or video recordings poses unique problems. Although Excalibur's Adaptive Pattern Recognition Processing technology (see Table 6.6, page 169) addresses certain aspects of this problem, the more usual route is to utilise the skills of a human indexer. To be effective the index must be able to reflect the relative importance of the various features in the image; this in turn requires

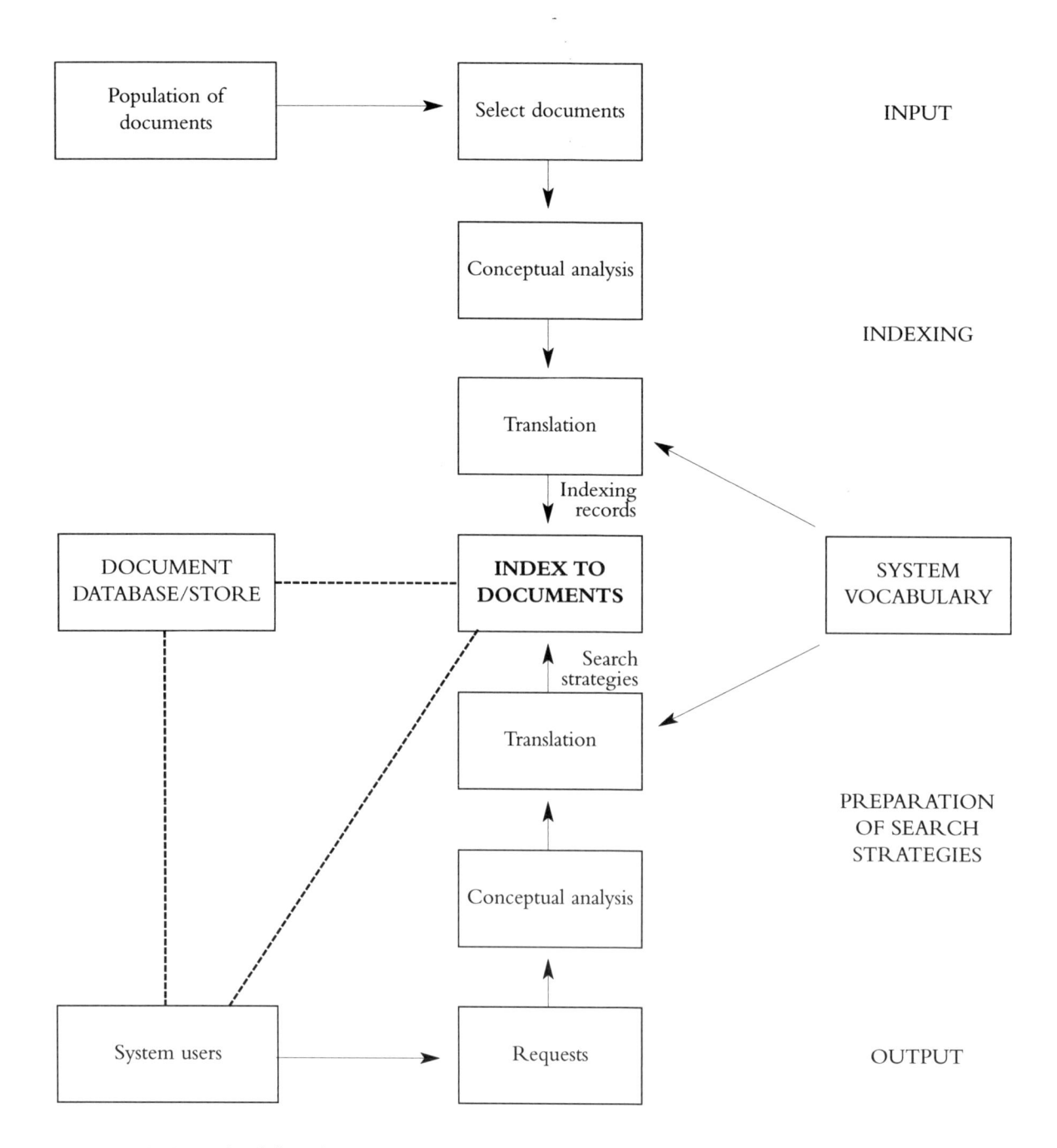

Figure 6.2 Generalised flow diagram for document indexing

that the indexer has knowledge of the interests of the information seeker and hence the types of query that will be posed. One approach is to adopt layered indexing[5] involving three layers – object, style and implication. The object layer defines the bare components of an image and the style layer records the purpose for which the image was captured. The implication layer is a short summary which addresses such questions as 'what is the point of the image?', 'why should someone want to look at it?' and 'what is unique or informative about it?'

6.6.4 Information retrieval facilities

Searching and retrieval of unstructured information such as text has, until recently at least, rarely been a requirement placed upon the traditional data processing department. Even now the concepts of IR, text retrieval and indexing unstructured data in general is often alien to IT managers. Because of the special nature of information retrieval, it is worth highlighting some of the facilities that such software may have in addition to the more standard features one would look for in database packages. These are summarised in Table 6.5.

FACILITY	EXPLANATION	COMMENTS
Word fragment searching	Searching for a particular string of characters irrespective of what other characters either follow that string or precede it, e.g. CORR* will find all information indexed by words beginning with CORR, such as CORRosion, CORRoding and CORRode, while *CORR will retrieve deCORRode.	A truncation facility helps find relevant information, particularly where a thesaurus has not been used. The required string may also be located in the body of the word, so that both forms of truncation are used. Improves recall of information.
Wild card searching	Where the precise spelling or format of the character string is not known, a so-called 'wild card' character can be inserted into the search string.	Depending on the type of wild card chosen, it may represent a single unknown character or any number of unknown characters.
Synonym control	Prevents scattering of synonyms across the database, typically by having preferred and non-preferred terms.	Usually found in thesaurus-based retrieval systems.[3] Improves recall of information.
Homograph control	Prevents irrelevant information being retrieved due to the search words having the same spelling but different meanings.	Scope notes used to differentiate. Usually found in thesaurus-based retrieval systems.[3] Improves the precision of searching.
Sound-alike	Ability to search for words or phrases which sound similar.	Improves the precision of searching.
Links and Roles	Used to prevent false co-ordination of search terms or incorrect relationships; e.g. an article on lead coating of copper pipes would not be relevant if one just entered the words as search terms but was seeking copper coating of lead pipes.	The terms are grouped or provided with role indicators at indexing time. Usually found in thesaurus-based retrieval systems.[3] Improves the precision of searching.
Date searching	Enables dates stored in different formats to be searched.	Dates are located regardless of the form in which they are expressed in the query or in the document. Ambiguity is resolved by reference to the regional settings.

Table 6.5 Retrieval aids (continued on pages 162 and 163)

FACILITY	EXPLANATION	COMMENTS
Range searching	Enables searching for information within a ranges of dates or numbers.	E.g. find documents dated between 01/01/1995 to 31/12/1998 or containing a value between £3 million and £9 million.
Phrase searching	Phrases, e.g. 'information retrieval', rather than the individual words are retrieved.	Improves precision of searching.
Stop word list	Avoids indexing common words such as 'and', 'the', 'a'.	List should be user-amendable.
Approved ('go') word list	Only indexes words that match a list of approved terms.	Facility may be provided by a thesaurus.
Boolean operators	Link search terms using the operators 'AND', 'OR' and 'NOT', e.g. find 'A' AND 'B' but not 'C'.	May be possible to combine operators into a more complex search statement by the use of brackets. However, the resulting query statement may be of such complexity that the result of the search may not be what was intended.
Proximity searching	This enables the user to specify the relative positions of search terms, e.g. the words must be next to each other, within a certain number of words of one another, in the same sentence or in the same paragraph.	Improves the precision of searching.
Fixed field searching	Searches can be limited to a specified field (such as an author field) or a set of fields (e.g. those containing subject term, i.e. title, keywords and abstract fields).	Used with structured databases; provides high degree of precision.
Hypertext	A linkage between related text, e.g., by selecting a word in a sentence, information about that word is retrieved if it exists, or the next occurrence of the word is found.	A navigation aid rather than a retrieval mechanism.
Hyperlink	A predefined linkage between one object and another. The link is displayed either as text or as an icon.	Browsers are used to navigate the Internet through a vast lattice of hyperlinks using HTML.
Concept tree	A user-definable hierarchical arrangement of subject terms to build up subject profiles reflecting the areas of interest to the enquirer.	Essentially a micro-thesaurus. Profiles may incorporate operators connecting terms to sub-terms, and weights to allow the retrieved information to be ranked in order of their relevance to the enquiry.
Summarisers	Automatic creation of reasonably accurate and intelligent abstract from the content of a document or set of documents.	Abstracts can be fed into full text retrieval software as a query-by-example.

Table 6.5 Retrieval aids (continued on page 163)

FACILITY	EXPLANATION	COMMENTS
Relevance ranking	The answers received to a query are ranked according to some measure of relevance to the enquirer.	Ranking may be based simply on the frequency of occurrence of a search term in the text or e.g. on a pre-stored subject interest profile coupled with statistical and linguistic analysis of the text – see 'Weighting'.
Weighting	Applying values to index terms or search terms to indicate their relative importance in documents or search programs.	May be found in thesaurus-based retrieval systems.[3] Improves the precision of searching.
Refining searches	Refining or expanding the previous search because the initially retrieved items may prove to be too great, or too few in number.	Most retrieval systems provide an indication of the number of items that have been found in response to the search query.
Saved searches	Completed searches are saved for future use, e.g. following an updating of the database.	Can be used to store a user's interest profiles which are run regularly against the database. User can be notified of, or sent the retrieved information (an example of 'push technology').

Table 6.5 Retrieval aids

Of particular importance is SQL (Structured Query Language), an English-like search language originally developed at IBM for its mainframe computers, and now a standard means for data independent querying of databases irrespective of the computer hardware and software on which they run. It is particularly suitable where there are large numbers of PC-based users wishing to access data across different types of computer hardware. Since the syntax of SQL is not readily assimilated by users, it is often hidden behind more familiar user interfaces.

Although the subject of an ISO standard,[6] there are several variants of SQL in existence, so there is no guarantee that SQL queries can be reliably communicated across different hardware and software platforms. Thus Z39.50 is an ANSI standard query language that is a simplified version of SQL used to search for documents on the Internet. DQL (Document Query Language) is an example of the commercial extension of SQL by the document management vendor Documentum. DQL is a superset of ANSI-standard SQL that aims to serve as a single, unified query language for all of the objects managed by a Documentum server. Using a built-in search engine, DQL provides full-text as well as attribute searching. It is stated to facilitate access to document, work process and business information.

As regards interaction with the retrieval system, there are two basic methods - command-driven and menu-driven. With the command-driven interface the user enters commands whose vocabulary and syntax are predefined for the particular database software. Knowledge and experience in using the commands is therefore necessary if the search process is to be conducted effectively and efficiently. A command-driven interface may therefore be best for the regular user and is typified by the direct use of SQL.

For occasional users, or those just starting to learn the system, a menu-driven approach is preferable and the most widely deployed. In this case the user selects from several options presented on the screen. Usually the menu system is structured as a hierarchy of menus and sub-menus. The user is guided through these until the required search query or other command specification has been entered. The system then takes the required action.

It is important that data entered into the system is not able to be accessed, altered, added to or deleted by those without the necessary approval. The ability to assign such privileges to different categories of users is important. Thus some users may only need to retrieve information for viewing. Others may have the right to amend and add, but not delete information. These rights can be applied very specifically, for example to specified document types or even individual documents. Such software features are particularly important when the system is to manage revision and version control of documents.

6.6.5 Indexing and retrieval performance

Aside from any system performance limitations introduced by the hardware, software and communication systems, the effectiveness or otherwise of the index and search facilities is critical.

At the outset, the ability to find the information, or the document it contains, depends on the completeness and accuracy of the original indexing process. The more limited the chosen indexing criteria, the greater the chance that the information will not be found if an error is made at the time of index entry. Thus if a document is only indexed by a reference code and date, then entering the wrong code will not enable it to be retrieved via the index. If, however, additional information is entered onto the computer, such as the name and address of the originator of the document, then even if that extra information is not in an indexed field in the database, at least there is the chance of retrieving the desired document by undertaking a serial search through the database records.

The accuracy with which the index data is entered can be maximised by double-entry indexing. This involves the index entries being repeated by a second person and comparing the results with those that were entered first.

The facilities of the computer and the database software can also be harnessed. Thus when entering an index code which will always have the same number and type of characters, the computer can be programmed to check that the number is correct, or always begins with the appropriate prefix. Most retrieval software enables approved lists of codes or index terms to be recorded on the system so that index terms entered at the keyboard can be automatically validated against them. Such a facility may be used in conjunction with a thesaurus.

As regards the performance of the retrieval system, a seeker of information usually has one of two basic objectives, either to find a specific piece of information or document, or to find information relevant to their information needs.

Searching an engineering drawing database by drawing number will find the associated drawing if it is in the database (and has been indexed correctly!). Thus the enquirer has found 100% of what they were looking for, and 100% of the required items (in this case one entry) in the database have been found. No other drawings are relevant to the enquiry. Put in terms in which retrieval performance is usually quoted, there has been 100% recall and 100% precision where:

$$\text{Recall} = \frac{\text{Number of relevant items retrieved}}{\text{Number of relevant items in the database}}$$

$$\text{Precision} = \frac{\text{Number of relevant items retrieved}}{\text{Number of items retrieved}}$$

If that same database is searched to find drawings containing a particular type of flow meter, it is likely that the only way these can be found is by searching the title field which contains a description of the drawing. Since such descriptions are usually 'natural language' there is no guarantee that a drawing relating to, or containing such meters, will have the type of meter named in the title field. Hence it is likely that not all the desired drawings in the database will be found (recall less than 100%), and furthermore some of the retrieved information will not be relevant (precision less than 100%).

In general, document retrieval systems are required to operate at 100% recall and 100% precision. However, when searching databases for relevant information rather than specific items (for example on-line bibliographic databases where one is dealing with unstructured text and natural language), achieving maximum recall with maximum precision is an aim which is rarely if ever achievable. Generally with such systems recall and precision tend to be inversely proportional to one another. Thus designing for maximum recall will reduce precision, but this may be acceptable if it is important to find the maximum possible number of relevant items.

The index design and retrieval aids employed (see Table 6.5) will depend on the particular application, but they should be selected to provide a suitable balance between recall and precision, and between indexing and search effort.

6.6.6 Comparative studies of search software

The use of the concepts of recall and precision, as introduced above, to test the efficacy of search software is only reliable if there is full agreement on what items of information in the collection being searched are 100% relevant to an enquiry and what proportion of the collection these relevant items constitute. This can realistically only be achieved under artificial 'laboratory' conditions.

In the real world there is no such predictability in terms of the information being searched and the type of question being posed. Hence for different types of query, a range of precision and recall measures will be obtained, given that opinions on the relevance of the information retrieved will vary.

As noted by the Gartner Group at the end of 1995 in one of their product guides: '*At this time, no reliable data exists to prove the value of natural language approaches. Therefore, clients should take claims in this area lightly, even though natural language understanding has been a fruitful area for research for more than 20 years*'. Furthermore they state that '*Although the IR (Information Retrieval) industry desperately needs a means to compare relevance performance across products, the complexity, level of effort and technical depth needed to judge text-retrieval engines is so great that there will be no common tests within the next five years*'. At the time of writing there is still no sign that such common tests are emerging.

A somewhat broader comparative approach based on consumer perceptions of service quality has been applied to Internet search engines.[7] Here the dimensions of service quality applied were:

- tangibles (e.g. the characteristics and functions of the search engines)
- reliability (e.g. ability to provide relevant and useful information)
- responsiveness (e.g. ability to provide prompt response to the query)
- assurance (e.g. ability to ensure that the results are accurate, recent and precise)
- empathy (e.g. provision of individualised attention provided to the customers).

The article includes a preliminary survey questionnaire which readers are invited to complete.

6.7 Software for information retrieval

As has been already noted, indexing is a separate process to that of the physical storage of the documents or information that are indexed. This means, for example, that the index may be held on a different computer to that which handles the access to the physical store, or may be provided by the same database that holds the electronic files or images.

As a generalisation two main avenues of software development for indexing and retrieving information emerged over the years, these being:

- Database management systems (DBMS) dealing with structured data
- Information retrieval systems aimed at searching less structured text-based information.

For DBMS systems there usually has to be an exact match between the query posed and the information stored to have a successful conclusion. DBMS have therefore mainly been used where such predictable conditions prevail, typically in transaction processing-type systems. The design of such databases is centred around the concepts of data and process modelling, and of structuring the data into related entities (e.g. customer, order, invoice). Various designs of DBMS software – principally hierarchical, network and relational - exist to provide the necessary linkages between the entities, the choice of design being largely dependent upon the nature, frequency and predictability of the search queries.

Information retrieval systems, on the other hand, are aimed more at unstructured information such as the titles and abstracts of bibliographic data in a library database or the full text in a document. They involve the use of more natural language than the somewhat artificial query languages often found in DBMS. Furthermore they do not rely on an exact match to achieve useful results. As an example, when seeking information on corrosion of North Sea oil exploration platforms, details may be found of corrosion of piers in the Atlantic ocean. Although this information is not precisely what was sought it may prove to be sufficiently relevant and therefore useful.

In broad terms, the basic distinguishing features of DBMS and information retrieval systems are shown in Figure 6.3.

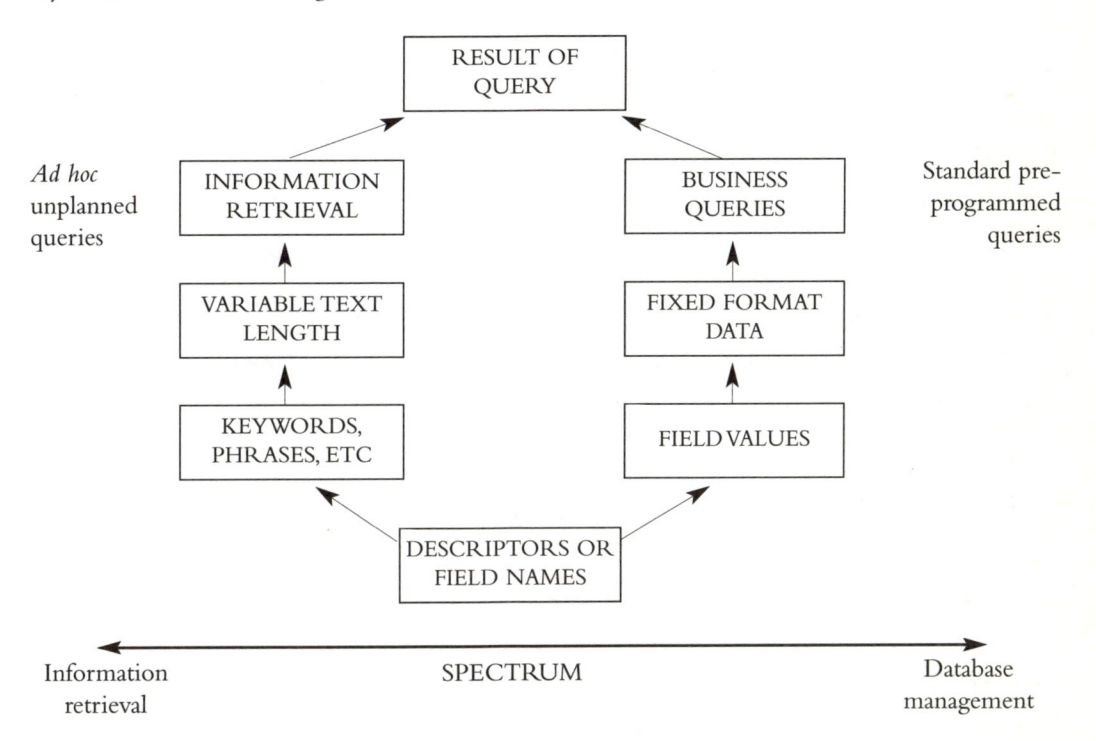

Figure 6.3 Contrasting DBMS and information retrieval systems

With the move to multimedia and compound documents (i.e. electronic documents holding not only text, but graphics, pictures, video clips, etc.) there is increasing interest in object-oriented DBMS (ODBMS) that manage objects (abstract data types). The Object Database Management Group (ODMG) was formed to promote standards for object databases and has provided programming extensions for accessing an object-oriented database. Although some relational DBMS products provide a large object (LOB) field for this purpose, they are not best suited to storing multimedia. Furthermore, the use of such facilities requires more computing power to drive them. An interesting exception is the BASIS software from Open Text which is a document database offering powerful information retrieval capabilities (see page 238).

The advent of client/server computing and unified access to corporate data has focused the interest of companies on the need for specialised 'warehouses' to facilitate queries on production data. Some companies are therefore deploying data warehouse-style environments with ODBMS acting as the object warehouse while production data remains in relational databases. Although the topic of data warehousing falls outside the scope of this book, it is an important element of building enterprise knowledge management.[8]

The aforementioned DBMS and information retrieval software designs largely predate the Internet and the WWW, the emergence of which saw the rapid development and commercial deployment of Web search sites. There are broadly two categories: one provides a subject-based directory (classification) of Web sites, while the other is based on pre-compiled index. Most search sites offer a mix of these facilities. The directory-based services use humans to classify information received about sites into the various subject categories. Search engines (variously called spiders, robot ('bot'), intelligent agent or crawlers) trawl Web sites and index Web pages to create extensive databases for users to consult. In general terms the directory services are likely to provide improved precision, but possibly lower recall than will be achieved by the search engines.

For an increasing number of applications, for example in the commercial and marketing area, and for enterprise-wide information retrieval, there has grown a need for a combination of all these approaches. This requires the ability to deal with both structured and unstructured information and all data types, using standard and *ad hoc* queries within the same system whether searching within one's organisation or accessing external on-line databases or the Internet.

When looking for retrieval software, whether for a small document collection or to support a Web-based enterprise-wide service, it should now be clear that there is a wide choice of software designs and products emanating from various sectors of the industry. It is easy to be confused and even duped by advertising blurb and the hype surrounding existing and new products that have emerged in the emperor's 'knowledge-management' clothes. It is therefore vital to probe behind the seductive words of the salesperson and seek out the real capabilities of the product, focusing on one's real business needs and drawing on the experience of existing users before contemplating even a pilot run.

Table 6.6 provides examples from the range of retrieval software on offer at the time of writing, i.e. the listing is representative, not comprehensive. The software is categorised broadly into three groupings: Internet search engines, vendors who are focusing on the burgeoning knowledge management market, and examples of other text retrieval suppliers who have established a presence for themselves in this software sector. Note that this division is somewhat arbitrary and subject to change from market forces. The table excludes document management (DM) products that may have this type of software embedded in them. Examples of DM products are provided in Chapter 8. A useful Website for finding CD-ROMS and commercial software products is Turbo Guide.[10] An overview of software packages for knowledge management was provided by Kibby and Mahon.[11]

CATEGORY	PRODUCT	VENDOR + WEB SITE	COMMENTS
Internet/ Intranet search engines (see reference 9)	Yahoo	Yahoo http://www.yahoo.com	Oldest Web site directory. Provides linkages to search engine sites.
	Excite	Excite http://www.excite.com	Provides traditional searching plus listings of sites by topic. Owns WebCrawler. Powers the Netscape portal site. BT has bought into UK subsidiary of Excite.
	Alta Vista	Digital (owned by Compaq) http://altavista.digital.com	Largest number of Web pages indexed; has a directory listing. Supports 'RealNames' providing keyword links (e.g. company names, trademarks) to corresponding sites.
	InfoSeek	Infoseek http://www.infoseek.com	Limited database; has separate directory listing and provides hand-picked (reviewed) sites.
	Lycos	Lycos http://www.lycos.com	Directory service plus search engine. Provides reviews of sites.
	Google	Stanford University http://google.stanford.edu/	New generation search engine ranking Web sites by how often they are pointed to by other Web sites. Akin to the Citation Index of old.
Search software focusing on 'knowledge management' sector	Knowledge Warehouse	Dataware Technologies http://www.dataware.com	Long-established supplier of information/text retrieval products (e.g. BRS/Search) now focusing on enterprise knowledge management. (See Sovereign Software below.)
	Agentware Knowledge Server & Agentware Knowledge Update	Autonomy http://www.agentware.com	Uses 'Concept Agents' employing range of statistical, information theory and neural network technology. Searches using natural language or user-supplied examples.
	Muscat empower	Muscat (70% owned by the Dialog Corporation)	Searches and correlates information based on concepts. Seamless interface to structured and unstructured data

Table 6.6 Retrieval software – representative products (continued on page 170)

CATEGORY	PRODUCT	VENDOR + WEB SITE	COMMENTS
	RetrievalWare	Excalibur http://www.excalib.com	Long-established information-retrieval supplier founded on its own pattern recognition technology and subsequently enhanced with semantic network technology it acquired.
	Knowledge Network	Fulcrum Technologies http://www.fulcrum.com	A text-retrieval vendor subsequently acquired by PC DOCS (a document management company). An early proponent of enterprise knowledge management.
	Knowledge Organiser for Information Server	Verity http://www.verity.com	An early developer of search technology and custom integration products, it is now focusing more on exploiting corporate knowledge via Intranets.
Text retrieval software	InQuery	Sovereign Hill Software	The Center for Intelligent Information Retrieval (CIIR) established Sovereign Hill to commercialise the InQuery retrieval engine which is deployed in many US government and educational establishments. Was acquired by Dataware Technologies in January 1999.
	ISYS	Odyssey Development http://www.isysdev.com	General full text indexing and search package for e.g. CD, hard disk, Web site or corporate file server. Has products for imaging and Web searching.
	ZyINDEX	ZyLAB International, Inc http://www.zyLAB.com	Full text indexing and retrieval package for electronic files. Has products for imaging and Web searching.
	BASIS	Open Text http://www.opentext.com	A database software in its own right for storing the documents and providing powerful text search and document retrieval.

Table 6.6 Retrieval software – representative products

As a postscript, the topic of retrieval software is not complete without reference to expert systems – arguably the ultimate example of knowledge management. An expert system is composed of three elements:

- ◆ a knowledge base containing facts and rules
- ◆ an inference engine which manipulates the knowledge base and
- ◆ a user interface to these first two elements.

The knowledge base contains a semantic map (akin to a thesaurus, but with more explicit relationships) and rules based on an 'IF..THEN' logic. Its success is based on the quality of the data and rules obtained from the human expert. Expert systems can work reasonably well in relatively closed systems such as for medical diagnosis, equipment repair and training. However, if even a simple problem is posed just slightly beyond their experience, they will usually provide a wrong answer, without any recognition that they are beyond their range of competence. Also such programs can not readily share their knowledge, as each represents its bit of the world in idiosyncratic and incompatible ways.

REFERENCES IN CHAPTER 6

1   *Design Criteria Standard for Electronic Records Management Software Applications,* DoD 5015.2-STD

2   *Suggested Index Fields for Documents in Electronic Image Management (EIM) Environments,* ANSI/AIIM TR40-1995

3   Aitchison, J., Gilchrist, A. and Bawden, D., *Thesaurus Construction and Use: a Practical Manual Third edition* (London: Aslib, 1997)

4   *BS 5723: 1987; ISO 2788, Guide to Establishment and Development of Monolingual Thesauri*

5   Schroeder, K.A., 'Layered Indexing of Images', *The Indexer,* Vol.21, No.1 April 1998, pp. 11-14

6   *BS ISO/IEC 9075: 1992, Information technology. Database languages. SQL*

7   Xie, M., Wang, H. and Goh, T.N., 'Quality Dimensions of Internet Search Engines', *Journal of Information Science,* Vol.24, No.5, 1998, pp. 365-372 (the survey questionnaire included in the article is stated to be available from URL http://www.eng.nus.edu.sg/ise/seq-survey.html)

8   *Data Warehousing & Business Intelligence Software in Conspectus,* March 1999, (Chorleywood, Hertfordshire, UK: Prime Marketing Publications, http://www.conspectus.com)

9   To keep up-to-date on search engines technology consult Mecklermedia's 'Search Engine Watch' on URL http://searchenginewatch.com

10 http://software-guide.com

11 Kibby, Peter and Mahon, Barry, 'Software Packages for Knowledge Management', *Records Management Bulletin* (of the UK Records Management Society), Issue 91 (April, 1999), pp. 13-17

PART 3

PROJECT MANAGEMENT AND SOLUTIONS – IDEAS INTO ACTION

7

DOCUMENT MANAGEMENT – THE PROJECT FOCUS

'I have frequently told you, amongst other absurd habits, that that of making drawings on the back of others was inconvenient; by your cursed neglect of that you have again wasted more of my time than your whole life is worth, in looking for the altered drawings you were to make of the Station – they won't do.'

Isambard Kingdom Brunel, quoted in Brunel and his World: John Pudney

The approaches outlined earlier in Part 1 of this book provide means for analysing various aspects of business performance. These means range from high level information systems strategy to more focused methods and methodologies concerned with processes, quality, human resources and, at the sharp end, documents and corporate records – a topic clearly of concern to Brunel early in the nineteenth century! The broad base of information technologies that can be integrated to help effect improvements in business performance was presented in Part 2.

In this part attention is directed to putting ideas for improvement into action by way of formal projects. It includes choosing the target area, and project justification. Project management is an unglamorous activity, but one that is a critical success factor for deploying document management with its numerous and disparate technologies.

7.1 CHOOSING THE PROJECT AREA

In the late '80s and early '90s a working group drawn from 20 organisations including commerce, industry, government, manufacturers, academia and service firms addressed the question of electronic imaging.[1,2] The aim was to clarify its definition, identify appropriate areas for application and consider costs, benefits, barriers and required actions. It concluded that the major strategic issues that needed positive management intervention were:

- ◆ ensuring organisational awareness of the technology and how to obtain value from it

- redesigning processes (not just improving work flow)
- targeting high opportunity applications
- managing the human side of the technology
- establishing a long-term architecture for imaging from design to implementation
- creating a strategy linked to the business and funded.

All of these issues are ones which arise to a lesser or greater degree when considering the introduction of any information technology. Management and staff must be suitably aware of technology so that they can make wise choices and smooth its introduction into the business. Appropriate application areas need to be chosen, and this should all be undertaken within the context of an overall knowledge/information systems strategy as was outlined in Chapter 2.

Arguably the most important issue is that of process redesign, a topic already referred to (Chapter 3), but which merits further emphasis. It is increasingly being highlighted that organisations who have embraced computing and other information technology developments over the years have done so without considering the effectiveness and efficiency of the underlying business processes which they perform. Even though they might have developed an information systems strategy, it has built upon existing practices, rather than upon a redesign which would help them not only capitalise on new technologies, but also wring greater benefit from the information systems already in place.

The survey published in 1995 of UK users (and prospective users) of document management systems[3] indicated the emphasis being given to business process re-engineering along with reviews on document and records management strategies and prototyping prior to initiating a document management project (see Table 7.1).

ACTIONS TAKEN	% OF USERS UNDERTAKING
Internal review of current document and records management strategy	81
Prototyping a proof of concept demonstration	76
Business process re-engineering	44
Audit of operations using external consultants	22

Table 7.1 Pre-project actions taken

While process redesign has always been a possibility, it has, until the emergence of electronic imaging, been constrained by the problem of integrating paper-based information with existing computer-based information. Document imaging helps address this problem. The need for imaging will decrease, however, as developments in electronic trading eliminate the use of paper at the very start of the information life cycle.

It is important that one's information systems strategy is not simply a document management strategy. The latter must be subsumed into the former if the management of information resources is to be optimised. In choosing the project area within the context of a portfolio of existing computer-based applications it can be helpful to consider a simple model of technology (Figure 7.1) based on the Boston Square - one of the techniques mentioned in section 2.7.2. Here the four segments represent technologies of different ages and potential. The technologies that have been mentioned, and their position in the grid will not be valid for all organisations. Nevertheless the concept of the grid is generally applicable.

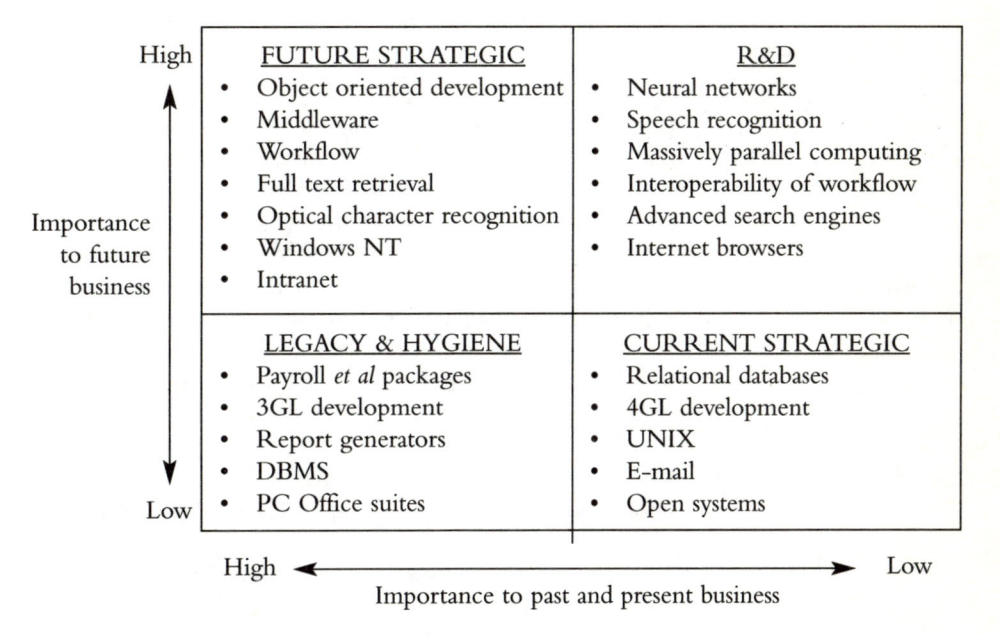

	Importance to past and present business	
High — Importance to future business	**FUTURE STRATEGIC** • Object oriented development • Middleware • Workflow • Full text retrieval • Optical character recognition • Windows NT • Intranet	**R&D** • Neural networks • Speech recognition • Massively parallel computing • Interoperability of workflow • Advanced search engines • Internet browsers
Low	**LEGACY & HYGIENE** • Payroll *et al* packages • 3GL development • Report generators • DBMS • PC Office suites	**CURRENT STRATEGIC** • Relational databases • 4GL development • UNIX • E-mail • Open systems
	High ←――――――――――→ Low	

Figure 7.1 Technology options

7.1.1 Where to look

Candidate areas for implementing document management may become apparent from:

◆ pro-active studies to achieve strategic or tactical benefits, for example:

- to support enterprise knowledge management initiatives
- improve customer satisfaction
- increase speed to market
- eliminate unnecessary tasks
- reduce costs

◆ reaction to business problems, for example:

- increased storage costs for documents
- difficulties in accessing and retrieving information from archives
- delays in dealing with customers' orders
- slow, bureaucratic document approval cycles
- need for simultaneous access to documents.

The more general techniques and methodologies outlined in Chapter 3, taken together with the records- and document-focus of *Infobuild* described in Chapter 4, provide a range of approaches for reviewing and analysing the business.

Candidate areas can also be identified by considering the types of applications that are seen as the main focus for document management implementations as exemplified by the categories shown in Table 7.2.

APPLICATION AREA	COMMENTS
Transaction or form processing	Based on handling single documents, e.g. as in bank cheque clearance and recording credit card counterfoils. The processing tasks and procedures are pre-defined, relatively simple and repetitive. Actions are not varied by the actual contents of the 'document' and usually consist of extracting data and transferring it to an alternative form for storage.
Case transaction processing	Involves accessing the accumulated documents linked to a specific key, for example a file concerning a named defendant in a set of such files handled by a lawyer, or an individual's records held by an insurance company. The reasons for accessing the file will vary but may involve undertaking standard tasks, e.g. to review renewal premiums, or for *ad hoc* research purposes.
Customer service enquiry	Oral or written requests are received from customers. Document retrieval provides the information for answering the query. The workflow element is minimal.
Corporate publishing	Typically associated with desktop publishing it may involve the integration of digitally generated images and scanned-in photographs
Quality management	Adherence to quality system standards and adoption of quality management systems involve the documenting of policies, procedures and possibly detailed work instructions. Document management coupled with workflow can facilitate the creation and maintenance of quality documentation.
Corporate administrative and management documents	Documents will include policies and procedures for the various business functions such as human resources and sales & marketing. The production and management of these documents will require the same kind of activities as those applied to quality management.
Records management	Retention scheduling of corporate records is incorporated into the document management system along with controlled archiving using appropriate storage media (e.g. online, near-line and off-line).

Table 7.2 Classification of document management applications (based on reference 3) (continued on page 179)

APPLICATION AREA	COMMENTS
Library services	Libraries are typically responsible for acquiring and managing externally published or sourced information. Commercially available systems have long existed for e.g. cataloguing, ordering, periodical (serials) management and loans management and for providing full text searching. Document management functionality is increasingly provided by these vendors, or as add-ons by third parties to help integrate this external information with other corporate information. Searching of the document collection is usually undertaken for research and reference purposes.
Office documentation	General office documentation such as word-processed correspondence, spreadsheets or scanned-in images from paper have long been candidates for document management systems. Access is provided by searching on structured indexes or occasional full-text searching. Links to work group scheduling applications can be important.
Engineering project management	Engineering document management systems have developed from the need to manage engineering project documents including large format drawings (e.g. up to A0 or larger) along with standard office sizes. For engineering projects such functionality as document version control, system access controls, user rights, controlled document distribution and approval and authorisation are key. Hence workflow controls are normally required. Retrieval of documents is normally satisfied by structured indexing (e.g. drawing numbers), although full text searching may be a requirement. Links to creation applications for documents (e.g. word-processing) and drawings (i.e. CAD) are important, as are communication links to external engineering contractors and the eventual beneficiaries of the project at the hand-over stage.

Table 7.2 Classification of document management applications (based on reference 3)

Additional information to help identify candidate project areas may be gathered from Chapter 8 which provides an overview of the supplier marketplace, and from Chapter 9 which provides examples of user experiences.

7.2 User needs and system functionality

A business need will not necessarily require all the functionality that can be provided by an integrated document management system, although the initial application area may be viewed as a pilot for possible roll-out and extension of functionality to other business areas.

There is often confusion amongst suppliers and users of document management about its scope and the technology deployed. It is therefore hardly surprising that the functionality associated with the technology can be similarly unclear. In this section a framework is presented for categorising the functions provided by products offered to the document management market, and in particular in relation to:

- ◆ storage of indexed documents in a secure vault (computer storage)
- ◆ acquisition of documents from outside the immediate organisation
- ◆ creation of documents within the organisation

♦ distribution of documents

♦ retrieval of documents

♦ support for business processes using workflow.

These elements are shown in Figure 7.2. (The numbers refer to the life cycle activities in Figure 2.12.) A more detailed breakdown of these functions is provided in Table 7.3, which can provide the basic criteria for developing a requirement specification and for analysing available products.

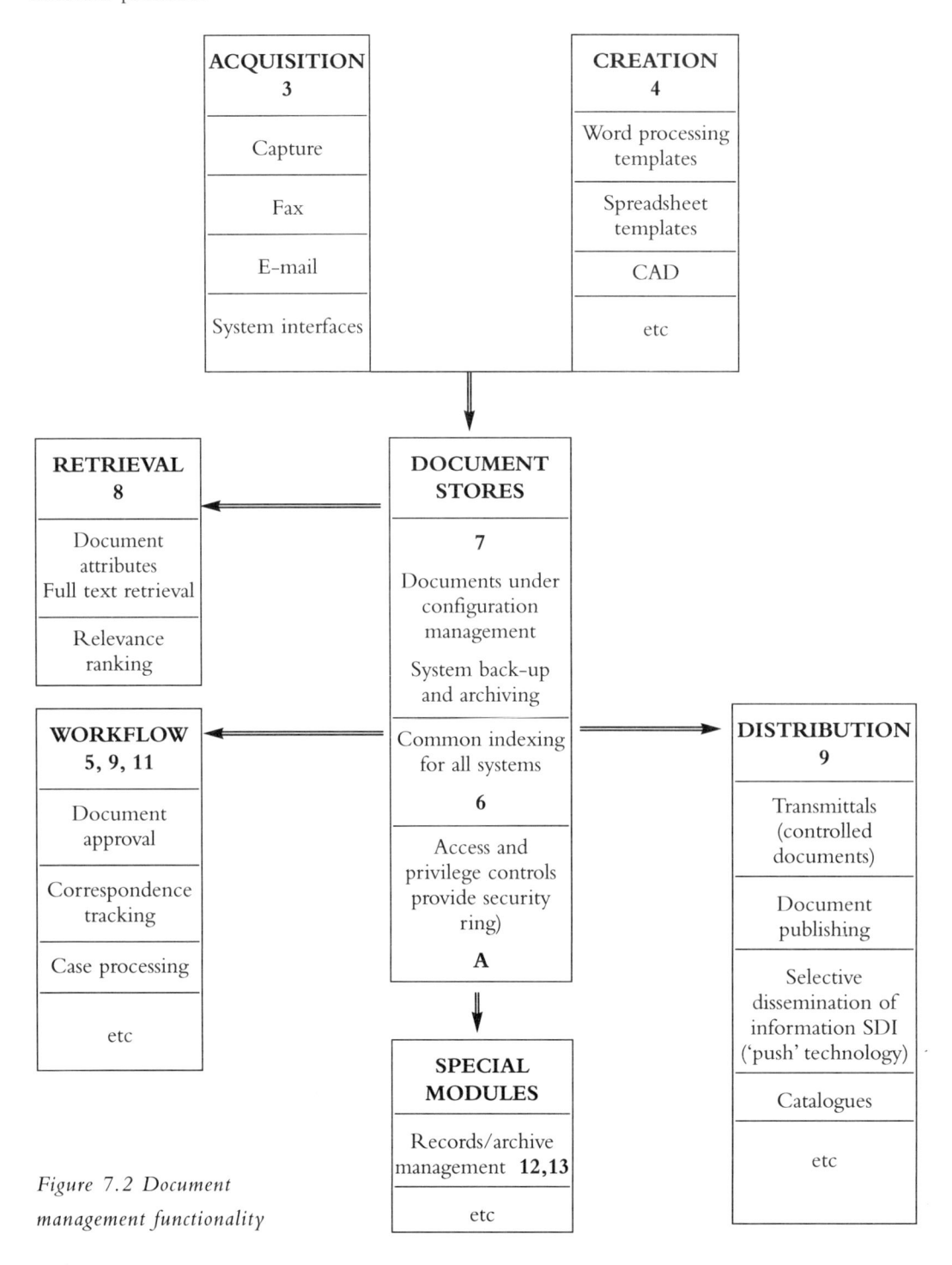

ACQUISITION 3	CREATION 4
Capture	Word processing templates
Fax	Spreadsheet templates
E-mail	CAD
System interfaces	etc

RETRIEVAL 8
Document attributes Full text retrieval
Relevance ranking

DOCUMENT STORES
7
Documents under configuration management
System back-up and archiving
Common indexing for all systems
6
Access and privilege controls provide security ring)
A

WORKFLOW 5, 9, 11
Document approval
Correspondence tracking
Case processing
etc

DISTRIBUTION 9
Transmittals (controlled documents)
Document publishing
Selective dissemination of information SDI ('push' technology)
Catalogues
etc

SPECIAL MODULES
Records/archive management 12,13
etc

Figure 7.2 Document management functionality

Functional module: *Acquisition*

SUB-FUNCTION	COMMENTS	LIFE CYCLE*
	Involves a range of approaches for acquiring documents external to the document management system and converting them so that they are able to be readily incorporated into the system.	3
Scanning	Capturing non-digital (analogue) information (e.g. paper, microfilm) and converting to a digital form. Colour and black and white scanning possible. Specific functionality to consider may include image processing, e.g. for de-skewing or image rotation.	3.1
Character recognition	Converting text in a digitised image file to revisable form so that it can be edited and/or used for indexing.	3.2
Voice recognition	Converting spoken words into digital form for direct entry into application software avoiding the use of a keyboard. Facilitates knowledge capture.	3.3
Bar code reading	Reading standard bar codes; useful for capturing indexing information.	3.4
Interfacing	Integrating into the system those documents that have been created within the organisation using its standard application software. The system should support the relevant software be it WP, DTP, CAD/CAM, spreadsheet or multimedia.	3.5
Importing	Acquiring digital information from sources external to the organisation and storing without conversion, however various intermediary checking and conversion processes may be required to render the documents acceptable to the system, e.g. vector or raster conversion.	3.6
Video capture	Incorporation of video (single frames or motion video).	3.7
Forms processing	Capturing information from forms or other structured layout for index entry or data processing.	3.8
Control/ Organise	The incorporation of documents into the system must be subject to system and user-definable approval/authorisation procedure.	A, B

*Table 7.3 Document management functional modules and sub-functions (continued on pages 182 to 185). *The life cycle references are to Figure 2.12.*

Functional module: *Creation*

SUB-FUNCTION	COMMENTS	LIFE CYCLE
	Document management systems are not usually provided with functionality for creating documents, and typically rely on interfacing with standard application software designed for that purpose. (For annotating and mark-up functions see 'REVISION' function.)	4
Authoring	Creation of textual information (e.g. using word-processors or desktop publishing).	4.1
Drawing	Creation of graphical information (e.g. CAD).	4.2
SGML/HTML/XML editing	Tools for marking up digital documents, e.g. to reflect their structure, provide means for embedding hyperlinks, aid indexing and render the documents suitable for use on the Internet or an Intranet.	4.3
Renditioning	Ability to create and manage different renditions of a document, e.g. *HTML, PDF*.	4.4
Control/organise	Any creation functionality must be subject to system and user-definable approval/authorisation procedures, e.g. with regard to version control, configuration management, check-out/check-in.	A, B

Functional module: *Indexing* (See Table 6.5 in Chapter 6 for more detail on indexing/retrieval aids)

SUB-FUNCTION	COMMENTS	LIFE CYCLE
	Appropriate attributes of the documents are recorded and/or index terms extracted from the documents to facilitate their retrieval and management throughout the life cycle.	6
Document profiling	A standardised set of attributes typically recording such information as ownership, retention schedule data and basic index information (title, author, creation date).	6.1
Structured indexing	Typically database fields of fixed length holding structured data where standard queries are posed and exact matches are sought on the information (e.g. document numbers, codes, dates). The data entered may be subject to pre-defined validation rules and entry into the fields may be defined as mandatory or optional for example.	6.2
Keywording	*Ad hoc* or predefined subject terms or phrases entered into specified fields. Their use may be controlled by a pre-defined authority list or a thesaurus providing logical grouping of terms (e.g. broader, narrower or related), and means for synonym control.	6.3
Full-text indexing	Uses all the words in the document (but usually excluding non-significant words such as 'and') to create an index for subsequent searching.	6.4
Subject filing classification	Logical grouping of subjects into a hierarchical filing classification which reflects the users' views of their subject matter for reference purposes.	6.5
Control/organise	Controls applied may include review and approval of indexing and validation using a thesaurus.	A, B

Table 7.3 continued

Functional module: *Storage*

SUB-FUNCTION	COMMENTS	LIFE CYCLE
	Ability to manage a range of storage media for holding digital documents.	7
Hierarchical storage management	Making appropriate use of storage media and devices available to the system, which may include magnetic hard disks, RAID, magnetic tape, optical disks.	7.1
COLD (computer output to laser disk)	Managing the indexing, mass storage and retrieval of documents (e.g. corporate computer reports and data) committed to laser disk. (Note, other storage media may be considered more appropriate.)	7.2
Control/organise	Controls to ensure effective authorisation as regards management of documents across a range of storage media including documents retained in paper and/or microfilm form.	A, B

Functional module: *Searching/retrieval*

SUB-FUNCTION	COMMENTS	LIFE CYCLE
	Encompasses retrieval of documents (or elements of a document), viewing and access control.	8
Searching - structured and free text	Software is available with a wide range of aids to maximise the retrieval of all relevant documents while omitting those that are not pertinent to the query.	8.1
Viewers	Provision of/support for file format recognition viewers and/or viewers for documents converted or existing in a single format.	8.2
Control/organise	User-definable access controls to information definable to various levels of granularity, e.g. document, index, field levels.	A, B

(Table 7.3 continued)

Functional module: *Communication*

SUB-FUNCTION	COMMENTS	LIFE CYCLE
	Digital and non-digital means for conveying and presenting documents to the user.	9
Network support	Ability to provide access via LANs and WANs.	9.1
Internet support	Provision of support for communication via the Internet and extension of document management functionality. May need to cover receipt and distribution of information.	9.2
Intranet support	Provision of support for communication within the organisation/closed community using Internet-technology and extension of document management functionality.	9.2.1
Interlinking	Ability to provide links to/from document-related associated systems, e.g. purchasing, asset management, personnel, ERP systems such as SAP.	9.3
Document distribution support	Ability to support/provide for distribution of documents using established proprietary formats and matching document sets against distribution lists. Audit trail and transmittal responses may be required.	9.4
Printer/plotter support	Ability to output to printers and plotters.	9.5
Display technology	The display technology must be suitable for the type of document being presented. For example higher resolution, larger screen sizes are required for large format, detailed drawings. Good colour definition will be required for coloured photographs.	9.6
Fax distribution	Support for fax including networked fax servers.	9.7
Electronic mail	Communication, receipt processing and filing of e-mail (in native format) integrated with other document formats.	9.8
Off-line distribution	Output to CD-ROM, diskettes, tape, etc.	9.9
Groupware support	Distributing digital documents through Groupware systems (e.g. Lotus Notes) which aim to improve co-operation between and the joint productivity of small groups of people.	9.10
Ad hoc workflow support	Communicating documents via *ad-hoc* casual workflow tools which use e-mail, forms and messages as the system infrastructure where information and work is sent out to people whether they need it or not.	9.11
Proactive workflow support	Communicating documents via higher-end workflow systems concerned with the proactive management of the flow of work between co-operating individuals and groups of people based on defined procedures and tasks. Graphical front ends to monitor and amend workflow. Typically associated with managing transaction documents	9.12
Control/organise	Suitable controls need to be in place and procedures documented and agreed to facilitate communication between consenting partners.	A, B

(Table 7.3 continued)

Functional module: *Revision*

SUB-FUNCTION	COMMENTS	LIFE CYCLE
	Effecting additions or changes to a document's content with the ability to audit the changes.	11
Annotation	Ability to annotate documents by way of notes, comments, mark-ups, etc., as text, graphics or voice.	11.1
Check out/check in	Controlled checking-out and checking-in of documents for revision, linked to user's access permission and rights.	11.2
Layer provision	Support for multiple, separately indexed, redline layers stored with, but separately managed from the document or drawing.	11.3
Redlining	Redlining tools for raster or vector files with 2D drawing and editing tools.	11.4
Text editing	Provision of integral editors or links to native applications.	11.5
Graphical editing	Provision of in-built tools or links to native applications for editing CAD or raster images.	11.6
Version control	Controls over access and making amendments to documents including such features as locking documents while being edited and notifying users of documents under revision.	11.7
Electronic signature	Support for authorisation by electronic signature.	
Control/organise	Appropriate version/configuration management controls need to be in place.	A, B

Functional module: *Monitoring and control*

SUB-FUNCTION	COMMENTS	LIFE CYCLE
	Various administrative and control functions to ensure the integrity of the information held.	A
Access control	Functions to control who can access the system and what rights they have (e.g. to view, annotate, edit particular types of document).	A1
Archiving	The removal of documents to cheaper and/or near-line and/or off-line storage according to pre-defined criteria, e.g. length of time during which the document has not been accessed.	A2
Retention	Ability to apply retention schedules regarding the retention and archiving of documents. This may be done at the indexing stage.	12
Disposal	Ability to manage the approved disposal of documents. Typically linked to retention criteria.	13

(Table 7.3 continued)

Although brief consideration is given below of the individual life cycle activities and some of the issues that need to be carefully thought about, the choice of target project area should take into account an assessment of the total life cycle and a prioritisation of users' needs in relation to their business processes. (Again, the numbered activities refer to Figure 2.12.)

7.2.1 Acquisition (Activity 3)

Acquisition is directed at information which already exists and is arguably a prime activity for the application of document imaging for documents in paper or microfilm form. Its importance is exemplified in the very title of the US Department of Defense's CALS initiative (Continuous Acquisition and Life Cycle Support). Acquiring the information in electronic form at the beginning of the life cycle provides the greatest flexibility for its subsequent management and use.

7.2.2 Creation (Activity 4)

Document management technology is not primarily focused on information creation in the way that word-processing and computer-aided design (CAD) are. However, electronic document imaging has an important facilitating role in such areas as desktop publishing by way of capturing existing information using scanners and enabling it to be edited, added to or incorporated in existing documents. Document management products can increasingly be integrated with standard 'commercial off-the-shelf software'.

7.2.3 Approval and authorisation (Activity 5)

In any business there are types of document which require some form of formal review, approval or authorisation, examples being:

- insurance claims
- engineering drawings
- invoices
- purchase requisitions
- quality plans
- standards/specifications
- audit reports.

Depending on the business application, the process of approval and authorisation may involve one or more persons undertaking relatively simple or complex review cycles. The degree of complexity, and the degree of standardisation of the process will be a determining factor in the choice of possible solution. Thus complex, standard review cycles may well merit the deployment of robust workflow software. Where the process is not standardised, but is *ad hoc* in nature, then groupware based on ubiquitous e-mail products or more sophisticated software are likely to be more appropriate.

7.2.4 Indexing (Activity 6)

It bears repeating - indexing is arguably the *most important* functional element of a document management system. Once the documents are in electronic form, the lack of an appropriate index can mean required documents may never be found. Careful thought must therefore be given to the type and level of detailed indexing that one requires, whether the documents have been created in electronic form at the outset or have been scanned in from paper or microfilm originals.

With the marked rise in interest in full text retrieval, there has been a tendency to see that technology as the answer to all indexing and retrieval needs. This is far from the truth as there is still the need for structured, database-type indexing. This enables key attributes such as title, author, date of document, customer name, customer address and so on to be recorded in database 'fields' (the particular attributes required depends on what the document is, e.g. a report or invoice). This topic and others relating to databases and text retrieval are covered extensively in Chapter 6.

7.2.5 Retention (Activity 12)

This is a key activity to be considered when deciding on the choice of storage medium. If a document and the information it contains is only of ephemeral interest following its creation - and there are no legal or historical reasons, for example, why it should be retained once it has been read - then the question of deciding on a storage medium is not a major concern. The medium for recording the information at the time of creation or for communicating it may have been important, but that is a different issue. An example of such a 'document' is a communication sent to confirm the time and place of a meeting taking place the same day. The memo may have been hand-written on paper, created and sent by electronic mail, or communicated by telephone and recorded on an answering machine. Once the recipient has read, or listened to, the communication it is unlikely to warrant further retention.

When retention is required, which fact should have been recorded in retention schedules, then choice of medium becomes important. Retention periods are usually assigned to records series. In the case of paper files, such series are physically located together. Hence at the time when destruction is due, the particular files are physically identifiable and can be easily extracted for disposal. The same situation can apply to microfilmed records, especially where unitised formats such as jacketed microfiche are involved.

The situation can be less clear with optical storage. Without proper preplanning to exploit the abilities of the image management software, the various documents making up the files may be scattered across several disks, thereby adversely affecting not only retrieval times, but also the management of the retention and associated destruction programme. If the storage system is managed to associate records series on the same physical medium, then proliferation of optical disks can itself be avoided.

Consideration must also be given to the life expectancy of the medium and ensuring that the medium itself can be accessed in the future as technology advances and particular designs of drive become obsolete.

The lack of a consistent, media-independent retention policy also has legal implications. Rarely do organisations have a consistent retention policy covering paper, microfilmed and digitally-stored records.

7.2.6 Storage (Activity 7)

Storage is in many respects the prime information life cycle activity. It is the means of ensuring that existing information is recorded in sufficiently permanent form to satisfy the requirements for retention and access, and in such a way that the legal acceptability of the records and documents is not compromised.

An important issue for paper documents, dealt with in section 6.5, is what is to be stored, the documents themselves, or the information they contain? If the complete documents are to be stored in image form as a substitute for paper as a medium, then either micrographics or electronic imaging are candidates. If, however, elements of a document are of particular importance and need to be extracted and manipulated, as might apply in some transaction processing applications, then electronic imaging coupled possibly with forms removal software, optical character recognition and an appropriate storage medium would be the likely system of choice.

On the other hand if certain key information, such as bibliographic information coupled with a summary as a document surrogate, is stored by information retrieval software, then this might provide sufficient information for the enquirer. Access to the actual documents will not then be so important, and these could be stored on microfilm. Depending on such considerations and on user priorities in relation to the other information activities, the storage medium chosen may be any one from the hierarchy of online, near-line or off-line systems. Choosing a storage medium is not a mechanistic process. It requires consideration of many inter-related factors throughout the information life cycle, as is clear from earlier chapters. Table 7.4 provides some guidelines that at least enable the selection process to be focused on those types of medium likely to be most suitable for particular requirements.

Table 7.4 Comparison of storage media for different requirements

7.2.7 Retrieval (Activity 8)

Two aspects are worth noting relating to the retrieval activity. First there is the question of what needs to be retrieved: is it information *per se*, or the documents which contain the information? This issue was addressed in section 6.4 where it was noted that, in general terms, transaction documents are associated with document retrieval, while non-transaction documents are usually identified with information retrieval.

Decisions on imaging systems and storage media must not be based solely on which of these document categories is involved. Nevertheless the added processing and manipulation flexibility provided by electronic imaging over micrographics can mean that it is a more suitable choice for non-transaction documents. This is because the importance of the information content and ready access to it transcends the fact that the information is contained within the format of a document.

The second aspect concerns access to the documents. If they need to be consulted frequently, and furthermore access needs to be rapid and simultaneous from different locations, then electronic imaging and storage systems are more likely to be suitable. Nevertheless such needs may be satisfied by providing duplicate copies of the documents on roll microfilm for local use on computer-aided retrieval systems, or on CD-ROM or

DVD-R. For irregular access where speed is not essential then microfilm-based systems may suffice.

7.2.8 Communication (Activity 9)

Access to and transfer of information relies on efficient and effective means of communication. The communication activity is at the heart of considerations of work flow and process redesign.

Multi-user, simultaneous access to documents does not necessarily imply implementing a networked computer system providing online access. Where documents need to be available at different locations and they are updated infrequently, then microfiche or CD-ROM provide an alternative medium for publication. The latter medium in particular has proved to be a commercial success in this regard.

If the dynamics of the situation require activities such as multi-authoring or frequent document revision, then the argument for computerised online systems is stronger.

Even if, for other reasons, documents are stored on microfilm, such as engineering drawings on aperture cards, rapid communication can be effected by digitising the analogue image and transmitting it by facsimile transmission.

7.2.9 Utilisation (Activity 10)

The way in which records, documents and the information they contain need to be utilised is a key factor in the design of an enterprise knowledge management system. Usage may range from simply consulting the document to amending it, copying extracts or merging it with other information.

Documents may only appear to be of interest to a particular function. On the other hand, that information may be important to others, but access is difficult. Thus a planning department of a chemical company may hold details of plant and equipment as part of an asset register. These details will be important to the maintenance function, but represent only one source of information it has to gather to perform its maintenance duties. Imaging systems, coupled perhaps with reorganisation of functional responsibilities, can be a way to address such problems.

Determining these and other usage patterns is important. Guidance on obtaining such information by way of a detailed information management survey was covered in section Chapter 3.

7.2.10 Revision (Activity 11)

Some types of document are subject to revision and may be re-issued as new revisions or versions (the meaning behind the terms 'revision' and 'version' can differ between or even within organisations). Key documents such as operational procedures, design drawings and standards will be subject to change during their life time. Failure to keep track of these changes can mean lives are put at risk, or at the very least time and effort is expended unnecessarily in tracing the latest editions or updating material which has already been so processed. Where the requirement is to manage and control these change processes and ensure users know what is current and what is superseded, it is essential that the document management system provides the functionality needed. Traditionally such requirements have arisen in the engineering and R&D environments. Hence document management suppliers who originally developed their systems for this sector, rather than for the general office environment, are more likely to address this need effectively.

7.2.11 Destruction (Activity 13)

There is a natural tendency to grasp at document imaging as a way to deal with the increasing storage, space and access burden placed on organisations by the use of paper. The 'film/scan and forget' approach neglects the need to purge the information of redundant, duplicate and superseded material, for example. If this is not done, system performance such as access and retrieval times can suffer, and the amount of unwanted information retrieved along with that which is required may increase to unacceptable proportions.

7.2.12 Monitor and control (Activity A)

While it is perfectly possible to establish and operate records and document management administrative functions as manual systems, irrespective of the storage media used, there are benefits in exploiting available information technology to support these activities. Thus if computerised indexing and retrieval systems are in use to enable document collections to be searched, there is obvious merit in integrating the records management functions with these systems. The aim should be to minimise the duplication of data concerning records management information. The complementary nature of records and document management (see section 4.3) argues strongly for this integrated approach.

7.2.13 Organise (Activity B)

There needs to be an overall organisational structure and set of policies and procedures for managing the life cycle of information. These should be an integral part of an organisation's enterprise knowledge management strategy in support of the business objectives.

In quality-oriented organisations one would expect to see these policies and procedures as part of the quality management system and documented (in electronic form!) in the corporate quality manual.

7.3 BUSINESS CASE AND JUSTIFICATION

Having identified candidate business areas, there may be several potential projects from which to choose and there needs to be some means of deciding between them. A business case may need to be developed for presentation to senior management. Irrespective of the formal nature of that business case, it is important to obtain 'buy-in' from management. Their support (whether they represent the users, the executives or the IT fraternity, for example) will be essential - particularly if the project is resource-hungry, high-cost, extends over many months and may hit problems later.

It is important to emphasise at this stage that the effort and resources applied to developing a business case, producing a requirements specification, formulating a tender document and evaluating tenders must be commensurate with the likely cost of the solution. For one client, a prospective supplier responded to an invitation to tender (ITT) congratulating them on the comprehensiveness of the document. However, it noted that if they complied with all the requests for information and the terms and conditions of the ITT, the cost to them would be several orders of magnitude greater than the profit they would make on selling the package! They therefore offered to let the client have the software to test themselves. The lesson from this is that if the required software package is of relatively low cost, then it may be more appropriate to 'beg or borrow' several competing products and evaluate them against one's requirements - which should still be clearly specified. The package that emerges best from the evaluation can then be tested more vigorously and selected or rejected on the basis of the test results.

7.3.1 External versus internal development

An important consideration is to what extent the development of the intended system is to be undertaken in-house as a software development project, rather than bought in as a 'packaged' solution (i.e. a turnkey system). These options represent the extremes of a spectrum of solution provision. In reality few software developments make no use of existing software solutions or components, while turnkey systems rarely involve no tuning, configuration or tailoring of the 'package'.

By far the most prevalent route adopted for document management projects is to opt for commercially established solutions. These comprise in the main the integration and configuration of a range of third party products (the provenance of which is often hidden from the user) around a core system from the chosen supplier. The benefits of a turnkey approach over bespoke (i.e. specially written) software are for example:

- ◆ support and maintenance should be more readily available due to the commitment the supplier has to its existing user base

- ◆ problems and wishlists can be discussed with other users outside one's organisation

- ◆ the user is not locked into a single-supplier (whether internal or external) who has delivered a solution unique to that user.

Unfortunately the document (and knowledge) management marketplace continues to be in a state of flux. Hence one can never be sure that the chosen supplier will be around in the same guise in succeeding years. With one client, all three suppliers shortlisted in 1994, including the vendor whose system was implemented, were subsequently taken over by competitors. It is nevertheless important to assess the commercial and financial soundness of a prospective supplier. These criteria should also be applied to internal solution providers – it is not unknown for in-house IT departments to be reorganised, downsized, outsourced or even disbanded: decisions that can have a devastating affect on users' plans for improving their information systems.

7.3.2 Business case

In developing a business case it is helpful to understand the nature of 'projects' whose attributes have been identified as follows:[4]

- they are non-repetitive

- they may have significant unique features likely to be novel to the management

- they carry risk and uncertainty

- they are approved in return for delivery of specified results within specified timescales, quality and safety and health parameters

- they are usually undertaken by a team which has a temporary existence and whose make-up and numbers may vary with time

- they may be subject to change as the work progresses

- events inside and outside the organisation may affect the outcome if the project is of long duration.

Hence in developing the business case it is important to ensure that these factors are addressed in the context of answering the types of question exemplified in Table 7.5.

QUESTIONS TO BE ADDRESSED	TOPICS TO BE CONSIDERED (examples only)
What is recommended?	• a description of what is proposed • references to business needs that are being addressed
Why should we do it?	• business rationale for the development (usually a qualitative focus) • business benefits (typically as cost benefits – a quantitative focus) • consequences of not doing it • alternatives considered and why rejected
How much will it cost?	• total cost covering, e.g. internal staff • external contractors • software licences or services • hardware/equipment • training • support/maintenance
When will it be delivered?	• deliverables by date • money spent over time • benefit delivered as money over time
How will it be achieved?	• with what training or other purchased assistance? • with what technology? • what are key risks and control measures? • what are key dependencies, impacts? how will we control them?

Table 7.5 Elements of a business case

7.3.3 Cost benefit

The business justification may have relied on strategic or tactical objectives being achieved. The former are often associated with 'soft', 'qualitative' benefits which can be difficult to translate into monetary terms. Nevertheless it is more likely that a project proposal will be accepted if, under robust examination, the cost of achieving the benefits are shown to be outweighed by the beneficial cost savings.

Views on what constitute strategic and tactical benefits and the relative importance of one benefit against another will differ depending on a number of factors (e.g. the business sector involved and the nature of candidate projects). A 'shopping list' of some possible benefits is presented in Table 7.6. These range from the ubiquitous space and furniture saving benefits to the less frequently quantified strategic goals that can deliver orders of magnitude of greater benefit to the organisation. Research undertaken in 1997[5] showed that over 70% of users had difficulty in cost-justifying document management. Improved service quality and meeting regulatory and standards requirements were the main benefits met, while increased revenue was achieved by the fewest of those surveyed.

	CATEGORIES	POSSIBLE MEASURES
Strategic	Quality	Customer satisfaction Reduced product defects Speedier document updates through configuration management
	Market attractiveness	Market share Differentiated price
	Management control	Staff reductions Reduced number of meetings Reduced need for formal audits
	Responsiveness to change	Time to market
	Regulatory compliance	Reduced audit failings
	Supplier relationships	Shortened delivery times
Tactical	Task improvement	Productivity increase
	Records management	Reduction in lost vital records % reduction in re-creating lost originals
	Retrieval	Speedier retrieval Improved precision through better indexing Simultaneous access by x no. users
	Consumables	% reduction in copying % reduction in filing boxes/folders, etc.
	Storage	Number of filing cabinets eliminated
	Furniture and fittings	Number of desks/chairs saved
	Communication	Increased speed of delivery to users Increase in concurrent working Reduced storage through just-in-time documentation
	Office accommodation	Floor space saved
	Equipment	Reduced number of photocopiers

Table 7.6 Typical target benefits

Financial evaluation normally involves undertaking the following:

- identifying net cash flow changes
- reducing these to a single index
- consideration of unquantifiable factors
- recognition of any uncertainties
- comparison of results for the competing projects.

The evaluation takes account of the time-related value of money. The particular method of measuring and presenting this will usually need to conform to the practice followed in one's own organisation. Typically the process involves calculation of one or more of the following:

- net present value (NPV)
- discounted cash flow (DCF) and
- internal rate of return (IRR).

The criteria used to judge the worthiness or otherwise of a project may include:

- speed of payback
- first year return
- overall percentage return on investment
- annual average rate of return on the original investment.

Generally the DCF method provides a more accurate indication for comparison between competing longer-life projects.

More information on this issue and the concept of earned value performance measurement for assigning a value to the achievement of project work is contained in reference 4.

7.4 PROJECT MANAGEMENT

A project is a business process and as such needs to have that process defined, agreed, monitored and controlled throughout its period of existence. The British Standard on Project Management[4] provides useful insight and general guidance, although it is not specifically focused on IT projects.

In a quality-oriented organisation it is customary to draw up a quality plan which is defined as a:

> 'document setting out the specific quality practices, resources and sequence of activities relevant to a particular product, project, or contract'.[6]

A simplified framework for a software quality plan for a typical software life cycle (Figure 7.3) is shown in Table 7.7.[6]

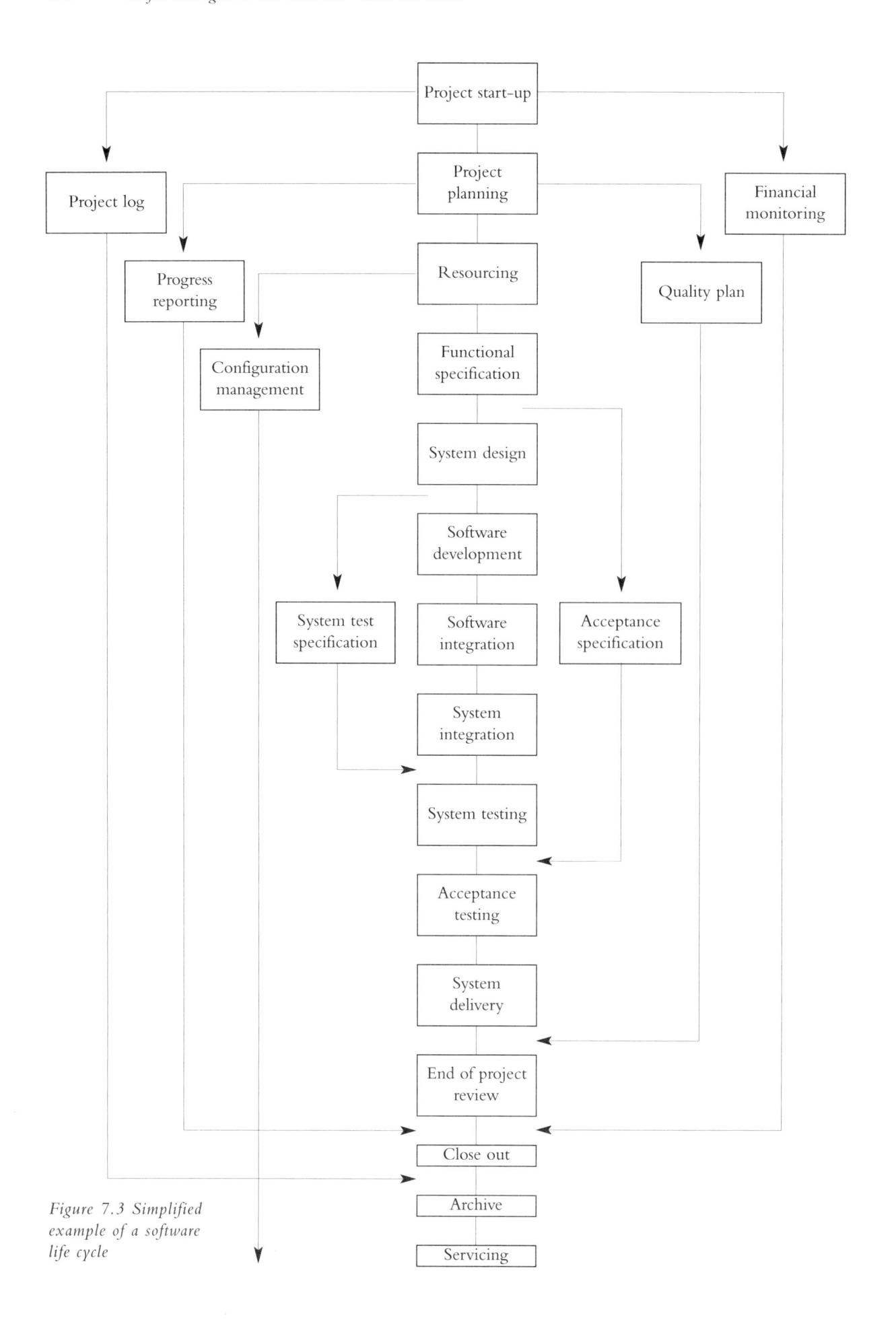

196   *Project Management and Solutions - Ideas into Action*

```
                          ┌─────────────────┐
                          │ Project start-up│
                          └─────────────────┘
                                   │
                          ┌─────────────────┐
                          │    Project      │
                          │    planning     │
                          └─────────────────┘
  ┌───────────┐                    │                    ┌─────────────┐
  │Project log│                    │                    │  Financial  │
  └───────────┘                    │                    │  monitoring │
                                   │                    └─────────────┘
  ┌───────────┐           ┌─────────────────┐           ┌─────────────┐
  │ Progress  │           │    Resourcing   │           │ Quality plan│
  │ reporting │           └─────────────────┘           └─────────────┘
  └───────────┘                    │
          ┌───────────────┐        │
          │ Configuration │        │
          │  management   │        │
          └───────────────┘ ┌─────────────────┐
                            │   Functional    │
                            │  specification  │
                            └─────────────────┘
                                   │
                            ┌─────────────────┐
                            │  System design  │
                            └─────────────────┘
                                   │
                            ┌─────────────────┐
                            │    Software     │
                            │   development   │
                            └─────────────────┘
       ┌─────────────────┐  ┌─────────────────┐  ┌─────────────────┐
       │   System test   │  │    Software     │  │   Acceptance    │
       │  specification  │  │   integration   │  │  specification  │
       └─────────────────┘  └─────────────────┘  └─────────────────┘
                            ┌─────────────────┐
                            │     System      │
                            │   integration   │
                            └─────────────────┘
                            ┌─────────────────┐
                            │  System testing │
                            └─────────────────┘
                            ┌─────────────────┐
                            │   Acceptance    │
                            │    testing      │
                            └─────────────────┘
                            ┌─────────────────┐
                            │     System      │
                            │    delivery     │
                            └─────────────────┘
                            ┌─────────────────┐
                            │ End of project  │
                            │     review      │
                            └─────────────────┘
                            ┌─────────────────┐
                            │    Close out    │
                            └─────────────────┘
                            ┌─────────────────┐
                            │     Archive     │
                            └─────────────────┘
                            ┌─────────────────┐
                            │    Servicing    │
                            └─────────────────┘
```

Figure 7.3 Simplified example of a software life cycle

REF.	ACTIVITY DESCRIPTION	PROCEDURE	COMMENT	ASSIGNED TO	APPROVAL AUTHORITY
1	Contract review	QM 5.2	Contract M&P	AMM	
2	Review plans	PMM 5.4		GT	
3	Requirements review	QM 5.3	Produce Doc. RS001	SME	
4	Design	PMM 5.6	Produce Doc. DS001	UT	
5	Design review	QM 5.6	Use expert review	SME	
6	Software implementation	SDM 5.6	Use C++		
7	Code review	QM 5.7	Produce Doc. CR001		
8	Unit tests	SDM 5.7			
9	System integration	SDM 5.7			
10	System test	QM 5.7	Use customer data		
11	Clear non-conformances	QM 5.7			
12	User acceptance tests	QM 5.8	Client witnessing only		
13	Technical transfer	PMM 5.9			

Table 7.7 Activities for a software quality plan (examples only)

Established organisations are likely to have in place formal project management procedures which will be suitable for document management projects. By way of illustration the following section covers PRINCE, a generalised approach for managing projects.

7.4.1 The PRINCE Method

PRINCE (Projects in Controlled Environments) is a structured method designed to help ensure effective project management. Originally aimed at managing projects in IT environments, its scope was expanded in PRINCE 2[7] to cover any type of project. Like SSADM (the Structured Systems Analysis and Design Method introduced in section 3.1) it was developed by the CCTA, the UK Government's Central Computer and Telecommunications Agency and has well-defined ways of binding together the development and management processes. PRINCE is 'publicly available' and has been adopted in organisations beyond the government arena. (Copyright in PRINCE is retained by the Crown and PRINCE® is a registered trade mark of CCTA.)

Like any project management method, it is open to criticism by some as being overly bureaucratic and complex. However, used sensibly it delivers benefit. The key features of PRINCE are stated as:

- its focus on business justification
- a defined organisation structure for the project management team
- its product-based planning approach

198   *Project Management and Solutions - Ideas into Action*

- its emphasis on dividing the project into manageable and controllable stages
- its flexibility to be applied at a level appropriate to the project.

It is based on a process model having eight management processes as shown in Figure 7.4. In addition the following eight components are applied to the processes:

- organisation
- planning
- controls
- stages
- management of risk
- quality in a project environment
- configuration management
- change control.

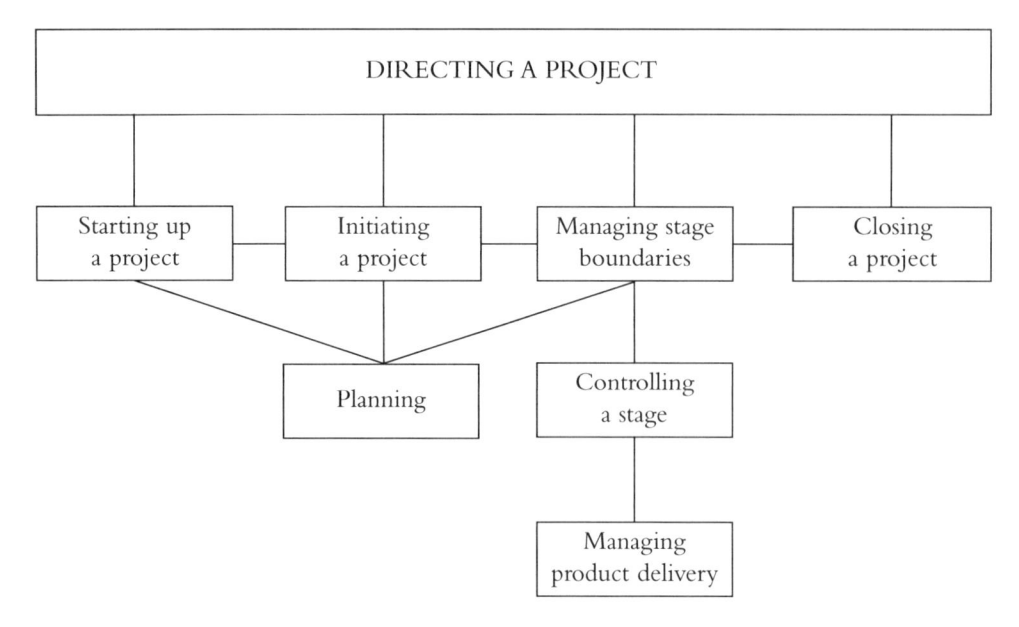

```
                    DIRECTING A PROJECT
   ┌─────────────┬─────────────┬─────────────┬─────────────┐
   Starting up    Initiating    Managing stage   Closing
   a project      a project     boundaries       a project
                        │
              ┌─────────┴─────────┐
              Planning    Controlling
                          a stage
                              │
                          Managing
                          product delivery
```

Figure 7.4 The PRINCE process model
(The UK Crown copyright material used here is reproduced with permission of CCTA and the Controller of HMSO.)

PRINCE is focused on the delivery of products, be they documents (e.g. covering system design or acceptance procedures) or, for example, software to provide specified functionality. It outlines an organisational framework in which the key players from the user, business and solution supplier communities can contribute effectively. This framework is shown in Figure 7.5.

```
                    ┌─────────────┐
                    │ Corporate or│
                    │  programme  │
                    │ management  │
                    └──────┬──────┘
                           │
        ┌──────────────────┴──────────────────┐
        │           PROJECT BOARD             │
        │  ┌────────┐ ┌──────────┐ ┌────────────┐ │
        │  │Executive│ │Senior user│ │Senior supplier│ │
        │  └────────┘ └──────────┘ └────────────┘ │
        └─────────────────────────────────────┘
                           │
   ┌──────────────┐        │
   │   PROJECT    │        │
   │  ASSURANCE   │────────┤
   │     TEAM     │        │
   └──────────────┘        │
                           │
                    ┌──────┴──────┐
                    │   PROJECT   │
                    │   MANAGER   │
                    └──────┬──────┘
                           │        ┌──────────────┐
                           │        │   PROJECT    │
                           ├────────│  ASSURANCE   │
                           │        │     TEAM     │
                           │        └──────────────┘
                    ┌──────┴──────┐
                    │    TEAM     │
                    │   MANAGER   │
                    └─────────────┘
```

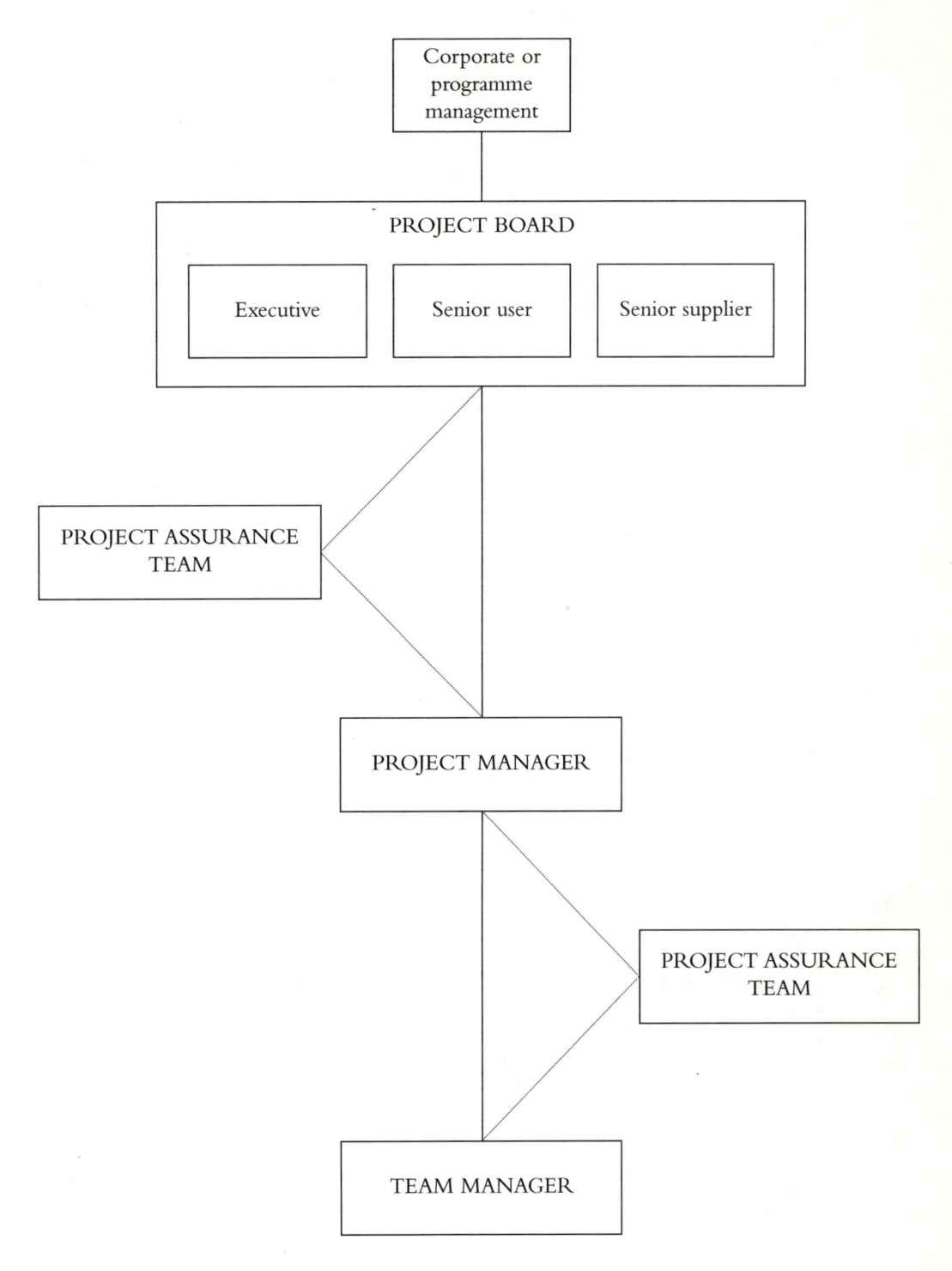

Figure 7.5 PRINCE project management structure (The UK Crown copyright material used here is reproduced with permission of CCTA and the Controller of HMSO.)

An indication of the roles and responsibilities of the organisational members is given in Table 7.8.

ROLE	KEY RESPONSIBILITIES
Project board	Commitment of resources. Approves all major plans and authorises major deviations from stage plans. Responsible for project assurance either directly or by delegation.
Executive	Ultimately accountable for the project. 'Owns' the business case. Provides the link to corporate or programme management.
Senior user	Accountable for products supplied by the users, e.g. ensures user requirements are clearly and completely defined; provides user resources; ensures project products and outcomes meet user requirements and expected user benefits. Responsible for project assurance from user perspective.
Senior supplier	Accountable for products delivered by the solution supplier(s) – e.g. a commercial vendor for the required document management system. Represents interests of those designing, developing, facilitating, procuring, implementing and possibly operating and maintaining the supplied products. (Multiple suppliers may require additional representation on the board.)
Project manager	Has day-to-day responsibility for managing the project throughout all its stages and within constraints laid down by the board.
Team manager	An optional role where the project manager requires to delegate responsibility for planning the creation of certain products to a team of specialists.

Table 7.8 Roles and responsibilities for a PRINCE project

The project board, through its executive chairman, will typically report to a corporate executive committee, possibly with organisation-wide responsibility for information systems. There are, however, no hard-and-fast rules for structuring reporting relationships; each organisation will differ in detail as to its approach. Suffice to say it is important that the business users and management for whom the system is intended, should be ultimately in control. The IT function in the organisation is there to provide a service and to advise on matters within their competence, such as corporate and industry standards for hardware, software and networking. Document management technology in all its ramifications is still, however, little understood by many IT personnel and management. Hence, it is important that all those who will be involved in the project (users, business managers and IT representatives) gain a common and sufficiently detailed awareness of the technology (scope, benefits, drawbacks, etc.) so that informed debate and decision-making is possible.

7.4.1.1 Project initiation

Having identified the business area(s) and business application(s) that are to be the focus of attention, the project needs to be formally initiated by way of a documented statement covering such matters as project objectives, resources and timescales. In PRINCE this is effected by producing a project initiation document (PID) for approval by the project board before any further work is undertaken on the project. Typical contents for the PID are:

- project definition (delineating the boundaries of the project)

- aims and objectives

- project priority

- organisation (identifying those connected with the management of the project)

- responsibilities (of each of the people named)

- project plans (broken into definable stages as appropriate)

- quality policy (control, reviews and standards)

- communication plan

- configuration management plan (creation, maintenance and controlled change of configuration data throughout the life of the project)

- control points (where formal reviews are undertaken at key points in the project, e.g. when project deliverables are due)

- reporting arrangements

- assumptions

- constraints

- risk management (e.g. security and business risks).

7.5 REQUIREMENTS DEFINITION

The key deliverable from a document management project is a system that satisfies users' requirements. While the term 'users' is usually associated with those who will gain business benefits from its deployment, there are other types of user, each with their own set of requirements as exemplified in Table 7.9. The titles given to user types may differ between organisations; however, the important point is to recognise that there is a spectrum of users with differing needs.

USER TYPE	EXAMPLE REQUIREMENTS
Business users	System should satisfy functional requirements.
Technology architects	The technology should be compatible with the organisation's IT standards (software, hardware and networking).
Technical support	Technology should be easy to support (e.g. upgrading to new product releases).
User support	System should be reliable and predictable (thereby placing minimum burden on first line support) and well documented.
System administrators	System should allow ready, but controlled addition of users. System should allow ready, but controlled changes in users' access rights.
Trainers	System should be easy to learn and have sufficiently comprehensive training manuals and online help.

Table 7.9 Types of user

Given this perspective it is important that requirements are properly identified, amplified, documented and agreed before significant project resources are deployed and costs are incurred. By all means adopt the 'laboratory' means for systems development (as noted in section 3.4.1) with its greater flexibility for embracing changes, but this should still be undertaken within a controlled project management environment that has accepted this approach within its configuration management plan.

7.5.1 Make-up of a requirements specification

The requirements specification, whether intended for use with in-house development or as part of a tender document for a prospective external supplier, should cover the needs of the various types of user and will typically be drawn from the following elements (commercial considerations are covered in section 7.6):

- ◆ business background
  - scene-setting
  - aims and objectives of the system

- ◆ functional specification
  - overview of functions required (see Table 7.3 for examples of what may be sought)
  - detailed list of requirements (categorised as mandatory or desirable)

- timetable for proposed phasing of delivery of functions

◆ Business models (see section 3.1 for more details)
- current (physical) data models
- current (physical) process models
- logical data models
- logical process models

◆ volumetrics (examples only here)
- quantities of documents – legacy and ongoing
- numbers of expected users
- access rates (helps to size the hardware and networks)

◆ current technology environment
- software
- hardware
- networks
- existing document-related information systems/applications

◆ required/planned technology environment
- standards/technical architecture
- user interfaces
- service performance
- service operational requirements
- security and access controls
- disaster recovery
- system support

◆ design methodology

◆ quality plan

◆ required deliverables (not all will be required for a particular project)
- hardware
- software
- networks

- documentation
- training
- project management products
- support services
- legacy data loading.

Where appropriate, the requirements should be referenced to relevant *de facto* and *de jure* standards and codes of practice (a topic largely covered in Chapter 5 relating to the technology of document management). This not only reduces the size of the requirements document, but also ensures that what is put in place as the eventual solution conforms to well-known and established practice.

7.6 THE INVITATION TO TENDER

If it has been decided to seek assistance from outside one's company, all the foregoing is directed towards producing some form of document for distribution to a set of chosen prospective suppliers who are invited to tender. The form that this document takes and the procurement procedure that is followed will depend on the practice followed by the procuring organisation.

For those organisations lacking any formal procurement procedures, and where the size of the envisaged contract in terms of complexity, resource allocation and cost is significant, then guidance on the structure and content of an invitation to tender (ITT) document will often be available from professional institutions. Thus the Institution of Mechanical Engineers and the Institution of Electrical Engineers offer a model form of general conditions of contract which, although slanted towards engineering projects, does address the needs of those procuring computer hardware and software.[8] A further publication from the IEE provides guidance on documentation of computer software.[9] Examples of the general conditions that one would expect to see in an ITT include:

- basis of tender and contract price
- warranty and performance
- contractor's (i.e. supplier's) obligations
- software and system acceptance
- title to the standard software (i.e. the contractor's standard software as listed in an accompanying schedule)
- title to configured and bespoke software (i.e. that part of the software to be developed by the contractor)

- purchaser's general obligations

- installation of hardware

- confidentiality

- source code deposit (e.g. via an escrow agreement to protect the purchaser in the event of the supplier going bankrupt for example)

- training

- manuals and user documentation

- defects liability.

These general conditions, which would be part of any ITT, are amplified by a series of schedules specially formulated for the particular project and detailing requirements and obligations. Typical schedules might include those headed:

- instructions to tenderers (e.g. detailing the format of response, specific questions to be answered by the tenderers and the basis on which the tenders will be evaluated)

- particulars and special conditions (amplifying and adding to those in the general conditions)

- requirements specification (see section 7.5.1)

- project management (covering project plan, resources, organisation and change control and incorporating consideration of risk, safety and quality issues)

- testing (covering more detail on the approach, responsibilities and acceptance criteria)

- training (details of those to be trained and types of training)

- form of tender (including any payment schedule linked to defined deliverables)

- software licences and maintenance agreement

- hardware maintenance.

7.6.1 Public procurement

There are special rules for procurement by 'public bodies' in the European Union. The EC Procurement Rules apply to public authorities (including, amongst others, government departments, local authorities and NHS authorities and trusts) and certain utility companies operating in the energy, water, transport and telecommunications sectors. The rules set out detailed procedures for the award of contracts whose value equals or exceeds specific thresholds, the values of which are subject to review and change. Further information on the main characteristics of the EC Procurement Rules is given in a guide from HM Treasury[10] and from the Treasury themselves.[11]

7.6.2 Evaluation of the tenders

It is important that all the tenders received are evaluated according to a predefined, auditable documented process using a set of evaluation criteria acceptable to the purchasing organisation. This approach should be outlined, at least in general terms, in the invitation to tender.

The evaluation procedure should:

- define the evaluation process itself
- identify the evaluators and their roles
- specify the evaluation criteria
- indicate the priorities/weightings applied to the criteria
- state who will review and approve the results of the evaluation.

Typical categories of requirements to which weighting may be applied are:

- functional
- commercial
- infrastructure (technical aspects)
- operational
- support
- training.

Within these categories the specific requirements can be individually weighted. For example, those that are mandatory will be more highly rated than desirable requirements. The first cut evaluation could be focused on the degree to which mandatory requirements are met.

As with other aspects of the procurement process, the make-up of the evaluation approach may well be dictated by established practice within one's organisation.

7.6.3 Contract negotiation and supplier options

Given that the evaluation process has resulted in the identification of preferred suppliers, the next stage is detailed contract negotiation. If it is a close call between two or more suppliers, it is sensible not to discard all but the one that came out on top. This provides a safeguard should contract negotiations fail with one's first choice. Although this topic is not central to the theme of this book it is worth noting that the aim of the negotiating process is to arrive at an agreement satisfactory to both parties. If you as the purchaser cause the supplier to leave the completed negotiations dissatisfied in some way, then it is more likely that they will stick strictly to the terms of the contract giving you no latitude should you default from your obligations under that contract. This is not to say that you should avoid striking a 'hard bargain', but both parties should be able to leave the negotiations feeling that they have achieved their objectives.

In parallel with the negotiation stage, and before contract signing, it may be required to produce a supplier options paper for senior management. The paper should revisit the project initiation document and any cost-benefit appraisal that was undertaken then, and present an appraisal of the current situation with recommendations of the way forward with the preferred supplier. This could be incorporated in a revised business case.

In estimating the time that a procurement phase may take, the negotiation stage is often allocated too little time. This is a critical stage of the procurement cycle and should not be skipped over lightly. Decisions made then become binding on contract signing and may be regretted later.

7.7 THE PROJECT FOR REAL!

The signing of the contract moves one from a somewhat artificial world of 'theory' to the real world of 'practice'. The project initiation document should have been revised to provide a springboard for action with inclusion of an updated project plan and the naming of the supplier/turnkey manager in the project organisation.

The details of the project plan will depend on the type and scale of the system envisaged, so no hard-and-fast rules can be laid down. The generalised project management process flow shown here in tabulated form in Table 7.10,[4] provides a checklist of the kinds of project activity to be undertaken.

ACTIVITY	PROJECT ACTIVITY
1	Obtain authorisation
2	Establish project team
3	Establish project plan
4	Develop project work breakdown structure
5	Assign accountable task owners
6	Develop statement of work for each task
7	Balance time, cost, specification and risk
8	Get commitments to do the task
9	Get formal agreement to do the task
10	Issue the plan
11	Prepare a budget for project funding
12	Secure management reserve and release funds
13	Instruct work to start, stop or continue
14	Monitor progress
15	Analyse and communicate results
16	Negotiate changes from whatever source
17	Modify plans, physical and financial
18	Go back to Activity 1

Time →

Table 7.10 Project management activities

The experience of those adopting document management technology for the first time has in the main shown that a phased or pilot approach to implementation offers the greatest chance of achieving the intended benefits. The knowledge gained from the initial system, with well-defined functionality experienced by a chosen group of users, provides the foundation for successful implementation of additional functionality or roll out to more users, or a combination of the two.

Those new to document management technology usually phase the introduction of the required functionality, and typically in the order:

- storage and retrieval of documents accompanied by the necessary indexes (enables users to gain early benefit through improved research and retrieval functions).

- distribution of documents, both *ad hoc* and via standard distribution lists, often under transmittal (auditable and managed control becomes a reality)

- document review and approval, either newly created or under revision, possibly supported by simple, *ad hoc* workflow or groupware procedures

- more complex workflow to support a variety of business processes (significant improvements in speed and quality can be achieved).

This phasing addresses at the outset the basic requirements of most users who seek access to and ready communication of documents. It enables users to build up confidence in the system from simple beginnings and avoids the risks associated with a 'big bang' implementation.

7.7.1 Getting and keeping commitment

The new system is being introduced to achieve stated objectives. However, to achieve these objectives the staff involved have to be convinced not simply that these aims are achievable, but more importantly that their new or revised functions and tasks deliver benefits to them as individuals. To arrive at this point requires proper involvement of the staff during the project phases so that they do not encounter any surprises, and can contribute positively and appropriately to the specification, design and selection of the systems they will eventually utilise.

A key to success is the continuing commitment of both users and business managers supported by IT personnel. The project organisation, if established along the lines outlined in PRINCE, helps ensure that all parties are involved at the key decision and product review points of relevance to them. Additionally instilling awareness of technological developments in the staff (and their management), coupled with specific training and visits to existing users of such systems at other sites, will help ensure a smooth transition from project to operational use. Another way of facilitating commitment is to establish internal user panels linked to the project assurance team. If the supplier has a user group for its product, user representatives should attend these meetings.

As the project achieves its various milestones, this success should be publicised to other parts of the organisation who may in some way have an interest. This can be effected in various ways, for example newsletters, 'open day' demonstrations, or via a corporate Intranet where one exists. All this education and awareness process should be set within the context of the broader business picture, so that participants can appreciate the significance and potential of new developments. Once fully committed, the staff 'at the sharp end' are often the main champions of the system and are best placed to wring further gains from it.

7.7.2 Post-project review

An oft-forgotten stage of a project is to prove that the system has achieved its objectives. This involves a post-project review timed sufficiently long after the system's formal acceptance and implementation to allow its steady-state performance and functionality to be more accurately assessed. This review will mean revisiting the original business case and justification (as may have been subsequently amended as part of the project's change control procedure) and undertaking a fresh cost-benefit analysis, this time based on real rather than projected operational experience. Naturally such an evaluation is not possible unless the same metrics have been applied both before and after the project timeframe.

If the project has been effectively and efficiently planned and managed, then there should be no surprises at this, the final project milestone.

REFERENCES IN CHAPTER 7

1 *Imaging: The emerging Tiger*, First Report of Research Working Group (1988-89) (Nolan Norton Institute, KPMG Management Consulting, undated)

2 *Imaging: Taming the Tiger,* Second Report of Research Working Group (Nolan Norton Institute, KPMG Management Consulting, undated)

3 *Document Management Strategy Report - The Virtual Opportunity; A guide for Users* (UK Document Management Suppliers' Group, 1995)

4 *BS 6079: 1996: Guide to Project Management*

5 Staunton, R., Tougard, J-F., Richardson, J. and Carnelley, P., *Ovum Evaluates Document Management – Guide to Understanding and Selecting Document Management Systems* (London: Ovum Ltd, 1998) pp. 39-40

6 *BS ISO 1005: 1995, Quality Management - Guidelines for Quality Plans*

7 *Managing Successful Projects with PRINCE 2 CCTA* (London: The Stationery Office, 1998)

8 *Model Form of General Conditions of Contract MF/1* (Rev.3), published for the Joint IMechE/IEE Committee on Model Forms of General Conditions of Contract (London: The Institution of Electrical Engineers, 1995); *Commentary on Model Form of General Conditions of Contract MF/1 - A Practical Guide for User of MF/1* (London: The Institution of Electrical Engineers, 1995)

9   *Guidelines for the Documentation of Computer Software for Real Time and Interactive Systems* (London: The Institution of Electrical Engineers, 1990)
10 *HM Treasury Central Unit on Procurement (CUP) guide no. 51*, available from Web site http://www.hm-treasury.gov.uk under 'Guidance' then 'Procurement'
11 Procurement Policy Room 219, HM Treasury, Allington Towers, 19 Allington Street, London SW1E 5EB. Tel. 0171-270 1647; Fax. 0171-270 1653

8

THE DOCUMENT MANAGEMENT MARKETPLACE

'Put on a bright face for your customers, and smile pleasantly as you hand them what they ask for! A stale article, if you dip it in a good, warm, sunny smile, will go off better than a fresh one that you've scowled upon.'

The House of the Seven Gables: Nathaniel Hawthorne

Document management is still a relatively youthful being with strong potential for growth, especially as organisations grasp the benefits to be gained from a broader-based approach to managing and utilising the information and knowledge available to them. It represents a coming together of existing and new technologies and skills from different and overlapping sectors of the IT industry. The successful development and implementation of a document management (DM) system can involve significant configuration of hardware, software and communication technologies usually involving the integration of some third party products. It is not surprising, therefore, that the types of supplier who have entered the field vary accordingly covering such fields as systems integration, image processing, text retrieval, recognition technology, CAD and workflow.

Most of the leading DM product companies rely on third parties to sell and configure their products for the ultimate customer. System integrators exemplify this situation. As their name implies, they provide skills to build systems based on hardware and software acquired from appropriate sources. System integrators encompass a wide range of sizes and types of organisations, from small software houses and consultancies, to large management consulting firms and specialised divisions of larger corporations.

Their contribution can be particularly valuable with emerging technologies where standards are lagging behind leading-edge developments. This is the case for much of the technology used in document management, although stabilisation of hardware and software round open systems, and the drive to firm up on storage media and format standards is helping to alleviate these problems. The initiatives being taken by the Workflow Management Coalition (WfMC) and the Document Management Alliance (DMA), as noted in section 5.9, will improve inter-operability between disparate workflow and document management systems.

At a more general level system integrators can usually offer skills, experience and services covering information system strategy and feasibility studies, system specification, design, construction, and support in the field of information management, computers and communications. Specialist knowledge of, and products relating to, specific vertical sectors such as government, defence, energy, industry and finance, may also be available.

Whether a DM supplier or a system integrator is to deliver your solutions it can be useful in addition to employ the services of an independent consultant well versed in DM projects, technology and your business environment.

He or she may provide, for example:

- quality assurance/mentoring role to the project board

- specialist advice at particular stages in the project

- project management guidance

- authorship for key deliverables such as the requirements specification.

8.1 INDUSTRY CONSOLIDATION

The last few years have seen an accelerating consolidation of companies delivering document management and related products, and an increase in industry acquisitions. Notable examples are provided in Table 8.1. Ovum sees the number of companies developing products for the document management repository market consolidating to less than 40% of the current level[1].

BUYER	BUYER TECHNOLOGY	ACQUIRED	ACQUIRED TECHNOLOGY
Adobe	Print architecture; Document Exchange	Frame Technology	Document creation tools; Document exchange
Alpharel	Imaging; Engineering document management	Trimco	Imaging; engineering document management
At Home Corp	Home Internet connection	Excite	Internet portal company (January 1999)
BancTec	Scanning; OCR/ICR	Recognition	Scanning; OCR/ICR, workflow; imaging
CP Software Group	Full text searching	Uniplex	Office productivity application

Table 8.1 Industry acquisitions (only more recent acquisition dates noted) (continued on pages 213 and 214)

BUYER	BUYER TECHNOLOGY	ACQUIRED	ACQUIRED TECHNOLOGY
Caere	OCR, Document Management	ViewStar	Imaging; workflow
Coopers & Lybrand	System integrator	Kinesis	Middleware for DM
Cornerstone	Display; document capture	Pegasus	Mass storage
Dataware Technology	Knowledge management; Text retrieval; CD Authoring	Status/IQ	Text retrieval
		Sovereign Software	Text retrieval (January 1999)
Documentum	Document management	Relevance Technologies	Content mining technology for unstructured information (July 1998)
		Workgroup Management, Inc	Expertise in solution provision for semi-conductor industry (October 1997)
Excalibur	Imaging; text retrieval	Conquest	Text retrieval
FileNet	Imaging; workflow	Watermark	Imaging (HSM)
		Saros	Document management
		International Financial Systems	COLD
Hummingbird Communications	Network connectivity and business intelligence products	PC-DOCS	Document management and text/knowledge retrieval (June 1999)
IBM	Just about everything	Lotus	Groupware; e-mail gateways; Image viewers; low end document management capabilities
Informix	Database	Illustra	Document management functionality
Inso	Universal file viewer	Electronic Book Technologies	Online document publishing
Interleaf	Document creation; exchange	Avalanche	SGML tools

Table 8.1 Industry acquisitions (only more recent acquisition dates noted)
(continued on page 214)

BUYER	BUYER TECHNOLOGY	ACQUIRED	ACQUIRED TECHNOLOGY
Kodak	Imaging	Wang Imaging	Imaging; workflow (Kodak formed Eastman Software)
Kofax	Image capture; image manipulation	LaserData	Optical management; Imaging
Microsoft	Operating system software	Firefly	Interest profile matching for search software
Novell	Networking	SoftSolutions (then owned by WordPerfect)	Document creation; document management (Soft Solutions)
Open Market Inc	Internet commerce	Folio	Information publishing
Open Text	Web-oriented full-text searching	Odesta	Document management capabilities
		Information Dimensions	Document database (BASIS); text retrieval
		Lava	Assets of Web-based document management company (January 1999)
PC-DOCS (see Hummingbird Communications)	Document management	Fulcrum	Text retrieval; embryonic knowledge management
SER	High volume scanning, archiving	PAFEC	Engineering document management (September 1998)
SDRC	Product data management	Some software from Altris	Document management (due to restructuring of Altris)
TMS	Imaging tools	Sequoia	Image enhancement
Wang (see Kodak)	Imaging; workflow	Sigma Imaging	Imaging; workflow
		Group Bull (part)	Imaging; workflow
		Avail	Hierarchical storage management (HSM)
Yahoo	Internal portal site	Geocities	Community site (February 1999)

Table 8.1 Industry acquisitions (only more recent acquisition dates noted)

With the coming maturity of the marketplace and the availability of product sets that can offer solutions without extensive configuration to the core product, it is rarely the case that the user can justify the creation of a bespoke system. Adopting this latter route invariably results in increasingly costly on-going maintenance and support, with the user being locked into a supplier whose core product will over time develop along quite different paths. The bespoke system becomes, in effect, the next legacy system from which the user must eventually migrate. Despite these potential drawbacks, there are companies who adopt the 'bespoke' route.

Although there is consolidation of the market, and an increasing move by the major players to address all market segments, the provenance of suppliers still has a bearing on their understanding of the needs of different sectors, and their ability to satisfy these needs.

Vertical markets for document technologies have traditionally been dominated by banking, financial services, insurance and government customers. The data IDC in the US collected from vendors regarding how their revenue breaks down by industry today supports this traditional view. While vendors have experienced growth in secondary and tertiary markets such as health care, process manufacturing, oil and gas, legal, and pharmaceuticals, these markets are still seen by IDC to pale in comparison to the money being spent by the traditional top four verticals.

This is due to the fact that document processes tend to be at the core of mission-critical activities such as mortgage loans, credit applications, insurance claims, customer statements and tax processing activities that carry such a high monetary value to insurance, government, banking and financial services enterprises. In addition, these services-based industries do not have the capital budgeting dilemmas of product-based enterprises, regarding plant and equipment expenditures.

Thus many vendors, such as PCDOCS and Documentum started business in these environments where document sizes are rarely larger than A4 and, at least at the outset, there was not always a requirement for stringent version control and configuration management. FileNet too started in the office electronic filing sector, with a particular focus on imaging. Other vendors, such as Altris and PAFEC - now part of SER, have come from the engineering sector with a background in computer-aided design (CAD) and project work. Here version control, approval procedures and configuration management are key processes to be supported. Generally the latter type of supplier should find it easier to address the needs of administrative offices than has the office document management supplier in satisfying the more demanding document control requirements of engineering projects, for example.

Almost without exception, nowadays, suppliers to the document management market are offering their functionality through the browser technology of the Internet. While existing DM suppliers have been adding browser functionality to their current products, more recently established 'start-up' companies have embraced Web technology at the outset and offer DM functionality through this interface. The use of this Internet/Intranet technology has re-directed the expectations of users who have become familiar with this means of accessing information via the World Wide Web.

The document management market is dominated by North American developers and suppliers whose business is fed by the demands of the US government and defence industry and the innovations from Silicon Valley. The perceptual and tangible differences on the two sides of the 'pond' have been neatly summed up (with tongue in cheek) as noted in Table 8.2.[2]

Despite these differences there is little doubt that what happens in North America in the information technology field eventually finds its way to Europe. The trends in key areas such as workflow, text retrieval and latterly knowledge management in the US are already impacting the UK and Europe.

WHAT THE EUROPEANS DISLIKE ABOUT AMERICAN VENDORS	WHAT INFURIATES NORTH AMERICAN VENDORS ABOUT EUROPE
Treating Europe as a single market The way business is conducted in Paris is significantly different to London, although you can drive between them in 4 hours	*The slow sales cycle* Think of a number of months and double it
Uplift The difference in the US dollar price and prices charged in local currency	*Targets* European sales staff claiming the market is different and not meeting their targets
Localisation Releasing international language versions of products months and even years after American/English versions	*All those holidays* Why do the French manage six weeks while we have two?
Imperial units The American habit of using old imperial units for paper sizes and dimensions	*Standards* Those Europeans refer to ISO this and DIN that, which puts up the cost
Support Lack of technical support during a significant proportion of the business day if it is provided from America	*Telecommunication costs* When imaging has to bear the cost of a new network

Table 8.2 Opposites attract?

8.2 SOURCES OF INFORMATION

Faced with a range of possible suppliers, it is helpful to turn to sources of information from those that specialise in 'watching the marketplace'. These include subscription-based consulting and research groups, industry bodies there to promote the technology and its benefits, academic-based organisations, publishers of directories and text books, and consultancies. A sample of these available sources is provided in Table 8.3.

A particularly detailed 'one-off' study[3] of document management systems for the construction industry, was undertaken by the Construction Industry Computing Association (CICA). The investigation was supported by the Construction Sponsorship Directorate of the Department of the Environment, Transport and the Regions. It provided an overview of document management principles and recommendations and presents the responses to a vendor and user survey.

NAME	CONTACT DETAILS	COMMENTS	EXAMPLES OF OUTPUT
AIIM/IMC	AIIM International 2 Crown Walk Winchester Hampshire SO23 8BB Tel: 01962 868333 Fax: 01962 868111 http://www.aiim.org	Association for Information and Image Management (AIIM) International and IMC (International Information Management Congress) agreed in November 1998 to combine.	Range of standards, technical reports, industry studies, white papers and conferences, for example - *AIIM Products and Services Guide* (annually); - *Managing Electronic Documents as Assets* by Rob Allen; - *State of the Document Technology Industry 1997-2003*
CIMdata	CIMdata Inc 3909 Research Park Drive Ann Arbor MI 48108 USA Tel: +1 (734) 668-9922 Fax: +1 (734) 668-1957 http://www.CIMdata.com/	Strategic technical consulting and in-depth market research on areas related to PDM, CAD/CAM, and technology and information exchange standards.	*PDM Buyer's Guide.* 500+ page reference which provides comprehensive reviews of Product Data Management systems offered by US and European vendors.
Cimtech	Cimtech Limited University of Hertfordshire 45 Grosvenor Road St Albans Hertfordshire AL1 3AW Tel: 01727 813651 Fax: 01727 813649 http://cimtech.herts.ac.uk	Provides consultancy, training, courses and directory and journal publications. Part of the University of Hertfordshire.	*Document Management Directory* (annual) covering products and services available in the UK. *Information Management & Technology* (bi-monthly journal) sponsored by CSF – see separate entry.
Computer Suppliers Federation (CSF)	The iT Centre 8 Canalside Lowesmoor Wharf Worcester WR1 2RR Tel: 01905 727610 Fax: 01905 727619 http://www.csf.org.uk	Supplier grouping focusing on specialist IT sectors in the United Kingdom.	Has a document management Forum for suppliers in document imaging, document management and workflow. Sponsors the Document Management Roadshow and the *Document Management Yearbook.*

Table 8.3 Sources of information on document management technologies (continued on page 218)

NAME	CONTACT DETAILS	COMMENTS	EXAMPLES OF OUTPUT
GartnerGroup	Tamesis The Glanty Egham Surrey TW20 9AW Tel: 01784 431611 Fax: 01784 488980 http://www.gartner.com	Subscriber-based authority on information technology with over 30,000 individual clients and 8,000 organisations worldwide providing publications, consultancy and training and product and vendor selection.	*Choosing Information-Retrieval Systems to Find Digital Information* Strategic Analysis Report 1995 *Ten Hot Reasons for Seeking a Single IDM System* Research Note 1998. European E-Work and Knowledge Management '98 Conference, Rome, March 1998
International Data Corporation (IDC)	IDC UK Ltd 6 Dukes Gate Chiswick London W4 5DX Tel: 0181 987 7100 Fax: 0181 747 0212 http://www.idc.com.	Provides data, analysis and advisory services to IT suppliers and IS professionals. Research and opinions are based on extensive end user surveys and analysis.	*Document Management Software: Midyear Market Review*, 1998. Amie White. Includes analyses of the markets for various document management sectors and products including Documentum, FileNet, Open Text, Lotus, document-centric EDM (Cimage and Netright), and full text retrieval (Verity and Excalibur).
Ovum	Ovum Ltd 1 Mortimer Street London W1N 7RH Tel: 0171 255 2670 Fax: 0171 255 1995 http://www.ovum.com	Independent research and consulting company, offering expert advice on IT, telecoms and new media.	*Ovum Evaluates: Document Management,* 1998. Loose-leaf publication covering understanding and selection, market and technology guides and product evaluations. *Knowledge Management : Applications, Markets and Technologies,* 1998
Strategy Partners International	Strategy Partners International Ltd Chappell House The Green Datchet Berkshire SL3 9EH Tel: 01753 592787 Fax: 01753 592789 http://www.strategy-partners.com	Provides consultancy and market analysis in key IT sectors, particularly EDM.	*EDM Europe 98.* Detailed analysis of the European Market for document management technologies in 1998 (sponsored by IMC)
Workflow & Groupware Stratégies (W&GS)	Workflow & Groupware Stratégies 37 Rue Bouret 75019 Paris France Tel: +33 1422 380802 Fax: +33 1423 380802 http://www.wngs.com	Undertakes consultancy in workflow, groupware, document management and Intranet and produces evaluative reports on workflow products.	*Workflow Comparative Study,* 1999. Available in paper or electronic form. Includes definition of workflow comparison criteria.

Table 8.3 Sources of information on document management technologies

8.3 SUPPLIER PROFILES

Profiles of a sample of document management suppliers are presented here based on published information mainly obtained from their Web sites. Most suppliers support Microsoft Windows and NT environments, but not all support UNIX. Because each prospective user company has its own information technology architecture requirements, no attempt is made here to provide sufficient information on which to base system selection. The inclusion or exclusion of a particular product or supplier does not signify endorsement or rejection. The information is intended simply to provide an indication of the type and scope of the technologies that were available at the time of writing. Ovum's estimation[2] of sales revenues in 1997 of those vendors they surveyed and which are covered in this section is shown in Figure 8.1.

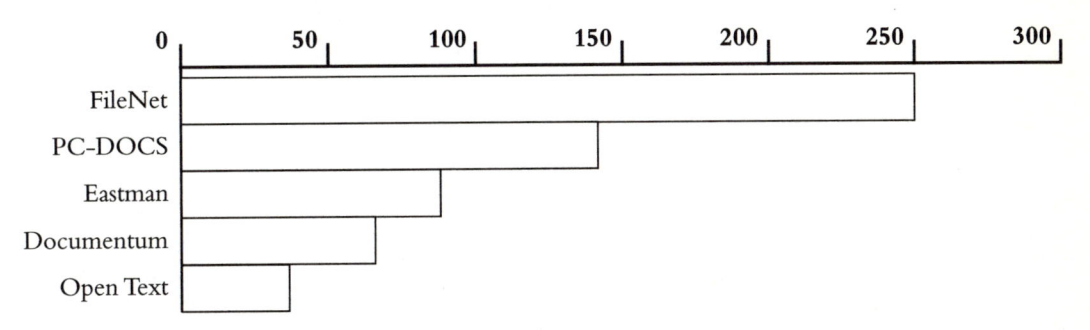

Figure 8.1 Sales reveues ($ million) of document management vendors

ALTRIS

UK Address	Altris Software Altris House 53-55 Uxbridge Road London W5 5SA
Telephone	0181-579 8788
Web site	http://www.altris.com
Company background	Altris resulted from the merger of Trimco Enterprises in the UK and Alpharel in the USA in 1995. Trimco was founded in 1988 and developed enterprise-wide document management system focused largely in the construction and engineering sector. Alpharel was formed in 1981 as an engineering research laboratory producing imaging hardware products. It was floated in 1987 and moved into document management in 1991. It has offices in the US, and is represented in more than 50 countries.
Application focus	Altris focuses solely on document management (although now advertises itself as a knowledge management solution provider). It has particular skills in managing large format documents such as drawings in an engineering environment.
Customer base	Supports solutions for the utilities, manufacturing, engineering and financial industries. Customers include: Agip UK Ltd., Avon Cosmetics, BNFL, Bournemouth & West Hants Water, BP Chemicals, Continental Airlines, Eurotunnel, Kent County Council, London Underground, Security Life Reinsurance, University Hospital Birmingham.
Products include	*Altris EB*: an integrated document management system for office and technical documents. It combines document indexing and searching, imaging, creation of office and CAD documents, workflow and COLD reports into one application, within one solid data vault. User interfaces include an out-of-the-box Windows application, Web interface, access from office applications through ODMA and custom designed interfaces. It uses a scalable 3-tier architecture with a comprehensive integration toolkit to allow customers to link documents from the secure EB data vault with other line-of-business applications. Staffware is used to provide the workflow functionality. *Altris FTR/OCR* automatically recognizes text from images. The resulting text can be loaded into a full text database. *Altris pro EDM*, an enterprise DM system that can work across multiple sites. *Altris pro CM* provides product information management, including creation, management, tracking and change control. *Altris CAD-Connect* links CAD departments with the DM system to provide an automated link between vector and raster files. *Altris WISDOM* a supplemental interface to Altris enterprise document management systems enabling access to these systems through Internet browsers now commonly found on user desktops.

CIMAGE

UK Address	Cimage Enterprise Systems Centennial Court Easthampstead Road Bracknell Berkshire RG12 1JZ
Telephone	01344 860055
Web site	http://www.cimage.com
Company background	A US-based pioneer in document management in 1989, Cimage became in 1995 part of the Tarmac Group, a UK onstruction and professional services companies. It designs, develops and distributes integrated document management systems through a direct sales team and a global network of value added resellers.
Application focus	Document management and workflow systems for manufacturing utilities, oil and process sectors.
Customer base	450 systems in 18 countries including Rover, British Telecom, Ford Motor Company, British Nuclear Fuels, British Energy, Texaco, Marathon Oil, Gillette and other major corporations in a variety of manufacturing, process and utility industries.
Products include	*Workflow Manager*. Workflow Desktop for Windows provides a Microsoft Windows 95 style user interface to Staffware Workflow and information managed by a Cimage DM Server. *ImageMaster*. View and markup any drawing or document. *DM Server*. Store drawings and documents centrally, manage revisions to drawings and documents, synchronise copies of drawings and documents between offices. *DM Desktop and DM-Net* (uses a Web browser): Find and retrieve drawings or documents fast, eliminate unwanted copies of drawings and documents, share drawings and documents with other users, anywhere. *DM for AutoCAD & DM for Microstation*: Integrate tightly with leading CAD packages.

DOCUMENTUM

UK Address	Documentum Software Europe 5 Roundwood Avenue Stockley Park Uxbridge Middlesex UB11 1NZ
Telephone	0181-867 3012
Web site	http://www.documentum.com
Company background	Documentum was founded in 1990 by technologists from Ingres Corporation, to develop a new class of enterprise document management systems that would offer dramatic improvements in business-critical processes. Documentum made a successful initial public offering in February 1996. It has 530 employees.
Application focus	High-end systems primarily used for building applications across large organisations. Links to enterprise resource products such as SAP.
Customer base	Emphasis on addressing vertical markets, initially pharmaceutical and subsequently in process and discrete manufacturing, and into new markets such as financial services. Customers include Arco, Brown & Root, Enron, Kvaerner, Barclays PLC, Bayer Corporation, Brown & Root, Ford Motor Company, GTECH.
Products include	*Documentum 4i* – a web-based application to support Web integration in Microsoft Office 2000. Includes *EDM Server* to to implement the *Docbase* knowledge repository and provide support for the document life cycle from creation and capture to routing for approval and publishing. *Developer Studio*, a graphical development environment. *Documentum Administrator* to facilitate managing and administering distributed servers and users. *Documentum 4i* is designed to replace the company's current offering: *Enterprise Document Management System 98 (EDMS 98)* which was announced July 13 1998 and is an enterprise application platform for automating the end-to-end life cycle management of business-critical documents.

EASTMAN SOFTWARE

UK Address	Eastman Software 661 London Road Isleworth, Middlesex TW7 4EH
Telephone	0181-231 3200
Web site	http://www.eastmansoftware.com
Company background	Eastman Software, a Kodak business, is a leading provider of Enterprise Work Management technology. It was formed in 1997 and has around 600 employees world-wide.
Application focus	Capture of paper documents and workflow particularly in Microsoft Exchange environments. Has coupled application to SAP.
Customer base	Been most prominent in finance and banking markets. Customers include Pennsylvania Life, Italiana Petroli SPA, Swiss Bank Corporation, Science Applications International Corporation.
Products include	*EASTMAN SOFTWARE Imaging* helps manage paper documents by turning a page of information into an electronic image. *EASTMAN SOFTWARE COLD* indexes and stores the information that critical business applications would normally send to print *EASTMAN SOFTWARE Workflow* electronically moves work through the organisation. Specific support for Microsoft Exchange is provided by a family of products: *EASTMAN SOFTWARE WorkFolder* for Microsoft Exchange lets teams collect, organise, manage and share information. *EASTMAN SOFTWARE Document Manager* for Microsoft Exchange provides enterprise-wide document management services. *Imaging for Windows Professional Edition* transforms paper documents and faxes into electronic documents to view, edit, and distribute via Microsoft Windows, Microsoft Exchange, Intranets, and the Internet. *Imaging for Windows*, Eastman Software's basic desktop imaging product, is included as an accessory in every copy of Windows 95 and Windows NT 4.0.

FILENET

UK Address	FileNet 1 The Square Stockley Park Uxbridge Middlesex UB11 1FN
Telephone	0181-867 6357
Web site	http://www.filenet.com
Company background	Originally a hardware producer, it moved into the DM software market with the acquisition of Watermark Software (a document imaging application), and the DM system supplier Saros during 1995 and 1996. It employs 1,400 people.
Application focus	Integrated document management focused across a wide range of commerce and government clients. Has developed applications with third parties, e.g. case processing for specific lines of business, links to ESRI's Geographic Information System (GIS), links to ERP systems (such as SAP), development of online plant manual systems, and engineering drawing system management.
Customer base	Has range of sectors including banking and financial services, government, healthcare, insurance, manufacturing and utilities, services and retail. Customers include Credit Suisse, Engineering Department of the United States Postal Service, SmithKline Beecham, Pacific Mutual Life Insurance, Amoco Corporation, Budget Rent a Car Corporation.
Products include	Introduced its *Panagon* family of products in 1998 providing integrated document management, all from within a Microsoft Windows Explorer or Internet browser interface. *Panagon IDM Desktop*: electronically view, manage, revise, share, and distribute documents. *Panagon IDM Document Services*: Information repository providing the foundation for Panagon IDM solutions. *Panagon Capture*: Captures, indexes, and stores virtually any document type. *Panagon Report Manager*: A client/server COLD application that eliminates printing and distributing of computer-generated reports and statements. *Panagon Visual Workflow*: Java-Based production workflow. *Panagon Web Publisher*: Manages the Web site and web content publishing process *Panagon Document Warehouse for SAP*. *Filenet Watermark*: document imaging and workflow product for departmental or small business applications.

KEYFILE

Address	Keyfile Corporation 22 Cotton Road Nashua NH 03063 USA	A partner in UK:	Dialog Imaging Hamilton House The Marlows Hemel Hempstead Herts HP1 1BB
Telephone			01442 401000
Web site	http://www.keyfile.com		
Company background	Keyfile Corporation, a privately-held company established in 1989, provides document management and workflow software. It is backed by private investors and leading venture capital firms. There are over 5,000 Keyfile servers installed (70,000 users) and 3,500 Keyflow servers (35,000 users) in over 50 countries.		
Application focus	Broad-based where paper and electronic documents need to be integrated. Now re-focused on e-mail applications.		
Customer base	Present in most sectors including manufacturing, financial services, retail, healthcare, government and transportation. Customers include Forest Heath District Council, BICC, Stratford on Avon District Council, AUDI AG, Airline Pilots Association (USA).		
Products include	*Keyfile Active Document Workspace:* integrates document management functionality with standard web browsers and provides transparent access to *Keyfile*'s document repository via Microsoft Outlook's public folders. *Keyfile Commerce*: automates e-commerce processes, transactions and customer relationship management by improving and integrating *Keyfile*'s document management, workflow and forms functionality. Integrates with Microsoft Office 2000. *Active Document Workspace* (ADW): automates storage and handling of document-related tasks. *Workflow Server* and *Workflow Designer*: work process automation.		

OPEN TEXT

UK Address	Open Text Webster House 22 Wycombe End Beaconsfield Buckinghamshire HP9 1NB
Telephone	01494 679700
Web site	http://www.opentext.com
Company background	Founded in 1991 it was an early developer of text-indexing software; it subsequently moved to Intranet-based document management and in June 1998 acquired Information Dimensions. Its stated strategy is one of internal growth assisted by strategic acquisitions. With the acquisition of Lava systems in January 1999, the combined company has around 700 employees and offices throughout North America, Europe and Asia. It claims a worldwide installed base of 2.5 million users in 3,500 corporations. An IDC study report, Document Management Software: Mid-Year Market Review, 1998, showed that Open Text captured 42.1% of the enterprise-centric EDM software revenue as of mid-year 1998.
Application focus	Web-centric systems to improve the efficiencies of key business processes and to release the full potential of applications and information sources for knowledge workers.
Customer base	Wide range of industry sectors, including financial services, high technology manufacturing, telecommunications, government and pharmaceutical. Customers include Unisys, First USA Bank, F. Hoffman LaRoche, HJ Heinz, QUALCOMM, UK House of Commons, Silicon Graphics, British Broadcasting Corporation, Hewlett Packard.
Products include	*Livelink 8* Collaborative Knowledge Management System for Intranets. Optional modules are available to address specific business solutions such as locating documents published on Web sites and retrieving them to be indexed; notification of changes in documents via e-mail; a scheduling system for enterprise-wide use; and highly targeted searches for business users. Modules include: *Livelink Forms, Livelink Prospectors, Livelink Desktop Activator* for ODMA, *Livelink Activator for BASIS, Livelink Activator for SAPR/3*, and a new version of the *Livelink Spider* for Windows NT. *BASIS 8.2 Document Management System*: (acquired from Information Dimensions) a document database specifically engineered for strong document control and high-throughput document search and retrieval. Has been integrated with Livelink. *TechLib* using BASIS with extended relational database structure optimised to manage text and documents in library environment.

PCDOCS/Fulcrum

UK Address	PC DOCS Group Europe Ltd Sherbourne House Croxley Business Park Watford Herts WD1 8YE
Telephone	01923 814700
Web site	http://www.pcdocs.com
Company background	Founded in 1990, and now part of Hummingbird Communications, PC DOCS, Inc, claims the largest revenue share in the document management market through its subsidiary PCDOCS/Fulcrum. It employs 400 people. It acquired Fulcrum, a text retrieval company in 1998. Claims over 700,000 end users and more than 3,500 user organisations.
Application focus	Document management solutions and the claimed widest range of language support of any DM product. Relatively new in large format document applications.
Customer base	Variety of industries including manufacturing, finance, government, insurance, legal and other professional services, e.g. Canadian Coast Guard, London Borough of Enfield, London Fire Brigade, Shotley Police Training Centre, Charles Schwab, Thomas Cook, Wells Fargo, British Steel, Denton Hall.
Products include	Knowledge Management: *DOCSFulcrum* knowledge-retrieval and analysis capabilities to tap corporate information repositories and the Web. *SearchServer* information-retrieval engine, used on its own or in knowledge-intensive software products. Server-based Document Management: *DOCSFusion* new-generation engine of PC DOCS/Fulcrum products; three-tier architecture to access, analyse and act on internal or external information from any location or platform. Its clients include *CyberDOCS*. With DOCSFusion functionality from a Web browser, operating over the Internet or an Intranet or Extranet. CyberDOCS is the Web window to DOCSFusion and DOCS Open libraries. *PowerDOCS* Windows-based client to full DOCSFusion document management functionality. Client-server Document Management: *DOCS Open* A client-server product to store, locate and manage information across a wide range of platforms and networks, regardless of location. Various DOCS Open add-ons available, e.g. for imaging.

SER (PAFEC)

UK Address	SER Systems Ltd 39 Nottingham Road Stapleford Nottingham NG9 6AD
Telephone	0115 935 7055
Web site	http://www.pafec.com
Company background	In July 1998 PAFEC was acquired by SER, the German software and systems company, to make the group the largest document management company in Europe. PAFEC itself was formed in 1976 from a research group at Nottingham University. Strong in CAD, it now develops, markets and supports computer solutions for electronic document management and geographic information systems.
Application focus (PAFEC)	Document management with strong emphasis on version control and audit trails and large format documents and drawings.
Customer base (PAFEC)	Construction, transport and utilities industries with customers including Alstrom, Scottish Hydro-Electric, Railtrack, Serco Raildata, Foster and Partners and Southern Water.
Products include (PAFEC)	*Document Manager* provides computer repository for all forms of information together with facilities for accessing and managing the data stored. *Work Manager* (its own product) provides workflow support for business processes. It controls the passage of information between people, groups and departments. *Distribution Manager* has been designed to manage the flow of information between organisations. *PAFEC EDM Internet/Intranet viewer* allows location-independent distributed access to managed documents. *Free Text Retrieval* of document content.

REFERENCES IN CHAPTER 8

1 Staunton, R., 'Divided by a Common Tongue', *Document World Issue 1* (March 1996), pp. 20-22

2 Staunton, R., *et al*, *Ovum Evaluates Document Management*, 1998. Produced in association with Strategy Partners International.

3 Wagner, D. and Winterkorn, E., *Document Management for Construction* (Cambridge: Construction Industry Computing Association, 1998)

(See also Table 8.3 for other sources of information.)

9

SUITABLE CASES FOR TREATMENT

'Well, new experiences are broadening. ... But where are all the victims?'
Anne of the Island: Lucy Maud Montgomery

This final chapter provides examples of published case studies to indicate the range of applications that have been addressed by document management and related technologies.

BROWN & ROOT ENERGY SERVICES' COMMON ENTERPRISE REPOSITORY FOR KEY DOCUMENTS SPEEDS TIME TO CONSTRUCTION, DELIVERS HIGH ROI

(Sourced with permission from Documentum – http://www.documentum.com)

Problem

- Inefficient processes for managing engineering and technical documents, and then assembling current documents into operations manuals.

Solution

- Automated system based on the Documentum EDMS that creates a common enterprise repository for all design and engineering documents related to a project.

Results

- Accelerated time to construction
- Improved plant operations

◆ Estimated 424%, three-year return on investment from lower costs of document communication, updating, and storage, as well as bids and proposals savings.

'Brown & Root has been able to virtually eliminate the costs of retrieval, transfer, and communication of information from design to operations. Instead of employing engineers to organise design operations manuals, the company can simply provide the operations group with access to the Docbase.'

Increasing dependence on offshore oil and growing environmental protection concerns have led today's oil producers to demand the most advanced technology in at-sea oil-recovery equipment. The job of designing, building, and maintaining the state of the art in offshore oil and gas production platforms falls to companies like Brown & Root, a subsidiary of the Halliburton Company and one of the world's largest integrated energy services and engineering construction firms.

The large volume of documents generated by complex engineering construction projects can pose major challenges to an engineering firm's ability to operate efficiently. Brown & Root needed a system that could manage all engineering and technical documents created during the design and construction phase of a project - a process that can involve many contractors with various systems not under its control. The company also needed a system to translate the design documents into operating manuals that could be instantly accessed by offshore crews. At the same time, it needed a way to ensure that all operations staff worked from certified drawings and documents and that any changes made by operations staff were recorded for future reference. The Documentum Enterprise Document Management System (EDMS) has provided the ideal solution.

Brown & Root's design process produces a variety of electronic and paper documents in several formats from different authors. Before the Documentum system, there was limited formal organisation or centralisation of electronic specifications for a project.

Once a production platform is operational, ongoing maintenance, repair and modifications are necessary to ensure that the platform operates efficiently and meets safety and environmental regulations. Operations personnel need access to all original design documents to ensure appropriate maintenance. Before Documentum, documentation assembly sometimes required a 10-person crew to spend up to two years locating the pertinent documents and then assembling and distributing the operations manuals. During this time, the platform would be in full operation. If repairs or maintenance were required, the operations group would have to search for documents still in the process of being compiled. If information on a certain part was not available, operations on the platform could be jeopardised until the needed manual was located and consulted.

CUTTING TIME AND COSTS

Following a successful pilot phase, the Documentum EDMS is now being deployed throughout Brown & Root. A Documentum Docbase™ repository is created for each new project the company undertakes. Petro-Canada's new Terra-Nova platform is an example of a project that is relying on a Documentum Docbase throughout its design, construction and operation. Brown & Root external suppliers are encouraged to submit technical documents in a standardised electronic format for entry into the system. The Docbase maintains records of changes and provides an accurate history that meets design, regulatory, and insurance requirements.

With the Documentum EDMS, all documents are tracked and managed through the design phase. At the end of the design phase, the documentation in the Docbase is made available to the operations group. The ability to immediately search all of the data required to operate the platform represents a vast improvement over the previous paper-only method, enabling operators to rapidly access just the current technical documents they need. As the operations of the platforms change, revisions to technical requirements can be immediately updated and distributed.

These qualitative benefits represent huge cost savings for Brown & Root. A recent study conducted by International Data Corporation (IDC) estimates that the company will receive a three-year return of 424% on its investment in the Documentum system. Brown & Root has been able to virtually eliminate the costs of retrieval, transfer, and communication of information from design to operations. In addition, the Documentum EDMS has helped Brown & Root reduce its document updating costs. When specification changes are made, the resulting design documents can be updated in the Docbase, ensuring that all who access them will have the most timely and accurate information. The organised structure of documents enables the design group to reuse portions of previous projects and save time on post-design organisation. This frees the staff to take on more projects and bid more competitively for potential new projects.

A PLATFORM FOR THE FUTURE

The success of Brown & Root's Documentum EDMS application has encouraged the company to explore other uses for the Documentum technology. Brown & Root plans to take advantage of the EDMS's workflow capabilities in order to streamline approval processes for engineers and designers. In addition, Brown & Root plans to provide suppliers, contractors, and other outside organisations with access to project Docbases in order to help reduce transaction costs in dealing with third parties.

At Brown & Root, the Documentum EDMS has provided new channels for feedback to the design process that were unavailable before. Because of these feedback channels, the company is finding that information from the operations phase can spur improvements in future designs. That is yet another way Brown & Root is gaining a business advantage from leveraging the knowledge in documents.

BP Schiehallion information management and the challenge of cultural change

(Sourced with permission from Altris - http://www.altris.com)

The biggest issue facing the North Sea's oil explorers today is that, to maintain the flow of gas and oil from this part of the world, they are being driven further and further offshore and therefore into ever deeper water. In the autumn of 1993 the semi-submersible drilling rig, Ocean Alliance, working in the deep waters of the North-West Atlantic, some 150 kilometres west of the Shetlands, discovered the Schiehallion oil field. (Schiehallion and the associated Loyal Field are estimated to have recoverable reserves of approximately 425 million barrels.)

To meet the challenges posed by operating so far offshore in deep and often hostile waters, BP and its five partners (Shell UK Ltd, Amerada Hess, Statoil, Murphy and OMV (UK) Ltd) have adopted an innovative approach to the development of the field. This involves the construction of an FPSO (Floating Production Storage and Offloading) vessel rather than a fixed production platform. Capable of processing 142,000 barrels of oil per day and with a storage capacity of 950,000 barrels, FPSO Schiehallion, which has been constructed by a consortium of companies, including Brown & Root, Harland and Wolff and SBM in Belfast, is the largest new build vessel of its type in the world today. As its description implies, the vessel is designed to extract the oil and store it on board until it can be transferred to a tanker and transported to the oil refineries ashore.

Everything about this facility is unique. It required an unprecedented number and range of documents during the design and build phases and subsequently for maintenance and development.

SIMS objectives

The task of designing and implementing the Schiehallion Information Management System (SIMS), which will be accessible from terminals aboard the FPSO as well as onshore, became the responsibility of Ms Nada Zdravkovic, Information Management Delivery Team Leader for the Operations Support Contractor, Brown & Root/AOC. Brown & Root are the project managers for the FPSO. The objectives were to:

- minimise offshore manning and maximise efficient operation (minimising offshore manning is as much a safety as a cost issue with Schiehallion)
- ensure safe and environmentally friendly operations
- provide up-to-date technical information quickly to enable offshore to
  - manage risk effectively
  - meet operating and production targets.

Mapping system to culture

Nada knew that one of her biggest problems would be to persuade the people who would be involved with the day-to-day operation of the FPSO to use the new system rather than, what was to them, the more convenient, if flawed, paper systems to which they were accustomed. Early involvement in the design process is, she believes, critical to getting this 'buy-in' from all the people who will eventually use the system - from management right through to the people who will physically maintain the vessel.

The key was understanding the importance of 'tag numbers'. These are similar to part numbers in other industries and each component of the FPSO is marked with the tag number. In this environment this is the starting point for operations and maintenance staff searching for documents or drawings. The problem was that document management systems are built around 'documents', not tag numbers. It would of course have been possible to effect some kind of 'fudge' in which tag numbers could have been added to documents as keywords but this would have been a less than satisfactory solution. The outcome would have been like settling for a flat file solution when a relational database which could interchange and cross reference information is the more efficient solution.

> *'Thinking through how your data works and fits together and making it accessible in a form which is acceptable to the people who will ultimately use it is critically important to being able to deliver a successful system. The earlier in the project you go through this process, the higher your chances of ultimately achieving your goals',* commented Nada Zdravkovic.

The tag to document relationship was fundamental to the selection process, but at first there seemed no obvious solution. There has traditionally been a demarcation line between the EDM and PDM vendors with the former concentrating on the needs of large paper-bound organisations such as banks, insurance companies, government, etc. and the latter on manufacturing and maintenance organisations with thousands of parts and sub-assemblies to track. Now here was a problem that required something from both cultures - an ability to manage changing and complex relationships between components of a structure and an ability to control a vast quantity of documents that would be presented in a variety of forms, encompassing everything from hand-written notes to CAD files. One of the ways in which this relationship has been realised is the ability of the Win-Track document management system to prevent a document being checked out of the system for change if that document has been placed under configuration management within the Pro CM system. This indicates that the document has many others dependent on it and therefore any changes have to pass through a formal change request procedure.

Reducing technology risk

Given that the SIMS system would eventually integrate the tag or asset register (built in Altris Pro CM), the document management system (Altris Win-Track document management software) and the maintenance management system (Engard from Indus) to provide a single source of electronic information accessible from the tag numbers, Brown & Root were keen to minimise the technological risk inherent in integrating three completely different systems on an *ad hoc* basis.

Fortunately Altris Software, already a preferred supplier of document management systems to BP, had recently completed the integration of Altris document management software with their own PDM system which is called Altris Pro CM. It is proving an ideal marriage. BP needed the technology that Altris offered in the market and Altris were looking for a prestigious customer who could help them prove to the world just what a powerful combination EDM and PDM are.

However, the stakes were high. BP and Brown & Root had to be absolutely certain that Altris could deliver what they promised and deliver it on time. SIMS is a critical element in achieving the highest standards of safety and environmental care to which BP are committed on the development of the Schiehallion Field.

The core review team had to be satisfied at a number of levels that Altris Pro CM was the right choice. At the first level they needed to be sure that Altris Pro CM could achieve the following:

- collate an integrated master tag register of all maintainable, operable and certifiable items
- collect sufficient technical information for effective use by operations
- navigate to and from the document register
- navigate to and from the maintenance system
- be accessible offshore and onshore
- provide effective change control management.

The team also reviewed Altris Pro CM at a very detailed level including assessing the system's ability to track and control change; its ability to interface to the EnGarde maintenance system and its compatibility with BP's future strategy.

The effort that BP, Brown & Root and Altris put into this preliminary stage was, however, vindicated by the delivery of the SIMS system integrating document management, the asset register and the EnGarde maintenance management system in time for the vessel sail-away early in 1998.

Commenting on the importance of this development to Altris, Director of Professional Services, Robb Liddell said:

> 'As far as Altris are concerned the project has been important not only because it reinforces our relationship with a long established customer but also because it has allowed

> *Altris to bridge a gap in the industry. Mature users of EDM systems, particularly in the manufacturing and engineering environments, have begun to experience limitations with those systems. Altris and BP have proved that these can be successfully overcome by the tight integration of EDM and PDM.*
>
> *The benefits of this approach are enormous. Not only does it allow systems to be built around the way people work, rather than requiring them to make dramatic changes, it also speeds and smooths the whole process of change management.'*

Where next?

The document management system, the first part of systems to be developed and implemented, is now almost fully populated with 'documents'. The link to the asset register - the tag number system - has been in place for some months and the link to Engard went live in November 1997. During the commissioning phase changes will be marked on documents and drawings to reflect any differences between the original designs and the vessel as it has been built and these will in turn be fed back into the document management system. After that process has been completed the vessel will be ready in mid 1998 for Operations with a full set of up-to-date electronic information.

The user interface, which will allow easy navigation between the Pro CM asset register, Win-Track document management and the Engard Maintenance Management System will also be fully implemented by mid 1998. System users will be able to enter a tag number into the asset register and with a single key depression go directly to relevant documents in the document management system or to appropriate parts of the maintenance management system. (Users can if they wish access documents directly, without going via the tag number and shore-based staff whose main role is the maintenance of the document database may indeed choose to do this.)

As far as Nada Zdravkovic is concerned the months of patient planning and the steady build-up of the system are beginning to pay off. Altris have been able to support her policy of building up the system in a very controlled fashion, starting with only basic facilities enabled and gradually enriching the system as seemed appropriate. For example, Nada asked Altris to disable the 'what if' capability of CM (a facility that shows all the consequences of making a change to one part of the construction before that change is implemented) during the development stage. (Nada comments that this type of option is not always possible with 'off the shelf' packages.) However, she knows that the most testing period is yet to come. Looking ahead to the next phase, she said:

> *'The people who will be using SIMS on board the FPSO will have varying degrees of familiarity with computer systems and they will all be used to a traditional system in which they rely on the P&IDs (Process and Instrumentation Diagrams) plus a subset of documentation which experience has taught them will solve most of their problems. Initially at least they will need frequent reminders that the objective of introducing SIMS is to help them to "work smarter" and more safely. They need to remember that a lot of accidents are down to people being unaware of changes because*

they're not using a full set of information or because that information has been updated since they made their copy of their documentation'.

'The importance of SIMS goes beyond meeting the objectives of this single project. It underscores the critical importance of being consciously aware of what information does to your business. It reinforces the case, if it still needs reinforcing, that the management of information today is as important as the management of those other major resources - assets, people and money.'

'It will not be easy to make comparisons with earlier projects. There has never been one quite like Schiehallion. However, all our experience to date, which includes a recognition that the system has been able to accelerate the change approval process during the design and construction phases, leads us to believe that the Schiehallion Information Management System will be a watershed in the industry.'

Technical details

During its development phase the SIMS system was running on a Sun SPARC server located in south London with PC access from Aberdeen and from Belfast. Following completion of development the system was moved to an NT server in Aberdeen, with a second server installed on the FPSO.

Both servers run Altris Pro CM, Altris Win-Track document management and Indus EnGard Maintenance Management software. The systems have been configured so that synchronisation between the servers allows two way update of documents and annotations. (The annotation system has the ability to compare annotations made independently both onshore and offshore and to produce a synthesised version.)

Currently some 67 users have been trained to use the system. Further training on the current system and a possible extension of the system to handle office documentation are likely to increase the total number of users.

Other hardware and software included in the system includes:

- Database – Oracle
- Scanners – Fujitsu and Océ
- Plotters/Printers – Océ and QMS.

BASIS – PUTTING POWER TO WORK

(Sourced with permission from Open Text - http://www.opentext.com)

Power Technology is the centre of engineering and scientific expertise for PowerGen PLC - a name recognised as one of the world's leading privately-owned electricity generating companies. As PowerGen's engineering research & development arm, Power Technology comprises 220-plus highly-skilled and experienced staff involved in work for operational power plants, new developments and complementary research.

Open Text's TECHLIB and BASIS software are contributing to this success. The modular software lies at the heart of an evolving library system that co-ordinates the many engineering reports and technical papers that make a unique and vital reservoir of knowledge for the organisation.

A wealth of information

Power Technology competes for business both within PowerGen and in the open marketplace. In addition to this objectivity, Power Technology has a world-class reputation as a source of authoritative and practical advice, tailored to clients' needs and supported by continual investment in evaluating and applying new technologies.

At the Department's main site - Power Technology Centre at Ratcliffe-on-Soar near Nottingham - Information & Library Services supports on-site staff in their engineering work for all PowerGen power stations in the UK and abroad. Elizabeth Day, Information Officer, is responsible for the library services: *'Our information helps tackle a broad range of issues at existing and future power plants, such as engineering, environmental and management aspects.'*

Search for a system

With the privatisation of the electricity generating industry and the formation of PowerGen in 1987, two existing libraries - a PC-based system at Ratcliffe and an ageing mainframe-based application at Southampton were amalgamated. It was an opportunity for the library services to reorganise its resources.

Power Technology wanted a software package that would provide all necessary library housekeeping, including cataloguing and circulation tracking but also possible future activities, such as handling periodicals and the purchasing of library materials. A multi-faceted application would help streamline the service and optimise staff productivity.

Elizabeth Day continues:

> *'The new software had to be installed with the minimum in-house work. It had to cope with reports, which are specific to this industry and make up the majority of the material in our library, and it had to be capable of coping with multiple levels of security. TECHLIB does all this as an integral part of the product.'*

> *'I took a close look at what was available on the market. After examining several possibilities, Open Text was the first company to understand the nature of our work and empathise with our requirements. Importantly, unlike some, Open Text did not suggest that having bought the software it could then be made to do what I needed - I needed it immediately.'*

Report support

> *'The ability to input a report number into a field and to give every person and every document each a level of security may sound straightforward, but it was surprising*

how few systems were able to meet all the requirements. In the end, it was a clear-cut choice: Open Text had what we wanted and TECHLIB scored on all points.'

TECHLIB uses the BASIS software, but is developed as a library package with complex indexing and search facilities. Power Technology staff search the abstracts – summaries of the individual articles – using assigned key words that are often unique to the power generation industry. Once the library chose TECHLIB, the decision was taken that future entries would all be made on the software and nothing further on the card catalogue. It was the beginning of a process that puts TECHLIB at the core of the library's activities.

The system matures

After attending courses in BASIS and TECHLIB, an external IT contractor started work with Open Text's integral Online Public Access Catalogue (OPAC), in the course of a year converting over 100,000 records from their old formats into BASIS then DOS-based system.

Elizabeth Day recalls:

'After installing the catalogue, we began operations with the Loans module. I simply gave the contractor the necessary parameters and he installed the package virtually overnight. The changeover was trouble free.'

In addition, the contractor maintained close contact with Open Text during this period and was able to train a member of the Power Technology's computing staff and leave excellent documentation to allow future development after the contractor's departure.

Staff at the Centre can search the abstracts and request material electronically from their desktop computers linked via terminal emulation to the VAX-based host system. The library service retains contact with Open Text – *'the UK helpdesk always get back to you'*, says Elizabeth Day – *'particularly as new aspects of the library system are developed.'*

Enabling Intranet access

When the system was installed at Power Technology, Elizabeth Day considered the next step. This goal was always intended from the start: to make the catalogue available online not only at that site, but to PowerGen staff from their desktops in PowerGen locations throughout the UK and, eventually, overseas.

The most serious concern was the security implications in widening system access. The Centre is TCP/IP-based, whereas the power stations run Novell networks, for example, a difference which could potentially compromise the firewalls as the information passed through the intervening routers. Elizabeth Day decided to run a test, sending a tape containing typical library records to Open Text experts who loaded it on a computer and classified each document according to a set routine.

It was vital that Open Text be able to show the library service - and to Power Technology's director Dr David Parry, in particular - that system security could not be jeopardised through allowing wide area, rather than the existing local area, network access.

> *'The perceived sensitivity of this type of data meant that an enquiry from a remote client, must not be able to view the library activities of any other user anywhere on the Intranet. Each client's information would remain its own, accessible only by its staff and the Centre library, unavailable to others,'* recalls Elizabeth Day.

To enable this level of security, every piece of library information, such as a report, is given an access code, detailing its accessibility, such as universal, management only or site only. Each of Power Technology's business units has its own code which, through simple on-screen drop-down menus, is assigned as the documents are typed and is also printed on the hard copy. The contents and classification of each report is agreed and signed for and checked each time before it is being issued to an enquirer.

Using the prepared data, Open Text successfully demonstrated the system, with its various access codes, to David Parry. This demonstrated that only where authorised could users see the abstracts and other entries according to their own and the document's classification. A user could then request hard copies of the reports, videos and other material.

Open Text then set up a pilot Intranet between the Centre and the nearby power station which included activating the full range of access levels, the most secure being the power station manager. *'What is reassuring is that we chose a system capable of the most complex security configurations which can be altered simply and quickly by an authorised system administrator,'* explains Elizabeth Day.

Sharing knowledge

During a routine meeting with managers from all UK PowerGen stations, David Parry explained about the new Intranet, stressing the security aspects. It was soon apparent that the climate of opinion among the power stations favoured a sharing of knowledge.

Parry explained:

> *'We have now disabled the more detailed restrictions, allowing UK power stations to view abstracts from their own and other locations, according to each user's and each document's authorisation. Should there be a need to revise this at any time, we can restore the restrictions that Open Text illustrated during the demonstration. The system has that flexibility.'*

Users at UK power stations now access the library system over the corporate Intranet, via a PC running a TCP/IP stack and a Web browser. Moreover, security is ensured as they interrogate only a server, not the VAX host directly.

Further expansion

An internal survey revealed that before the Intranet a high percentage of users relied on contacts at Power Technology and the telephone to access library resources. These haphazard methods have been replaced by direct access to the library abstracts.

The next phase is to migrate to full-text access to internal reports and linking overseas plants to the system. Engineers at PowerGen's sites in India, Australia, Portugal, Hungary and Indonesia would obviously benefit in the speed of response if they could obtain information through their own interrogation of the system via the network, particularly where decisions have to be made quickly.

The library is currently considering having diagrams and photographs, as well as the text of internal documents, in electronic format. Users could search on this material in addition to the abstract, requesting a book, video or picture for delivery as hard copy and 'hot linking' through a mouse-click for the full text of the article on screen instantly.

'We are liaising with Open Text about how our library systems can integrate with the necessary electronic document systems, but prior planning by Open Text has ensured it can be achieved without difficulty,' says Elizabeth Day.

She concludes:

> *'Our users do not have to be computer experts or spend inordinate amounts of time on the system. We wanted it to be as simple as opening a filing cabinet, but with all the browsing and data dissemination advantages of an Intranet. This is the added value - in terms of future-proofing, simplicity and security - that we were looking for and that BASIS continues to deliver.'*

TWO-HUNDRED SEAT PAFEC EDM SYSTEM GATHERS SPEED AT RAILTRACK PROPERTY

(Sourced with permission from SER Systems Ltd - http://www.pafec.com)

For large projects such as those in the rail industry with high value, often low margins and high risk, electronic document management (EDM) systems are essential to enable projects to run to time, cost and specification. They not only provide full document control but just as importantly they provide the documented evidence that control exists.

Railtrack's Property Directorate have been using PAFEC EDM for eight months and in this time the system has grown significantly and is now well established with 200 seats. Steve Lewington of Railtrack Property explains:

> *'The system has been tremendously successful, and is very popular with the user population. This is partly due to our policy of risk reduction by selecting industry standard software. PAFEC EDM is already well established within our own organ-*

isation, and is being used, albeit for different tasks by West Coast Main Line Route Modernisation Project and other Railtrack Departments.'

Railtrack PLC was formed in 1994 to be the custodian of Britain's railway infrastructure. As well as the running and upkeep of track, signals, stations, depots, arches, bridges and viaducts, the company has one of the country's largest property portfolios, including over 40,000 commercial property units and thousands of hectares of land. The rail industry has undergone one of the most radical changes in its history and Railtrack's Property Directorate has evolved to reflect these changes. Based in their new offices in London and Manchester the Property Directorate focuses on all rail related property activities and is responsible for the management and development of one of the country's largest property portfolios. Railtrack Property are currently involved in a £2.5 billion station refurbishment and construction programme.

The Directorate's property facilities are diverse. From freight sites to wayleaves and easements, from advertising hoardings to an investment portfolio worth in excess of 200 million pounds, from garden extensions to shooting rights. The sheer scale of the task of managing over 40,000 separate lettings is enormous. It is the responsibility of the Property team to find hidden value for both Railtrack and its customers and partners and to enhance facilities to encourage rail usage.

PAFEC's DM software has been tremendously successful within the rail industry, capturing some 60% of the market, and being used on an estimated £7 billion of rail projects world-wide. PAFEC's rail customers include a number of Railtrack's Departments such as WCML Route Modernisation; together with other leading rail organisations including Hong Kong Mass Transit (MTRC), HSL's Rail link in the Netherlands and a number of service organisations such as Serco Raildata and Railpart.

The EDM system is being used for the management of maps and other related site documentation for Railtrack's 2500 stations and associated property. At present the system holds three distinct categories of plans of all 2500 sites. The first is a clean up-to-date Ordnance Survey map of the station and its surrounding area. The second is a copy of the first plan showing the current freehold ownership boundary of the company by a broken black line. The final plan is the current station lease plan as agreed in the station lease document to the Train Operating Company. The same lease plan also exists for the freight and depot sites and over the coming months the blank and boundary versions will also be added along with the arch estates documentation.

Railtrack Property initially envisaged holding the scanned images electronically at the site of each drawing office and distributing it to users by CD. It was quickly realised, however, that by holding this information in a central store the system could be 'live' to all users across the Directorate and potentially corporately. Needless to say Railtrack now make use of a central server situated at Crewe which currently serves seven Railtrack offices, with each of the users having instantly available information on their desktop. This principal also rigorously enforces document management processes in order to control use and validity of the data. A CD browser solution has also been developed to enable those users away from the network to have access to the information.

Scanning equipment is situated within each office which allows the scanning of documents and associated attributes which will allow the subsequent retrieval of the correct information. A team of System Administrators have been established to provide guidance in the use and application of the system and ensure that the business procedures are adhered to. They also have the responsibility of controlling input of both new and updated mapping and estate documentation as well as managing the access rights to the system. They have a further task in controlling the creation and release of information on CD to outbased users.

The system has been tailored to meet the needs of Railtrack Property, so that on entering the system the user may choose to search on any of the customised criteria. Search options currently include: property reference number, the location name, the type of plan, type of property, the Zone, the Regional Manager responsible for the area, and the railway tenant and any other content of the plan itself. Once the desired image has been identified it can be viewed using a raster viewer that has again been modified to enable Railtrack Property to work more effectively with map based images. Standard windows tiling methods can be used to position a number of images on the screen at once. Tools are also available that give the ability to zoom in and out of areas of the image as well as pan, once zoomed in.

Steve Lewington of Railtrack Property concludes:

> *'The introduction of the PAFEC system has enabled more efficient working practices within the Directorate. For example the inclusion of a highly accurate measuring tool within the software enables users to accurately calculate distance measurements within various property plans much more quickly and accurately than conventional manual methods would allow. This frees skilled technicians from laborious administrative tasks, so enabling them to concentrate on more important surveying and draughting activities which in turn will have enormous benefits for Railtrack Property.'*

GRANADA GHIA – GRANADA MEDIA'S SWITCHED-ON VIEW OF INFORMATION RETRIEVAL

(Sourced with permission from *Information Age,* February 1999, pages 32 to 33 – a report by Jane Barber)

Digital television and satellite expansion in the international marketplace present a huge challenge to programme makers and broadcasters. They transform the prospects of companies like Granada, representing a tremendous opportunity to increase programme and footage sales.

Granada Media is the television division of the Granada Group, established in 1954. One of Britain's largest and most successful commercial television companies, it owns Granada Television, London Weekend, Yorkshire, Tyne Tees, Granada Sky Broadcasting and 50% of Ondigital. Granada's assets are the footage and programmes in demand among various broadcasters and video production companies in the UK and overseas. To make the most of the opportunity, it has had to resolve an escalating problem.

Granada needed to reorganise its management of information to trace critical production documents, carry out sales and locate contractual and legal confirmation of royalties related to productions. Finding all this data was affecting the bottom line. Manually searching through the vast array of archives was taking too much time.

Ian Whitfield, head of IT development, and his colleagues were increasingly aware of the difficulties of efficient data retrieval. To keep the company at the forefront of the industry and capitalise on its growing sales potential, Whitfield knew the problems needed to be resolved.

He explains: *'Personnel were having sometimes to contact up to eight different departments to retrieve the data required to carry out the job in hand and this was proving both labour intensive and prohibitive.'* For example, if a specific programme synopsis needed to be found, staff would not necessarily know whether it would be in the library at Tyne Tees or Yorkshire. This resulted in a long process of liaising with colleagues in different departments in different locations, until the footage was finally recovered in the appropriate section.

Whitfield had fielded a number of questions from his staff about the possibility of an information retrieval system. After looking into it, he concluded that there were, initially, four key departments that could benefit from a fully integrated information management system across the whole of Granada Media: extract sales, rights management, research and the archive librarians.

The extract sales division is responsible for sales of productions to video production companies and broadcasting organisations. The key to efficiency here is the rapid identification of the asset a buyer is interested in. For instance, a satellite production company may be interested in televising particular episodes of *Cracker*. The extract sales department would need to find the footage and associated information as efficiently as possible or the sale might be lost. The division was finding the task increasingly difficult; only an estimated 80% of all data was retrievable and it all took time.

The rights management department handles vital contractual rights information. It has to work out whether or not the company will make a sufficient profit from the sale of a production, once all the artists' royalty fees have been taken into consideration. If Granada were to produce a period costume drama and a broadcasting company wished to buy it, this department would assess the total cost of all royalty fees to all associated parties -

including script writers and musical directors as well as actors. If it decided there was little or no prospect of a profit, the sale would not go ahead.

Vast archive

Granada Media houses a UK archive library second in size only to the BBC and the company also runs a public service. Members of the public can contact the librarians to ask for copies of particular footage of their favourite programmes. The footage is subsequently sent to their home addresses for a nominal fee. The primary job of the librarians, however, is to find particular footage for other broadcasters or departments - a current affairs programme might want archive footage of a celebrity to support a news item, for example. There are over 70,000 productions on file. A librarian would have to search manually through millions of rows of videotapes.

Whitfield assessed only one other potential solution before he selected Excalibur Technologies' knowledge retrieval software RetrievalWare. Its Adaptive Pattern Recognition Processing allows the rapid automatic indexing of digital data from a variety of sources, including paper, electronic and sound, and is based on conversion of information to binary patterns. In retrieval, Excalibur searches for an underlying pattern from the digital data, not for specific words. The semantic network technology is concerned with narrowing the search through word meanings. *'It's a sophisticated search engine,'* says Whitfield. *'The product allows us to do concept searches. For example, if we type in BSE, it would pull out everything that has "mad" and "cows" in it.'*

Whitfield piloted the Excalibur software in the four key departments. *'The system has been up and running for about three months,'* he says. *'Initially we've got 50 users and this should grow to about 100. It's used in Newcastle, in Leeds, Manchester and London.'*

The users are enthusiastic, he notes. *'Although we haven't actually done any calculations, the system has led to huge time savings. For example, researchers might have had to make eight or more calls to locate material. Now they just do a search and find out whether the material is available.'*

Getting data into RetrievalWare has been a major part of the project. *'The information is actually stored on a core artists' rights information system, Paris,'* says Whitfield. *'We do an extract into the Intranet database on a nightly basis and download the information into the Excalibur technology.'*

As for programme details and synopses, a group of students is retyping a brief synopsis of every episode of every programme ever made within Granada Media. So far, the job has taken three months and it is expected to take two more to complete. The finished compilation will probably run to 'a couple of gigabytes.' Whitfield explains: *'The number of tapes or productions made by Granada is 70,000. Associated with each production we have a synopsis about 100 words in length. It is quite a brief synopsis, but if you multiply it by 70,000, we're talking about several million words.'*

The main lessons from the project, he says, *'are not untypical of any large project. The challenges were more organisational than having to do with the technology. The actual collation of data was the biggest challenge we faced.'*

The result, Whitfield says, is that information on documentation and video and immediate retrieval of synopses and scripts. Interested buyers can be told more quickly whether the production exists and the corresponding episodes are available, reducing the risk of lost sales.

The rights management department has been able to pinpoint contractual details and hence make faster and more accurate decisions.

Future plans

The jobs of researchers and librarians have become far less labour intensive, time consuming and frustrating. Staff can ascertain in an instant whether or not footage is obtainable from the archive library.

'Already we're seeing that people would like to extend the functionality,' Whitfield says. *'For example, it's one thing for researchers to identify the material we've got, the next thing is to locate it within the organisation. So, we're considering downloading additional information which will tell us where an item is.'*

Granada Media would eventually like to see RetrievalWare as a feature of the desktop suite for all personnel. Whitfield believes the system could benefit the business as a whole, not just certain departments. Staff in other departments have expressed an interest in Excalibur as the retrieval of documentation and information is an integral part of the service they provide, whether it be to the public or prospective clients.

For the moment, its RetrievalWare system is text-based, but it is looking into the possibility of video searches.

The company also plans to reorganise the archive library by categorising and numbering footage by row numbers to provide a physical location marker.

Whitfield says, *'We required a faster, more accurate system, as we didn't feel in control of our assets. What we have seen so far fulfils our criteria and has given us food for thought regarding the future prospects of the technology within our company'*.

He concludes, *'We are more confident about the retrieval of vital information in an important situation and, effectively, this application will add value to our bottom line. Ultimately, that is why we are all in business.'*

INDEX

Acquisition of information, information life cycle function 67, 68, 70, 180, 181, 186
Agents and the Internet 168
Analogue transmission 92
Application areas for document management 175-179
Approval and authorisation, information life cycle function 180, 186
Asynchronous communication 93
Asynchronous Transfer Mode 94, 95, 96
ATM, *see* Asynchronous Transfer Mode

Bandwidth 92
Bar coding 106
Baseband 93
Baud 92
Benefits, strategic and tactical 194
Bitonal images, *see* Images, bitonal
Boolean operators 162
BPR, *see* business process re-engineering
Bridges 91
Broadband 93
Buses and interfaces 98-100
Business case 191, 193
Business excellence model 50
Business performance, improving 41-61
Business process re-engineering 54-57, 176
Business process, definition of 51

Cabling, *see* Network cabling
CALS, *see* Computer-aided Acquisition and Logistic Support
Cameras, digital 106-107
Cameras, microfilm 116
CASE, *see* Computer-aided systems engineering
Case studies 231-247
Cataloguing 156, 180
CBA, *see* Cost benefit analysis
CD-ROM 119, 189, 190
Classification, conceptual and file 66, 73, 74-76, 80, 81, 84, 154, 156
Classification, aid to subject indexing 158
Clients, fat 89
    thin 89

Client-server technology 88-90
Coaxial cable, *see* Network cabling
COLD, *see* Computer output to laser disk
Colour images, *see* Images, colour
Commitment, getting and keeping 208-209
Common Object Request Broker Architecture 91, 131-132
Communication, information life cycle function 70, 184, 190
Competitive advantage, gaining 13-15
Compound document, *see* Document, compound
Compression, *see* Standards, compression
Computer-aided Acquisition and Logistic Support 98, 132, 135, 186
Computer-aided systems engineering 42-44, 59
Computer-Output-to-Laser-Disk 183
Computer systems, multi-user 190
Concept tree 162
Continuous tone images, *see* Images, continuous tone
Contract negotiation 207
Contrast, in electronic imaging and microfilming 113, 116
Controlled language indexing, *see* Indexing, controlled language
Co-operative working technologies 143-145
CORBA, *see* Common Object Request Broker Architecture
Cost benefit analysis 194-195, 207, 209
Creation of information, information life cycle function, 67, 68, 70, 180, 182, 186
Culture, organisational 59, 60

Data, as compared with information and knowledge 19-21
Data management 32-33
Database management systems, compared with information retrieval systems 166-167
Databases, full text, *see* Retrieval, full text
    object-oriented 167-168
    relational 167-168
Desk-top publishing 109
Destruction, information life cycle function 70, 191
Digital transmission 92
Digital video disk, *see* DVD

Display technology, 184, 126-127
Dithering, scanning 113
DMA, see Document Management Alliance
Document Management Alliance, specification
DMA 1.0 137
Document management, application areas,
see Application areas for document
management
Document management, potential of 3-4
risks 4-5
significance of 2-3
suppliers, see Suppliers, document management
Document retrieval, compared with information
retrieval 152-153
Document storage, compared with information
storage 154-155
Document viewers 142-143
Document, compound 1-2, 130-135
Document, types of 73
Documentation, online, authoring 142
Documents, characteristics of 72
non-transaction 153
retrieval data 154
transaction 152
Downsizing, organisations 12, 21, 58
DVD, variants of 120, 190

e-commerce 13-14
E-mail, see Electronic mail
EDI, see Electronic data interchange
EISA, see Enhanced Industry Standard Architecture
EKM, see Enterprise knowledge management
Electronic data interchange 14,106, 136, 143, 145
Electronic imaging, see Scanning
Electronic mail 102, 144
Enhanced Industry Standard Architecture 98
Enterprise knowledge management, definition
of 23-24
Ethernet 94
Extensible Markup Language 133

Facsimile 130
Fat clients, see Clients, fat
FDDI, see Fibre Distributed Data Interface
Fibre Distributed Data Interface 94
Fibre optic cabling, see Network cabling
File classification, see Classification, conceptual and
file
Financial evaluation, techniques 195
Firewall 102, 146
Forms management 76-77
Frame Relay 96
Free text, see Full text
Full text databases, see Retrieval, full text

Gateways 91, 102
GIFF, see Graphic image formats
Gopher 101-102
Graphic image formats, see Image formats, graphic
Groupware 143-145

Hand-held computers 105-106

Handwriting recognition 105-106
HTML, see HyperText Markup Language
HTTP, see HyperText Transfer Protocol
Hubs 91-92, 145
Hyperlinks 133, 143, 162, 182
HyperText links, see Hyperlinks
HyperText Markup Language 102, 132-133, 136,
141-142, 162
HyperText Transfer Protocol 91, 102, 138

ICR, see Intelligent character recognition
Image capture 109-110
Image formats, graphic 127-129
raster 2,112, 114, 128-129, 134
vector 2, 112, 128-129, 134, 155
Images, bitonal 110-112
colour 110-112
continuous tone 110-112, 130
Indexing, information life cycle function 180, 182,
187
controlled language 153, 158-160
depth of 155
natural language 154, 158-160
Industry Standard Architecture 98
Infobuild, an information life cycle management
approach 33, 67-72
Information, as compared with data and knowledge
19-21
distinguished from system 21-22
strategic importance of 15-16
transactional 15
type of stored 154
value of 151
Information age, management challenges 12
Information assets 22, 23, 25
Information life cycle, activities 35-38, 67
Information management, compared with knowledge
management 22-24
Information model 27
Information resources, managing 16-24
Information retrieval, compared with document
retrieval 152-153
software, facilities 161-164
systems compared with database management
systems 166-167
Information scene, Rich Picture of 18
Information sciences 33
Information storage, compared with document
storage 154-155
Information systems, development of 31-32
Information systems strategy, development of 25-31
stages of 26-28
planning, problems encountered 28-29
planning, techniques and methodologies 30
Input devices 104-116
Integrated Services Digital Network 96, 97
Intelligent character recognition 107, 108
Interchange standards, see Standards, interchange
Internet, description of 101-103
Internet, hardware for 102-103
Intranets 103-104
Investors in People 49, 58-59

Invitation to tender 204-207
ISA, *see* Industry Standard Architecture
ISDN, *see* Integrated Services Digital Network
ISIS (Image and Scanner Interface Standard),
    see Scanners, control software,
ISO 9000 50-51

Java 89, 102, 131, 132, 140, 141
Jukeboxes 116
Justification for project 191, 194, 197, 209

Keyboards, for information input 104, 105, 106, 108
Knowledge, as compared with data and information 19-21
Knowledge management, constituent elements 24
    see also Enterprise knowledge management

LAN, *see* Local area networks
Legal admissibility 123-125
Life expectancy, storage media 121-122
Local area networks, technologies 94-95
Local bus 98

Magnetic storage, *see* Storage, magnetic
Mail Application Program Interface 91
Management, challenges in information age 12
MAPI, *see* Mail Application Program Interface
MCA, *see* Micro Channel Architecture
Micro Channel Architecture 98
Microfilm cameras, *see* Cameras, microfilm
Microfilming and microfilm scanning 115-116
Middleware software 90, 91
Modem 93, 96, 97
Monitor and control, information life cycle function 185, 191
Monitors, *see* Display technology

Natural language indexing, *see* Indexing, natural language
Network computer 89
Network topologies, *see* Local area networks
Network cabling 96-98
Non-transaction documents, *see* Documents, non-transaction

Object-oriented databases, *see* Databases, object-oriented
Object-oriented programming 140-141
Object Linking and Embedding 91, 106, 131
Object Management Architecture 132
Object Management Group 131
OCR, *see* Optical character recognition
ODA, *see* Open Document Architecture
ODBC, *see* Open Database Connectivity
OLE, *see* Object Linking and Embedding
OMA, *see* Object Management Architecture
OMG, *see* Object Management Group
Open Database Connectivity 92
Open Document Architecture 133-134
OpenDoc 131, 132
Operating system software 139-140
Optical character recognition 107-108

Optical storage, *see* Storage, optical
Organisation, model of 11-12
    of information life cycle function 35, 38, 191

Paperwork Reduction Act 25
Parallel communication 94
PC Card 99, 118, 189
PCI, *see* Peripheral Component Interconnect
PCMCIA, *see* PC card
PD drive 120
PDF, *see* Portable Document Format
Pen computing, *see* Hand-held computers
Peripheral Component Interconnect 98
Pointing devices 108-109
Portable Document Format 137, 143, 155, 157
Post-project review 209
PostScript 126, 133
PRINCE (project management methodology) 197-201
Process improvement, tools and techniques 52-53
Procurement, public 205-206
Product data, Standard for the Exchange of 134-35
Productivity, contribution of technology 13
Programming software 140-141
Project initiation 200-201
Project management 195-209
Proximity searching 162
Public procurement, *see* Procurement, public

Quality, approaches for improving business performance 48-54
    plan 195, 196, 197, 203
    records 53-54

RAID, *see* Redundant array of inexpensive disks
Raster image formats, *see* Image formats, raster
Records, definition of 63
Records and document survey and analysis 67
Records management, benefits of 66
    compared with document management 66-67
    data 73-74
    description of 63-67
    need for 64-65
Records manual, contents of 83-84
Records storage and retrieval 81
Records system design 74-76
Redundant array of inexpensive disks 118-119
Refining searches 163
Relational database, *see* Databases, relational
Relevance ranking 163, 180
Reports management 77-79
Requirements definition 201-204
Resolution, scanning 111-114
Retention, information life cycle function 187-188
Retention and indexing criteria 53, 71, 156
Retention schedules, devising 37, 79-81
Retrieval, full text 81, 167, 182, 187
    information life cycle function 180, 183, 189-190
    performance 164-165
    software suppliers, *see* Suppliers, retrieval software
    speed of 152

Index

Revision, information life cycle function 185, 190-191
Rich Picture 1 6, 17, 44, 45, 46
Root definitions 45, 46, 55
Routers 91, 92

Satellite transmission 90, 98
Saved searches 163
Scanners 109
    control software 110-111
Scanning 109-115
Scanning resolution, *see* Resolution, scanning
SCSI, *see* Small Computer Systems Interface
Searching, information life cycle function 183
Security of information 145-147
Serial communication 93-94
Servers, types of 88
SGML, *see* Standard Generalised Markup Language
Small Computer Systems Interface 99-100
SMDS, *see* Switched Multimegabit Data Service
Soft Systems Methodology 30, 44-48
Software development life cycle, *see* System development
SONET, *see* Synchronous Optical Network
Sources of information 216-218
SPDL, *see* Standard Page Description Language
Specialists, contribution of 17-19
Speech recognition 104-105
Spiders 168
SQL, *see* Structured Query Language
SSADM, *see* Structured Systems Analysis and Design Method
Standard Generalised Markup Language 102, 132-133, 134, 135
Standard Page Description Language 133, 134
Standards, compression 111, 112, 128, 129-130
    document management 1 36-138
    interchange 133-135
    storage media 117-121
STEP, *see* Product data, Standard for the Exchange of
Storage, information life cycle function 68, 70, 183, 188
    magnetic 117-119
    optical 118-120
    technologies 116-121
Strategy, information systems, *see* Information systems strategy
Structured Query Language 163-164
Structured Systems Analysis and Design Method 30, 41-44, 55
Summarisers 162
Suppliers, document management software 219-228
Suppliers, retrieval software 168-170
Suppliers, acquisitions (industry consolidation) 212-216
Switched Multimegabit Data Service 96
Synchronous communication 93
Synchronous Optical Network 95

System development, external versus internal 192-193
System development life cycle 32

Tagged image file format 128
TCP/IP, *see* Transmission Control Protocol/Internet Protocol 91,100
Technology options 177
Tenders, evaluation of 206
Thesaurus 158, 159, 161, 162, 163, 164, 170
Thin clients, *see* Clients, thin
Three tier architecture 89-90
Threshold, scanning 113
TIFF, *see* Tagged image file format
Token Ring 94
Total Quality Management 48, 49, 51, 53
TQM, *see* Total Quality Management
Transaction documents, *see* Documents, transaction
Transmission Control Protocol/Internet Protocol 91, 100
TWAIN (Toolkit Without An Important Name), *see* Scanners, control software
Twisted pair cabling, *see* Network cabling
Two-tier architecture 89-90

User needs, system functionality 179-185
Users, types of 202
Utilisation, information life cycle function 37, 70, 190

Value chain 14, 30
Vector image formats, *see* Image formats, vector
VESA Local-BUS 98
Viewers, *see* Document viewers
VL-but, *see* VESA Local-BUS

WAIS, *see* Wide Area Information Server
WAN, *see* Wide area networks
WebDAV, *see* Web Distributed Authoring and Versioning
Web Distributed Authoring and Versioning, standard 138
WfMC, *see* Workflow Management Coalition
Wide area networks, technologies 95-96
Wide Area Information Server 101, 102
Wild card searching 161
Wireless networks 98
Word-processing software 141-142
Word fragment searching 161
Workflow 143-145
Workflow Management Coalition 138, 211
World Wide Web 100-102
WORM, *see* Write-Once-Read-Many
Write-Once-Read-Many 120
WWW, *see* World Wide Web

XML, *see* Extensible Markup Language

Copyright Theft

John Gurnsey

An Aslib/Gower Title

Copyright was developed to protect the printed word. In the late twentieth century can it and does it realistically serve to protect authors of audio, video and electronic products that are the vehicles of information supply in our multi-media age?

Systematic copyright theft forms part of a multi·billion dollar international industry, which is able to thrive partly because it is easy to overlook what is known to be theft when the original material remains intact. But what was a 'cottage industry' 30 years ago has now become much more sophisticated, so that pirate books printed in Taiwan flood the markets of West Africa, and audio tapes printed in the Far East appear in Saudi Arabia, Australasia and even Europe. The threat to publishers is alarming, and increasing. The burgeoning of the electronic information industry today makes copyright theft an urgent issue.

John Gurnsey has reviewed all forms of copyright theft, from commercial to domestic, gathering the experiences of a wide range of organizations across book and electronic publishing. Book, electronic, database, audio, video, games and multimedia publishing are all considered along with the question of whether existing laws can effectively serve such a rapidly changing industry.

Copyright law is an extremely complex area: this book is about the abuse of it, rather than the law itself. In helping publishing companies understand more about copyright theft, it might help them to avoid it in at least some of its forms.

Gower

Gower Handbook of Library and Information Management

Edited by Ray Prytherch

This *Gower Handbook* is an authoritative guide to both the traditional and newer aspects of library and information management. Edited by Ray Prytherch, it brings together the insight of a range of respected contributors, who offer advice on the management, storage, retrieval, analysis, marketing and delivery of information.

The book begins with Part I analysing the context and trends of the information world. In Part II, Strategy and Planning, the information environment is explored in more detail, with Chapters 3 and 4 presenting the main issues and principles of financial planning and strategic planning. Part III, The Service Infrastructure, looks at customer care, the role of performance measurement and research in service improvement, and the influence of copyright law in the delivery of information products to customers. Part IV, Managing Resources, includes five chapters on strategic management, information auditing, human resource management, preservation and disaster management. The last part of the *Handbook,* Part V, Access and Delivery, focuses on the potential of electronic systems with chapters on subject gateways and Z39.50, electronic publishing, intranets and new models of access and delivery. Each part of the *Handbook* begins with an introduction by the editor and the book concludes with a directory of organizations, including useful URLs, and a glossary.

Flexibility and adaptability are crucial for information professionals if they are to maintain their skills at the right level to provide the services needed by both information-rich and information-poor. In this one book librarians from all backgrounds, information managers and officers, document and records managers, and network and Web specialists will find answers to a wide range of questions that confront them in their working day. The *Handbook* will become a standard reference on best practice for professionals and students. It will be of interest to information analysts, knowledge managers, and others, including publishers, involved in information maintenance and provision.

Gower

A Guide to Image Processing and Picture Management

A E Cawkell

The value of convenient picture management has been appreciated for many years, and many useful books and articles have been written on the subject. However the advent of an electronic means of managing pictures and 'images' has drastically changed and improved the possibilities for such management. The rapidly falling costs of the technology means that electronic image management is now within the sights of most libraries, art galleries and museums, and is being considered by many organizations new to the field. This book explains the astonishing progress, increasing complexity, and the pervasive jargon of the technology, and is aimed at those with some but not a detailed knowledge of information technology. Armed with this valuable information on the current state of technology and its implications, the potential buyer and user of picture management equipment will face decisions in this area with confidence, and therefore be able to manage images more successfully.

Applications include:

- image processing
- image compression
- multimedia
- hypertext
- CDs
- indexing
- picture systems
- databases.

There is also a useful glossary and list of acronyms.

Gower

Practical Information Policies

Second Edition

Elizabeth Orna

Practical Information Policies offers readers a straightforward way of working out what their organization needs to know to survive and prosper, what information it requires to 'feed' its knowledge, and how people need to interact in using knowledge and information.

Readers of the first edition commended it for its practical and reliable guidance. The new edition keeps this emphasis on the practical, while taking full account of key developments in ideas, practice and technology. It includes new chapters on:

• People and technology: battlefield or creative interaction?
• What the organization values; the contribution of knowledge and information in creating value
• Knowledge and information for managing change.

A complete new set of 14 case studies from the UK, Australia and Singapore illustrates and supports the principles set out.

This new edition of an established classic will enable general managers, information managers and others responsible for any kind of organizational information resource to put their understanding of their organizations to work as a powerful tool in developing effective knowledge and information management strategies. For students of the information management disciplines, it will make a bridge between theory and practice as they prepare for their careers.

Gower

Records Management Handbook

Second Edition

Ira A Penn, Gail B Pennix and Jim Coulson

Records Management Handbook is a complete guide to the practice of records and information management. Written from a multi-media perspective and with a comprehensive systems design orientation, the authors present proven management strategies for developing, implementing and operating a "21st century" records management programme. Where most available titles are biased toward dealing with inactive records, this book gives a balanced treatment for all phases of the record's life cycle, from creation or receipt through to ultimate disposition.

The *Records Management Handbook* is a practical reference for use by records managers, analysts, and other information management professionals, which will aid decision-making, improve job performance, stimulate ideas, help avoid legal problems, minimize risk and error, save time and reduce expense.

Special features of the second edition include:

- new chapters on record media, active records systems and records disposition
- new information on management strategies and programme implementation
- revised guidance and material on records appraisal and record inventorying
- expanded and increased information on retention scheduling, records storage and electronic forms.

Gower